P9-CLB-495

First Comes
Love,
then Comes
Malaria

First Comes *Love,* then Comes *Malaria*

How a Peace Corps Poster
Boy Won My Heart and a
Third-World Adventure
Changed My Life

Eve Brown-Waite

BROADWAY BOOKS
New York

BROADWAY

Copyright © 2009 by Eve Brown-Waite

All Rights Reserved

Published in the United States by Broadway Books,
an imprint of The Doubleday Publishing Group,
a division of Random House, Inc., New York.
www.broadwaybooks.com

BROADWAY BOOKS and its logo, a letter B bisected on
the diagonal, are trademarks of Random House, Inc.

Library of Congress Cataloging-in-Publication Data
Brown-Waite, Eve.
First comes love, then comes malaria : how a Peace Corps
poster boy won my heart and a Third-World adventure
changed my life / Eve Brown-Waite.—1st ed.
   p.   cm.
   1. Ecuador—Description and travel. 2. Uganda—
Description and travel. 3. Brown-Waite, Eve—Travel—Ecuador.
4. Brown-Waite, Eve—Travel—Uganda. 5. Peace Corps (U.S.)—
Ecuador—Biography. I. Title.

F3716.B76 2009
918.66—dc22
[B]

                                                    2008022034

ISBN 978-0-7679-2935-6

PRINTED IN THE UNITED STATES OF AMERICA

10 9 8 7 6 5 4 3 2 1

First Edition

Dedicated to my Prince Charming,

for the happily ever after,

and to Jeremiah and Sierra,

for coming along

Author's Note

This memoir is based on actual events—some of which happened twenty years ago. But I am blessed with an excellent memory, so everything I wrote here is true and happened exactly the way I said it did, though others may disagree—but they should write their own books!

Naturally, I've had to reconstruct a lot of the dialogue. But as I said, I do have a very good memory (although sometimes I forget to feed the dog, and where the hell did I put my glasses . . . ?) and really I can often remember exactly what a person said and what the weather was like on a certain day, even if it was twenty years ago. And like I said, if you disagree, then just go write your own book, John.

Anyway, in the rare instances where maybe I could not remember the exact details of an event or precisely what a person said, I did what all writers do, and I filled in the blanks—because if I didn't, this book would be much shorter and you'd be bored. But I did stay true to the intent of each conversation and in no way meant to portray anyone in an unfavorable light. (So if you cringe when you read about asking John if he was *shtupping* me after our first date, Mom, you have no one to blame but yourself!)

The letters that appear in the book are all taken from actual letters I wrote, although they are edited quite liberally and in some cases were originally written to people other than to whom they are addressed in this book. I did this because, let's face it, some letters are like the contents of your nose, lots of bothersome useless stuff, but every once in a while, something of interest. I picked the interesting stuff out for you.

Everyone who appears in this book is real and for the most part I use their real names, except in a few cases to protect their privacy and because one person really, really smelled. But I am indebted to everyone who appeared in my life and who appears in this book—even the person who really, really smelled. And I thank them all for being a part of this amazing journey and for letting me write about them.

The book is funny, but malaria is not. More than a million people in Africa die from malaria each year, and it's the number one killer of children under five years old in Uganda. We can do something about that. Ten percent of my royalties from *First Comes Love, Then Comes Malaria* are being donated to organizations doing malaria prevention work in Africa. I invite you to join me by making a donation to one of these fine organizations that are working on malaria—and other much needed health issues—in Africa:

CARE/USA
151 Ellis Street, NE
Atlanta, GA 30303

African Medical and Research Foundation (AMREF), USA
4 West 43rd Street, 2nd Floor
New York, NY 10036

Médecins Sans Frontières (Doctors Without Borders) USA
P.O. Box 5030
Hagerstown, MD 21741–5030

First Comes
Love,
then Comes
Malaria

Part
One

Chapter One

In the Beginning (There Was John)

"So tell me why you want to join the Peace Corps." John looked across the table at me with his emerald eyes, and my heart danced a jig although my boobs stayed firm in their minimizing bra. I was moved by how earnestly he seemed to want to know. Okay, he was the recruiter and it was his job to ask. But, still, I was flattered by his attention. I was glad I had chosen to dress in safari chic for my interview. I thought my flowing bias-cut skirt, green canvas boots, and waist-hugging floral blouse had a certain I-may-be-going-off-to-the-jungle-but-I-still-look-damn-cute quality to them. That, and I knew the blouse showed off my breasts.

"I honestly can't tell you why I want to join the Peace Corps," I answered. "Just that I have always wanted to." I looked around the conference room at the University at Albany that had been set up as a Peace Corps recruiting office for the day. Smiling down at me were posters of Peace Corps volunteers in quaint fishing boats, dilapidated schoolrooms, and mud and thatch villages. The volunteers exuded a sheen of sweat and satisfaction, and they were all surrounded by happy, grateful villagers. *Them,* I wanted to say. *I want to be like them.* Well, maybe not so much the sweaty part.

"Well, I can understand that. Growing up, my family had me pegged to become a priest. I'm the middle of five Catholic boys. One of us had to be a priest." John laughed. "But helping others was never a religious thing for me. It's just what I think we were put here to do.

Y'know?" He smiled and I couldn't help but notice his straight white teeth and sweetly freckled face. Cute, I thought, if you go for that clean-cut look, which I didn't. I'd always had a hazy but persistent notion that I'd end up with a man who'd be tall, Irish, and look a bit scruffy in his red beard. My mother added her own notion that I'd probably meet him in the Peace Corps.

But this definitely wasn't the guy. When we first spoke on the phone to arrange the interview, I hadn't cared for John at all. I was expecting someone more hippielike than businesslike, and this guy was all business. My first look at him confirmed my earlier impression. John seemed far more prep school than Peace Corps.

I crossed my legs underneath the table, accidentally kicking the wicker hamper that I'd stashed there.

"Can I ask about the picnic basket? It's just a bit unusual for March," John said.

"It's actually my sewing basket. I'm making a quilt. I usually bring it along wherever I go. That way I can keep busy in case I have to wait."

"Oh, sewing is the kind of skill that would be great in the Peace Corps," he said enthusiastically.

"Great," I said, less enthusiastically. I was definitely not the Suzy Homemaker type the quilt made me out to be. I had only recently taken up quilting to pass the time on the nights I volunteered to stay home and take calls for the Rape Crisis Hotline. Fortunately, we didn't get many calls. Unfortunately, my roommate and I couldn't afford a television, and I was bored stiff on my volunteer nights. I got some fabric and a book on how to make a quilt, which recommended starting out small, by making a pot holder. But I didn't need a pot holder, and I didn't believe in doing anything small.

"So, what other skills do you have that would be useful to people in developing countries?" he asked, the pen in his left hand poised over a yellow legal pad with "Candidate #14—Eve Brown" scrawled across the top.

"That's a good question. Let's see. I was a political science major in college. With a women's studies minor," I added quickly.

"Uh-huh." John looked at me expectantly, pen not moving.

"And I was president of the Student Association." He didn't write that down either, so I didn't bother to add that I had championed such causes as free transportation to antinuke rallies and keeping the legal drinking age from being raised to twenty-one. "I guess there's not a lot of transferable skills there." *Nor in the fact that I can make a mean banana daiquiri,* I thought.

"Well, tell me about what you do now," he prompted.

"Like I said on the phone, I teach sexual assault prevention in elementary schools."

"Teaching, that's a great skill. Host countries are always requesting teachers," he said, writing. Having spent the last two years in the company of every snot-nosed kindergartener through sixth grader in a five-county area, I was hoping to get away from teaching. I was thinking more along the lines of organizing the oppressed. Helping them to rise up, claim their due, and perhaps win myself a Nobel Peace Prize along the way. But I didn't quite know how to communicate this to my recruiter.

"What did you do in the Peace Corps?" I asked John, hoping it was more exciting than teaching English.

"Economic development," he replied.

"So you exported capitalism to the Third World?" I could practically hear my socialist great-grandparents heave a collective *"oy vey"* from beyond the grave.

"Well, I worked with farmers to build an irrigation system so their crops wouldn't fail and their families wouldn't starve when there was a drought." He stood up. Quite tall, I noticed. He took off his sports coat and hung it over the back of his chair. "I helped families put fences around their farms so animals wouldn't eat their livelihood." He sat back down. "I helped plant a grove of mango trees so there'd be fruit in my village in ten years. And I helped women set up businesses as seamstresses so they would have money to buy medicine for their children. I don't know," he said, rolling up the sleeves of his somewhat faded blue button-down shirt. "Does that count as exporting capitalism?"

"No, that sounds wonderful, actually." He had the most adorable red fuzz on his arms that matched the glints of red in his slightly wavy brown hair. "Tell me more about your experiences." I wondered if batting my eyelashes was a skill that would be useful to people in developing countries. At the moment, I was proving to be a master at it.

"I lived in a village called Bomboré in Burkina Faso, which is one of the poorest countries in the world. Every volunteer is assigned to a community, a host country partner, and a primary project. But you can find your own secondary projects to work on. You get settled in your village, make friends, and then you look for opportunities to do other stuff. For me, that was the best part."

As John talked, I could almost see the dusty, brown village he loved. I could smell the smoke from the clay stoves he built to help women conserve wood. I could hear the delighted squeals of the barefoot children as they played soccer with the tall, friendly stranger. And I could see John a little tousled and scruffy around the edges. I was beginning to find the whole thing—the Peace Corps and its poster boy—more and more attractive. I could just imagine John and me together on some tropical island. Granted, it was all probably more Club Med than Third-World slum, but this whole Peace Corps thing was looking more appealing by the minute.

So I told John about my political awakening in the student senate of the State University of New York College at Oneonta. How I had discovered that I had a passion for politics and a natural ease as a public speaker and had gradually begun to take on more and more serious issues. I told him how, as Student Association president, I had won a class action suit that gave students the right to vote in their college towns all across the state. I told him of my involvement in local politics and my growing concern about America's involvement in the guerrilla wars of Latin America. I told of getting arrested the summer before for participating in a sit-in at my congressman's office, and of the ten days I spent in jail for that. And I told him that I hoped to go on to do something that would meaningfully impact people in the rest of the world.

"Thank you, Eve," John said, rising and shaking my hand at the end of our two-hour interview. "Thank you for being different from the other thirteen candidates I interviewed today. I think you'd make an excellent Peace Corps volunteer. I'll forward your application, along with my letter of support, to the placement office in D.C." Then he said something about medical clearance and forms, but I just kept thinking how nice my little hand felt in his big, strong hand. "The process can take a while, so be patient," he said. "In the meantime, call me if you have any questions."

"Um . . . I am a little worried that my jail time might be a problem." A criminal record, I was pretty sure, can keep you out of the Peace Corps.

"I think between what you wrote in your application and what I've learned about you," he said, tapping his pen on the yellow legal pad, now quite full, "we can adequately explain your time in jail. Spending ten days in jail for a civil disobedience charge shows that you are committed to your beliefs." He smiled. I didn't try to disabuse him of his noble image of me by informing him that I could have gotten out of jail by paying the $50 fine, but that the ten days in jail got me a lot of publicity, and like I said, I didn't like to do anything in a small way.

"Well, maybe I could call you in a week or so, just to check?" He said to call if I had any questions, and I was going to have lots of them.

"That'd be fine," he said. "And call me if you ever come down to the city. We could meet for lunch or something."

Yeah, or maybe we could pick out names for our children, I thought.

Driving home that evening, I wondered if I really would go through with this. Joining the Peace Corps someday had always been part of my plan. As in "I hope to join the Peace Corps someday," which is what I said when I won an all-expense-paid trip to Israel as a high school exchange student. And "I'm thinking of joining the Peace Corps someday," I said ever so coolly the fall I came back to college after spending the summer picking apples and scraping up chicken shit on an Israeli kibbutz. And "I'll be joining the Peace Corps in a couple of years," I answered when asked my long-term plans when I interviewed for the job I had now at the Rape Crisis Center.

So I had long been about the Peace Corps—in concept. After all, it never failed to get an approving smile and an admiring "oh, isn't that wonderful" when I said it. But the reality of the Peace Corps—the sweating in a bug-infested jungle and being deprived of creature comforts—well, that I wasn't so sure about. But I knew that eventually I'd have to poop or get out of the latrine. The I'll-be-joining-the-Peace-Corps-someday line was just going to seem pathetic if I was still muttering it while pregnant with my third child and toting the other two around in my Chevy Suburban.

But now it was two years since my college graduation. I was still living in Oneonta and still dating the sweetheart who was supposed to be my last college fling. He and I had a wonderful relationship, but as much as I loved him, for a reason I just couldn't put my finger on, I knew he wasn't THE ONE. Just as I knew that I had to get out of Oneonta in order to get on with my life. It was join the Peace Corps or go to law school. And when faced with two equal options—one being what would be expected of a nice Jewish girl and the other being somewhat outrageous—well, for some reason, I always choose the one that would make my Orthodox Jewish grandmother roll over in her grave.

It had taken me nearly a month to fill out the Peace Corps application. I was surprised by how thoroughly they investigate their applicants. I was *volunteering* to go to some god-awful country, live in a shack, and dig latrines for world peace. Obviously, I was insane. Wasn't that what they were looking for? But apparently they wanted their recruits to be insane *and* well qualified at the same time! We were required to have a college degree or be highly skilled, be in excellent health, have no potentially troublesome wisdom teeth, nor any romantic or financial entanglements.

I was asked to list all the courses I'd taken and what grades I'd received. I hoped to make up for my barely B average with my interest in all things international, as documented by my three consecutive semesters banging on coconut husk bongos in Javanese Gamelan class. I assumed that I was healthy enough to live in less developed countries, because at that time, I had not yet ruined my health by years of living in less developed countries. Since my wisdom teeth had never even come in, I figured that would pose no problem.

It was only the question about romantic entanglements that worried me, since The Oneonta Sweetheart and I were still entangled at the time. The fact that I had a boyfriend was not something I wanted to lie about, since it clearly stated that lying would lead to immediate disqualification and possible prosecution. Besides, I had listed the Sweetheart as one of my half-dozen references. He told them nice things about me and I told them I'd break up with him to go into the Peace Corps. Good enough, I guess, because I was invited for an interview.

I had long imagined that joining the Peace Corps would be like being ushered into a fraternity of like-minded peaceniks. I was sure that my history as a college radical and my present do-gooder job would grant me automatic entry into their club. I figured as soon as they heard about me, we'd all be holding hands and singing "Kumbaya." But there was no hand-holding when John had called and insisted I come to New York City for an interview.

"I can't possibly come to New York City. I work for a rape crisis center, traveling around upstate New York teaching elementary school kids about sexual assault prevention." Hadn't this guy read my résumé? "You know, 'good touch–bad touch,' 'say no, then go, then tell'?" The silence on the other end was not encouraging.

"Anyway, it's a really tight schedule. I have to cover forty different schools and we are scheduled right through the end of the year. So if

I miss one or two days, the whole schedule is thrown off." I didn't bother to add the part about my having to waitress at night so I could afford to keep my low-paying, do-gooder day job.

"Well, then, I'll assume you are not all that interested in joining the Peace Corps," said John, in his clipped Boston accent. *Did this guy even know "Kumbaya"?*

We reached a compromise when John offered to give me the last interview on an upcoming recruitment day at the University at Albany. For the entire ninety-minute drive there, I kept reminding myself that I didn't need to like my recruiter. I simply needed to get past him in order to get into the Peace Corps. But now, driving home, remembering the excitement in his voice as he talked about his little village in Burkina Faso and recalling how good my hand felt in his, I realized that I liked him very much. Now I wondered if I would have to actually go into the Peace Corps in order to get the recruiter.

> *Answering machine, beep:*
> *Hi, Mom. I'm calling to fill you in on my Peace Corps interview. It lasted for two hours, and, well, I'm still not sure about going off to live in the jungle. But I am definitely going to marry my recruiter!*

Chapter Two

One Day, We'll Tell Our
Grandchildren About This

Several weeks after our interview, I was still thinking about John. I hadn't gotten even the slightest romantic encouragement from him, and I really didn't expect to. He seemed far too reasonable a man to be interested in someone who: (a) was otherwise involved; (b) lived two hundred miles away; and (c) he was determined to send off to the Peace Corps for two years. So I had no choice but to take matters into my own hands.

When schools were closed for Easter vacation, I told The Oneonta Sweetheart that I was going to see my parents. I did go to see my parents, and then I went down to the Peace Corps office in Times Square. But first I paid a visit to my local Salvation Army and picked up some khaki cargo pants and a pair of Birkenstocks. With my backpack on my back, I thought I looked as if I were already in the Peace Corps. And I hoped that just might be enough to win John's heart.

"Um, the medical office is insisting I have my wisdom teeth removed," I told John when he asked me if I was having any problems with the process. "My dentist says my wisdom teeth are so far below my gums that he'd have to break my jaw to get them out." Apparently the Peace Corps wanted to avoid problems later on when I was "in country," should my delinquent teeth finally decide to arrive, and then arrive impacted. This seemed like an awful lot of certain trouble (and pain) to go through in order to avoid potential trouble later on.

"They always throw up roadblocks to see how badly you really want to go. Just have the dentist write a letter. I called down to Washington to check on your status and everything is moving along."

I wasn't really worried about the progress of my application; I was worried about the progress—or lack thereof—of John's interest in me. And as I looked around at his colleagues, all neatly dressed in business suits and skirts, I now worried that if in an effort to impress John, I had landed in the fashion no-man's-land between hippie and bag lady. But John invited me to lunch, which I thought was a good sign, although the restaurant he chose was awfully dark, which maybe was not a good sign.

"The funny thing about my Peace Corps service is that I went to Upper Volta," he told me while I picked at some kind of skewered meat. This might have been a good time to fess up to the fact that I was a vegetarian, except that Peace Corps volunteers are expected to eat whatever is put in front of them and I was determined to convince John that I was perfect volunteer material. "But I came home from Burkina Faso!" I tried to nod knowingly. Immediately after our interview, I committed Burkina Faso to memory and quickly found this tiny sub-Saharan country on a map of Africa. But until that moment I'd never even heard of Upper Volta. How many small, Third-World nations did this guy expect me to keep track of?

"A few months into my service, Upper Volta had a coup," John explained. "Thomas Sankara took over the government. Everyone called him the 'People's President.' He called us his 'comrades' and promised to give power back to the people. We loved him. He was going to help save this little piece of Africa." John was animated as he spoke and I was reminded of all the Che Guevara wannabes that I had been infatuated with in college. Only John was more hygienic than most of them.

"Wow! What did you do during the coup?"

"Oh, I was fine." John's green eyes crinkled as he laughed. "My neighbors took care of me. We stayed close to the village, and we were all fine."

"But weren't you in danger? Shouldn't the Peace Corps have evacuated the volunteers?" I knew that volunteer safety was the top priority. I had faithfully memorized the reams of paper I'd received from the Peace Corps so far. Ever the good girl, I was going to be ready in case there was a pop quiz.

"The thing about the rest of the world, Eve, is that no one else has the comfort and security that we Americans do. We have things pretty cushy, you know." He said this as if he was sure that I knew this too. "In Africa, no one counts on things going smoothly. You have to get used to a certain amount of uncertainty and discomfort and even insecurity."

"Were you glad to get back to America?" I asked.

"Oh, I'm happy here. I'm happy to be closer to my friends and family and to drink cold beer." John smiled again and I knew that I was staring into the handsome face of a man who could be happy anywhere. "But I miss Burkina a lot. I miss the people who became like family to me. And over there life is simpler and it somehow feels more real."

"Do you think you'll go back?" I asked, half dreading his answer.

"I'm here now. I love being a Peace Corps recruiter. It lets me relive my experience every day. And I get to meet some wonderful people . . . like you, for instance." He looked into my eyes and my heart raced. "And I'm planning on starting a master's program in International Development at Columbia University soon," he continued. "But eventually I want to go back. Maybe to Africa. Maybe somewhere else." He popped a piece of unidentifiable meat into his mouth and smiled.

"So, what does your boyfriend think about you going?" he asked after he'd swallowed. I had no idea if he was being a recruiter trying to gauge if I would really end a relationship in order to go wherever the Peace Corps deemed me suitable, or if he was asking as a man, trying to gauge my availability.

What boyfriend? I wanted to say. *He and I are just killing time.* "Oh, he's very supportive of me going."

"Really?" John raised his eyebrows.

"I mean, it's not like I'm going to marry him or anything." The Oneonta Sweetheart and I had actually talked about marriage, but as much as we loved each other, it never felt exactly right.

"Well, that's good, because most relationships don't survive the two-year separation. Either that, or the volunteer doesn't last the two years."

Before The Oneonta Sweetheart, I had been infatuated with a series of ponytailed and ponchoed hitchhikers. Guys who'd spent months sleeping in hammocks in the Yucatán or who had just rolled in from India still smelling of cardamom and cloves. I took a long look at John and no matter how I squinted I just couldn't imagine him in an alpaca poncho with a braid down his back; I inhaled deeply and smelled nothing but soap and water.

"I'm sure it's not the case with you or anything," John continued. "But you'd be surprised at how many people go into the Peace Corps committed to spending two years, but after a few months they quit and the biggest reason is because they left someone back home."

"Yeah, that would be hard." But I wasn't thinking about The Oneonta Sweetheart.

"Tomorrow a bunch of RPCVs—that's returned Peace Corps volunteers," he explained, "will be getting together in the office. Why don't you come by if you're free? It'll give you a chance to hear about a lot of other people's experiences."

"I'll try to make it," I said, sounding casual. But in my mind I was already scanning the clothes I had brought with me, picking out what I would wear. I was still determined to strike the perfect balance between total adaptability and irresistible adorability.

It turned out not to matter what I wore the next day because I felt totally invisible among the group of RPCVs. They looked ordinary enough, except for a woman whose hennaed feet poked out from beneath the batik print she had expertly wrapped around her waist. She was every bit as white and ethnically bland as I was, yet she seemed so much more interesting. They all did, laughing and reminiscing about drinking warm Zairian beer and eating *fou-fou* with their hands. They told of run-ins with merchants, bedouins, and soothsayers in places like Timbuktu, Tierra del Fuego, and Zanzibar. John's face lit up when a blonde woman jangling her clunky wooden bracelets began a sentence with "When I was in Ouagadougou during the coup . . ." Oh, how I wanted to be a part of this worldly group, forever bonded by malaria dreams, gamma globulin shots, and wiping my butt with the pages of my Peace Corps–provided *Newsweek* magazine, and also able to convincingly wear exotic clothing.

I couldn't help but wonder if John was romantically interested or already involved with someone in the group. Surely, these people were more his type than someone who regularly drooled over the Banana Republic catalog. Maybe after three years in West Africa John had a thing for hennaed feet.

As the RPCV group was breaking up, John invited me to meet him after work for a tour of Covenant House, the shelter for homeless teens where he volunteered one night a week. *Oh, c'mon,* I thought. *Can this guy be for real?* Or maybe the real question was *Can this guy be single? Or straight?* And again, I wondered if the invite was an indication of his personal interest in me, or just another thing that a good recruiter does to impress a recruit. But I certainly was not going to pass up an opportunity to spend more time with John.

The reception he got from everyone at Covenant House—from the guard at the door, to the director, to the teens themselves—convinced me that John really was as nice as he seemed. But as we said good-bye, I still didn't know if he was single, straight, or the least bit interested in me. And even if he was single, straight, and interested, I had no idea if there could be any hope of a relationship between a recruiter as dedicated as he was and a recruit as seemingly dedicated as I'd made myself out to be. And John wasn't giving any hints.

Worse, he seemed about to send me on my way and I wasn't sure how many more excuses I could come up with to visit him at the recruiting office. Of course, there was always the chance that the medical office would tell me I needed to have my appendix removed. But I couldn't count on that.

Luckily, an angel whispered into my ear just then. *Touch the small of his back,* it said. And of course, you may wonder what the hell an angel was doing involving herself in such a base affair, when she ought to have been saving a child about to fall from a sixth-story window or a preoccupied pedestrian in danger of being flattened by a bus. But there is no other explanation for what occurred to me just then or for what I did.

"Well, thanks again for making time for me," I said, reaching out my right hand to shake John's. He took my hand, and, as we shook, I pulled him slightly toward me. I extended my left hand and, ever so gently, touched the small of his back.

"You know, Eve, I'm meeting a friend for drinks after work on Friday," he said. "Why don't you join us?" *Just as if he had thought of it all by himself.*

We met outside of his office after work on Friday and walked a few blocks to the bar. I was struck by the obvious fact that he was a good foot taller than me. Of course, I had noticed his height before. But now, as I struggled to keep pace with him while keeping up my end of a witty conversation, I wondered if size really did matter to men.

I feared that in the battle to win John's heart (which might or might not be up for grabs), I now had two strikes against me. One, I was not a member of the international jet set, as witnessed by the fact that I didn't look natural in a sarong, serape, or sari and wasn't keen on drinking warm beer, Zairian or otherwise. And two, he'd have to bend way down to kiss me, assuming that he did, indeed, ever want to kiss me, of which there had been depressingly few signs up to this point. Then again, there was the fact that I was slated to go away for two years and he was the guy trying to get me to go. But if I figured that into the equation, I'd have three strikes against me. And though I have never been a sports fan, I definitely still wanted to be in this game.

It was obvious before we even set foot inside the bar that the ongoing Times Square beautification project had yet to reach this particular joint. It took my eyes a few minutes to adjust to the musty darkness inside, and I wasn't sure I really wanted to see it all that clearly anyway. But John strode over the sticky floor to the nearly empty bar, pulled out and wiped off a stool for me, and greeted the bartender like he was an old friend.

"I don't recommend the mixed drinks here," John said in a low voice. "But the bottled beer is safe." I had yet to be in a place where the bottled beer wasn't safe, but figured that was just another of my lacking Third-World experiences.

"I'll have whatever you're having," I said with a shrug.

"Well, here's to you," John said, handing me a beer. "And here's to the Peace Corps."

John's friend, Andy, joined us a few minutes later, and the two men hugged each other warmly.

"Andy, this is Eve," John said.

"So, going into the Peace Corps?" Andy extended his hand. *He knows about me! Does he know about me because John called him to say, "I'm bringing this wonderful woman to join us for drinks tomorrow?" Or does he know about me because John brings all his recruits here to toast their impending departures?*

"I remember when this guy was on the big sleep," Andy said, patting John on the shoulder. "That's what we called John's three years in Africa."

"You've known John since before he went into the Peace Corps?" I asked.

"Oh, Johnny-boy and I go way back to our freshman year at UMASS," Andy said. I found myself hoping that John would need to go to the john, so that I could pump Andy for information. But several beers later, all I knew was that John and Andy were best friends, had had some wild times in college, and that John seemed to have an iron bladder.

Andy looked at his watch and announced, "I've got to go meet my girlfriend."

"Oh, you have a girlfriend?" I asked, sensing an opening. *Does John???* I tried to ask telepathically.

"A fiancée, really," Andy added. I thought it was a good sign for me that John's best friend was both heterosexual and capable of a committed relationship.

"Well, it was nice meeting you, Eve. You two have fun."

"Hey, would you like to go back to Brooklyn with me for dinner?" John asked soon after Andy left. "I need to make a quick stop at my apartment before dinner, if you don't mind." *Now we are getting somewhere,* I thought as we took the subway to Brooklyn.

"Excuse me, I've just got to use the bathroom," John said as soon as we got to the third-floor brownstone apartment that he shared with two roommates. "I just hate public restrooms." So he didn't have an iron bladder after all, just a thing about using public bathrooms, which seemed a little odd since he obviously didn't mind using outhouses. But I was willing to overlook the toilet issue, since it had gotten me into his apartment. It was a nice three-bedroom apartment with lots of the original wood detailing and a fireplace in the living room. Clean enough that I could imagine spending time there, but not so neat, or so well decorated, that it said "gay man" or "resident girlfriend."

By the time we were sharing sushi and hot sake at a nearby Japanese restaurant, I was pretty sure we were on a date. Back at his apartment afterward, John leaned in close. "May I kiss you?" he asked. *I don't know what it says in the Peace Corps rulebook about that,* I thought, *but I was beginning to think you'd never ask.*

"Would you like to sleep under my African blanket?" John asked a few hours later.

"You bet I would," I purred. He led me to his bed, covered with a scratchy orange and black checkered blanket, and said he'd be fine on the couch.

"Wouldn't you like to come to bed with me?" I asked. I was hooked, and I thoroughly intended to hook him too. I don't care what your mama says: SEX, not food, is the surest way to a man's heart.

"Well, Eve, I kind of have a rule about sex. I only make love with someone I love."

Like it or not, you've got to respect that. So John tucked me under his African blanket, kissed me good night, and left the room.

Five minutes later, he was back.

"But I have the feeling I'm gonna love you soon," he said, crawling in next to me and covering us both with the African blanket.

When John went out the next morning to get breakfast, I looked through some of the photos on his dresser. There was John, looking exactly as he did now, amid a tuxedo-clad group of men at a wedding. They looked enough alike for me to assume this was John and his four brothers. They were all tall, handsome, and clean-shaven. Except for the slightly scruffy brother with the red beard. I panicked and wondered if I had slept with the wrong brother! But when John came back with coffee, bagels, and the *New York Times,* I forgot all about the red-bearded brother. After all, food—not SEX—was the surest way to my heart. Well, that and the fact that after breakfast he suggested we take a long ride on his motorcycle.

"Hey, let's go out to Staten Island. We can stop in at my mom's house," I suggested. In retrospect I can see that it would have been saner to suggest walking barefoot through downtown Brooklyn. But clearly, my better judgment was clouded, and besides, the round trip to my mom's meant nearly two whole hours snuggled behind John on his motorcycle. And I couldn't think of anyone else to visit on Staten Island.

"So," my mom said within five minutes of meeting my newly beloved, "are you *shtupping* my daughter?" I, of course, hadn't met John's Irish Catholic parents, but I sincerely doubted that they would ask me—in any language—if I was screwing their son. It is the type of thing my mother would, and did, do. But I had to give her some credit for at least being tactful enough to say it in Yiddish. John, who no doubt did not speak Yiddish, just smiled politely and nodded.

"Excuse us for a moment." I grabbed my mother and dragged her into the bedroom. "Be nice," I hissed. "I'm crazy about this guy."

"He's nice," she said. "Too nice. I don't trust him."

It belatedly dawned on me that it was way too early for John to meet my mom (especially if I had any hopes of marrying him). We declined my mom's invitation to stay for dinner. Back in Brooklyn, we held hands and strolled around Park Slope. We had dinner in a Mexican restaurant and spent the rest of the night—together—under John's African blanket.

I didn't hesitate the next day when John offered to take me on his motorcycle to get my car, which I'd left at my dad's house. My dad had always been as restrained as my mom was expressive, possibly explaining their divorce ten years earlier. So I didn't think he'd ask any embarrassing questions. Besides, how could I possibly turn down another chance to snuggle behind John on his motorcycle?

On the Long Island Expressway, a car slowed down beside us, the passenger pointing frantically behind us. I looked back and saw stuff—my stuff—strewn like confetti on the highway. My bag, which had been bungeed onto the rack at the back of the bike, had come undone.

John pulled off onto the side of the road and we walked back, picking up the bits of my life. We found everything—wallet, license, credit card, keys—everything except the picture I carried of The Oneonta Sweetheart. I thought this might be tremendously significant, as I was already thinking about whether or not to hyphenate my name when John and I got married.

We got back to the motorcycle and saw that our helmets were missing and that a car was pulling away. It had never occurred to John, still fresh from Africa, or me, living in sleepy Oneonta, that someone might actually pull over on the Long Island Expressway and steal the helmets off of our motorcycle. It is illegal, not to mention suicidal, to ride a motorcycle without a helmet in New York. While we might have been high on pheromones, we weren't scofflaws, so we found a pay phone, called the police, and then waited for them to come and lend us riot helmets for the ride home.

"You know," John said, "one day we'll tell our grandchildren about this."

My mind reviewed all the extraordinary signposts of our budding relationship: the intense connection at our interview, the glorious weekend, the lost picture, and now the mention of our grandchildren. Did John, too, sense that we were meant to be? Or did he simply mean that this story was so unbelievable that one day he'd tell his grandchildren about it and I'd tell mine?

Answering machine, beep:

Hi, Mom. You said that John was either gay or too good to be true. Well, he is definitely not gay. Now all I've got to do to convince him that I'm the woman of his dreams is to go off and live in a Third-World jungle for two years without him! That shouldn't be too hard, right?

Chapter Three

I Love You, You're Perfect, Now Leave

I may have been headstrong and starry-eyed, but I wasn't a two-timer, so I broke up with The Oneonta Sweetheart as soon as I got home.

"I'm sorry," I said. "But I think I've met the man I'm going to marry."

"Oh?" he said, his huge blue eyes opened wide.

"It's my Peace Corps recruiter," I explained. We had both known a breakup was inevitable; it was just a matter of when.

"Well, what about you going into the Peace Corps?" he asked. "You've been talking about this for a long time."

"Oh, yeah. I'm still going into the Peace Corps," I said, hoping to sound more convinced than I actually was. "Of course, I'm still going."

Yeah, there was no doubt about it. I was going into the Peace Corps. Until John called.

"Hey, the weather is supposed to be beautiful this weekend. Why don't I ride my motorcycle up to Oneonta?"

With John in town, I avoided the hangouts where The Oneonta Sweetheart and I had been regulars. We had broken up but remained friends, and I didn't want to flaunt my new boyfriend in front of him. Also, half the people in Oneonta were mad at me for breaking up with the sweetest guy in town.

So John and I took long motorcycle rides out of town, and I

cooked him my favorite hearty vegetarian recipes, which he ate with abandon. While it was clear that we had moved into a romantic relationship, I still felt a bit like I was applying for something. Perfect Peace Corps material or perfect mate; I was determined to prove to John that I could be either. It seemed to be working.

"This is Eve," John said, introducing me to his entire family when he took me to Massachusetts for his grandparents' anniversary party that June. "She'll be leaving for the Peace Corps soon."

As kind and welcoming as they were, they must have been as quietly confused as I was. Only John seemed to think nothing of the fact that this woman he was now introducing to his entire family was supposed to be leaving soon for two years. We spent the weekend in the house where John and his brothers had grown up. The walls of the comfortable three-story house were covered with pictures of growing boys and family events.

"This is Stephen, the oldest," John said, pointing to a picture of a brother who looked amazingly like John. "And here's Tommy and Joey and Jimmy," he said, pointing out more photos. All of them had boyish good looks—not a murderer in the bunch, as my grandmother would say. But they looked enough alike that I really couldn't tell one brother from the other. And there it was again, even bigger—that wedding picture with the mysterious, red-bearded brother.

There would be no premarital *shtupping* in John's parents' house, and just to be sure, his mother escorted me to a guest room on the third floor, while John got settled in his old bedroom on the second. On the bureau were several framed photos, and my jaw dropped when I looked at one of them.

"What a nice picture," I stammered. I knew I was looking at the ruddy-bearded face of my future husband. "Which son is this?" I was almost afraid to ask.

"Why, that's John when he was in Burkina Faso," she said.

"Oh, then in the wedding picture downstairs. The one with all the boys in tuxedos? The one with the beard, is that John too?"

"Yeah, he looks just like Stephen now that he's clean-shaven, doesn't he? But that was John when he'd just gotten back from Africa. I think he looks much better without the beard, don't you?" Far be it from me to argue with my future mother-in-law, so I just smiled. In fact, I smiled through the rest of the weekend and returned to Oneonta on Monday ready to give up everything to be with John.

"I'll be going into the Peace Corps," I told my boss when the school year and my teaching job ended a few weeks later. Then I moved down to New York City.

I hadn't received my invitation yet. But the medical office had cleared me—my wisdom teeth and appendix intact—and my application was now in the placement office. This meant that as soon as there was an opening for someone with my skills, the Peace Corps would send me an invitation. It could take a few months for the invitation to come through, and once I got it I'd have two months to prepare. And until I left, I wanted to spend every minute I could with John.

John hadn't exactly invited me to move in with him in Brooklyn. So I moved into my mother's guest room on Staten Island. I got a job running a YMCA day camp in downtown Manhattan and split my nights between my mom's apartment and John's. I loved being back in the city and loved the challenge and bustle of my new job. And every day I fell more in love with John. I wondered if somehow we could forget about the whole Peace Corps thing and just go on this way forever. *Maybe if I just don't bring it up,* I thought.

For a few blissful months it was easy to ignore the topic because my paperwork was stuck in the Peace Corps placement office and it seemed like it might stay there forever. I still hadn't heard anything from them by the time summer ended, so I took a job coordinating volunteers in Central Park. It was late in the fall by the time I got my big, fat manila envelope from the Peace Corps inviting me to Ecuador. By then, John and I had been together for seven months and I wasn't nearly as interested in spending two years sleeping alone under a mosquito net as I was in spending the rest of my life sleeping with John under his African blanket.

But I was too far in to back out now. John had proclaimed me perfect Peace Corps material and given me a coveted "outstanding" rating, which he'd only ever given to one other recruit. And while it was obvious that he loved me, I wasn't sure how much of that was *because* I was such outstanding Peace Corps volunteer material. A big part of what he loved, I was convinced, was the bold, adventurous woman—boobs and head held high in safari chic—that he had met at our interview.

"I will not be the person who stands in the way of your dream," he told me anytime I tried to hint that maybe I shouldn't go. Of course, I didn't have the nerve to tell him that my dream now was that he'd actually beg me to stay. More than anything, I wanted to stay with him. But if I didn't go, I wasn't sure that he'd even want me around.

"Eve, if we were meant to be together, then it will all work out," he'd say when I asked how, exactly, our relationship was going to work once I left.

"Well, does that mean you are going to wait for me? Not see anyone else while I'm away?" I knew I was breaking a cardinal rule of dating: Never push a guy into a commitment. But I just couldn't help myself.

"I can't promise you anything other than if it was meant to be, it will work out." I didn't have John's damn optimistic faith. I didn't believe it was going to work out if I left for two years. But I couldn't see how it was going to work out if I didn't go. I was caught between the proverbial rock and hard place.

So I made all my final preparations in a quiet state of dread. I tried to appear excited as I went shopping for my appropriately rugged sleeping bag, my Peace Corps–recommended duffel bag, and my sensible shoes. But all the while I was feeling like a virgin about to be sacrificed to the volcano gods. I tried to be perky and upbeat whenever I talked about my impending departure, but it was difficult to speak on account of the boulder-sized lump in my throat. It was hard work hiding how I really felt. Only when I was alone at my mom's apartment would I allow myself to cry out loud. But there were a few nights, after we'd made love and John was fast asleep, when I'd lie curled against him and cry ever so quietly, swallowing the enormous, pent-up sobs that rattled my entire body.

"Hiccups," I told him one night when I accidentally woke him.

There really seemed to be no way out. It wasn't just John I was afraid of disappointing. My mother had been crowing to anyone within earshot about how proud she was of her daughter who was going off to "save the world." Then she threw me a going-away party. A going-away party in a rented hall, packed with people and balloons and food and drink. A going-away party with a cake that had my face superimposed on the Peace Corps logo, and balloons that read "The toughest job you'll ever love, meet the best recruit you'll ever have." It was the kind of going-away party that makes one obligated to, well, go away.

Friends and family came to the party and brought me gifts. Thoughtful, appropriate gifts, like a black Swiss Army knife, because every other volunteer was going to have a red one, and a travel alarm clock that showed the time in two time zones. There were bandanas, inflatable water bottles, and Imodium pills. Clearly, I had no choice but to leave the country.

My brother's band played at the party, and for the last set they sang a pair of songs by the Mamas and the Papas. With an angelic voice like Natalie Merchant, but with better diction, the lead singer sang, "Just hold me tight and tell me you'll miss me, While I'm alone and blue as can be . . ." And the tears began flowing. Just a few drops at first, which is probably exactly how it is when they first start the Chinese water torture. Sure, you think, I can take this. I smiled wanly, and she went on to the next song in her sweet and lethal voice: "While I'm far away from you my baby . . . Whisper a little prayer for me my baby . . ." And I lost the last shreds of whatever bravado were holding me together.

Right then and there, amidst the cake, the balloons, and all my guests, the floodgates opened. John scooped me into his arms and did his best to comfort me, while I prayed fervently that he would end my suffering by admitting that he couldn't live without me. But for a smart guy, he was proving pretty slow on the uptake. Either that or he was dead serious about the Peace Corps recruiters' version of the Hippocratic oath, which I imagine went something like "I vow to reel them in and send them away." Or maybe there was a prohibition against recruiters falling in love with their recruits and begging them to stay. At least that's what I hoped, because it was either that or I was in this head-over-heels love affair by myself.

He held me tight. "Ecuador's not that far. Next summer, I'll come visit you" was all he said.

Two days later, on a dreary February morning in 1988, I got on a plane. "I'm going into the Peace Corps," I sobbed to my bewildered-looking seatmate. Dizzy, dehydrated, and hyperventilating, I looked more like a dishrag than an eager recruit for the cause of world peace.

"You don't seem all that happy about it," my seatmate observed.

When I finally stopped crying, I was somewhere over Florida. I started thinking about how I could get home. How long would I actually have to stay, I wondered, to convince myself—and most importantly, John—that I had given it a good try? I'd heard you could get out of the army by shooting yourself in the foot. That seemed drastic, and I already had a hard enough time keeping up with John's long-legged strides with two good feet. Besides, I was pretty sure they weren't going to give us guns in the Peace Corps.

Our first stop on the way to Ecuador was a three-day "staging" in the Little Havana section of Miami. And although we hadn't even left the country yet, it was amazingly like we were already in the Third World. The Peace Corps managed to put us up in a part of Florida where no one spoke a word of English. The purpose of staging is to introduce you to the three-dozen or so other equally stunned folks with whom you will be sharing the next two years of your life. It's also one last chance, I suppose, to turn back before it's too late.

Possibly to get the really squeamish folks to say "uncle," staging is also when you have to get vaccinated against anything and everything you might encounter in your country of service. I had worried just a bit about getting sick in Ecuador, but clearly not enough. On day one of our staging, each of us was flanked by a pair of nurses, each one armed with an arsenal of multiheaded inoculating guns and needles. The nurses jabbed us in both arms simultaneously, injecting us with as much protection as they could get against the illnesses, plagues, and parasites that apparently roam the streets of Ecuador in search of foreign *touristas* and other expatriate hosts. When the nurses finished with us that day, they promised to reload and return the next day.

The next morning we were lined up and ushered one by one into a little room and told to drop our pants. It was time for the dreaded gamma globulin shots that we would each receive every three months for the rest of our Peace Corps service. If ever someone was teetering about whether or not to quit the Peace Corps, what feels like a burning drill bit burrowing into their butt would push them over the edge—and it did too; three or four recruits dropped out on the spot. I can't imagine that the hepatitis these shots were supposed to protect us from was all that much worse.

Those of us who survived the shooting gallery were initiated into another facet of Peace Corps life: using our rudimentary Spanish skills to find vast quantities of alcohol. By day two, staging had turned into a giant booze fest. This, as it turned out, was an apt introduction to Peace Corps life. Social butterfly that I am, I dove right in, and things began to look up.

After three days in Little Havana, the whole group boarded a plane for Ecuador. All my earliest memories of Ecuador are slightly blurry and out of focus. That could be because I had been crying so much. But it also could be because, like much of the group, I arrived in Quito very hungover. But hungover or hyperventilating, it didn't matter. We all stepped out of the airport and stared, slack-jawed, as if we had just stepped into a postcard. There they were, the Andes Mountains looming unbelievably huge and majestic over absolutely everything.

As the Peace Corps chartered bus descended into Quito, those mountains engulfed us. Exquisite white-capped peak after peak after peak, all haloed in cushions of clouds, burst out of the watercolor sky like in a children's pop-up book. Our bus took twists and turns past tiny mountain villages, gated suburban estates, dirty slums, and finally into the bustling heart of Ecuador's capital city. And the mountains were the breathtaking backdrop to all of it.

I caught my breath and started crying again. It was clear I wasn't in Kansas, I mean New York City, anymore.

Dear Mom,

Well, so far the Peace Corps is a bit like summer camp, and just like when I went to summer camp, I've spent most of the first week here crying. I have no idea how I am going to survive two years without John.

My fellow trainees are a hoot, though. We are "Omnibus 56" in Peace Corps lingo, but we call ourselves "The Misters," because all the kids on the street yell at us, "Hey, mister, give me something!" The forty of us are a lively group, having already found ourselves in hot water, for being found, literally, in hot water, uninvited in the ambassador's hot tub. In a few days we'll be going down to the training center and then we'll each go live with our host family. My guess is that they're hoping to housebreak us!

Be sure to save all my letters. I'm going to want to remember this.

I'll keep you posted,
Eve

Chapter Four

How a Tampon Made a
Peace Corps Volunteer out of Me

No matter where in the world they serve, all Peace Corps recruits go through three months of training before being sworn in as volunteers. This provides volunteers with the language, cultural, and technical skills they will need once they get to their work site. Our training was held in Tumbaco, a small town outside of Quito. During training, the forty of us in "The Misters" were parceled out to host families who were responsible for our care, feeding, and Spanish-language immersion.

"Do you like sports in general and basketball in particular?" asked the Peace Corps staff person who matched trainees with host families.

"No on both counts," I told her. *Although the boyfriend I left behind is a big sports fan,* I might have added, but I was afraid to even talk about John for fear that the floodgates would open again.

"Well, that's too bad because for the next three months you're going to be living with a family of sports lovers, whose two teenage daughters play basketball." *Splendid,* I thought. *This just keeps getting better all the time!*

It was a bit awkward when my host family came to collect me from the training center. The sum total of my Spanish at that point consisted of what I had gleaned from riding the New York City subway system. No matter how I tried, I just couldn't seem to work *No se apoyo contra la puerta* (Don't lean on the door) or *No salga sin protecíon* (Don't leave home without a condom) into any of our conversations.

Our first exchange was conducted in sign language and theatrics. I'm pretty sure they asked if I played basketball, to which I answered an incredulous "No!" When they asked me why not, I pointed to my five-foot-tall frame and tried to pantomime that I'm too short to play basketball. This seemed to surprise them. It was only then that I noticed that nearly everyone around me hovered comfortingly right around my height. I realized with joy that I had been assigned to a country of short people!

My new family walked me home, the five of them carrying all my belongings. My father hoisted my duffel bag, my mother slung my backpack over her shoulder, the fifteen-year-old grabbed my daypack, her twelve-year-old sister daintily carried my fanny pack as if it were a purse, and having nothing left, I handed over my hat to the five-year-old boy. They chattered at me like incomprehensible birds as they led the way. I nodded politely, and squelched the urge to warn them not to leave home without a condom. Their house was conveniently located just off the town square, a short walk from the training center. The girls grabbed my hands as soon as we walked in the door and led me through the house out into an enclosed courtyard and back into a second part of the house that consisted of two adjoining bedrooms. They put my things down on the single bed in the smaller of the two bedrooms and then plopped themselves down on the double bed in the larger room, chirping away the whole time.

"*¿Mi casa?*" I said, grasping the concept although not knowing the word for room.

"*¡Sí, sí!*" they shouted gleefully, as the rest of the family joined us and piled all my belongings on my bed. My mother opened a small wardrobe and several empty drawers, chattering all the while. I understood that this was where I was to put my things. Then the family led me back to the courtyard.

"*¡La lavandaria!*" Mama exclaimed as she walked over to an imposing cement basin with a water spigot coming out of the top that seemed to be the centerpiece of the courtyard. I looked around nervously at the walkway and open doorways that surrounded us. Sensing that I wasn't quite getting the picture, my two new sisters walked over and began scrubbing imaginary clothing against the corrugated bottom. The children's song "This is the way we wash the clothes, wash the clothes, wash the clothes" began playing in my head. *All right,* I thought. It was definitely not the way I washed the clothes, but I was relieved to understand that this was not where I was meant to bathe.

The father pointed to a small room off the walkway opposite the *lavandaria* and said, "*El baño,*" a word I immediately grasped, as I'd always believed in the importance of knowing how to say both "beer" and "bathroom," in every language. I was greatly pleased to see that the *baño* had a sit-down flush toilet and a shower. Our trainers had prepared us for the possibility that we could live in homes that had neither. Clearly, I had hit the bathroom jackpot.

Father pulled aside the flimsy curtain that was the only thing that separated the bathing space from the rest of the bathroom. He pointed to a small box with Frankenstein-looking lights and switches that was attached to the showerhead with exposed wires. "*Agua caliente,*" he proudly proclaimed, which I immediately translated as "death trap" and vowed to take only cold showers from here on in.

The family walked me through the rest of the modest but comfortable house. The small kitchen was jammed with a refrigerator, stove, sink, counter, and plenty of pots, pans, and cooking implements. Just off the kitchen was a dining area with a large table and family pictures adorning the walls. Across from the kitchen was a cramped bedroom that the parents shared with their young son. Our tour ended at the front of the house in a room lined with overstuffed chairs and a couch, and a fancy shelving unit that showed off all the family knick-knacks. All the seats faced what was obviously the main feature of the room.

"*La televisión,*" the five-year-old said as if he were unveiling the grand prize on a game show.

As sweet as my family was, that first weekend with them were the longest and loneliest days of my life. I had no one to speak to in English and my subway Spanish proved to be of no use whatsoever. With no real ability to communicate, I had a lot of time to think about how much I missed John and to question the sanity of sticking out two years in this self-imposed exile. Just as unappealing, however, was the prospect of quitting and going home to face a disappointed John.

Upon returning to the training center on Monday, I learned however, that I had fared better than several of my fellow trainees. Aside from the ones who would be sharing bedrooms and living without indoor plumbing for the next three months, some had fallen victim to hospitality hell. Host families were warned about our potentially tender tummies and instructed to boil our drinking water and go easy on the lard and oil, which seemed to be a staple ingredient in many Ecuadorian dishes. We trainees, in turn, were warned not to waste food and to try to graciously eat whatever was put in front of us. My family, having hosted a trainee before, was highly conscious of my American stomach. My mother served me mercifully small portions of usually delicious or at least recognizable food, never pressuring me to eat more than I could handle. But other trainees were forced to dig right in to huge servings of traditional Ecuadorian fare, featuring things like guinea pig heads and cow hooves.

Privacy is not a popular concept in Ecuador. That became obvious a few weeks later, when I returned from training to find that my two sisters had gone through my drawers and were now arguing over what my tampons were for. The older one asked, hopefully, if these were the miraculous things that she had heard about that let American women have sex but not have babies. *No, that's birth control,* I thought. *Which here consists of sharing your bedroom with a five-year-old.* The younger girl was determined to prove her sister wrong by shoving one up her nose to demonstrate that they were used to stop nosebleeds.

I thanked God that they had not unearthed my diaphragm and did my best to explain, in faltering Spanish, what tampons were actually for. When they refused to believe that my tiny little o.b.'s could really perform such a function, I took them outside to the *lavandaria* and demonstrated by stopping the flow of water from an inverted bottle of Fanta. I could see the lightbulb flash of enlightenment in the girls' eyes. I had used ingenuity and the tools at hand to bring knowledge to those without access to modern-day feminine care products! Okay, it wasn't exactly lifesaving technology or a giant step toward world peace, but I truly felt like a Peace Corps Volunteer.

It quickly became apparent that Ecuadorians equate being alone with being lonely. The members of my host family did their best to *acompañarme* at all times. My sisters spent most evenings in my room, the three of us doing our homework side-by-side on my bed, munching on salty *choclo*—a tasteless but strangely addictive toasted corn snack. Various cousins, grandparents, and in-laws were called in to *acompañarme* when the members of my immediate family were otherwise engaged. With all this togetherness, it didn't take long for my family to figure out that I was not totally thrilled to be there. My host mother brewed great batches of "grief tea," and despite our language barrier she pretty quickly parsed out the cause of my sadness.

"*¿Usted lo ama?* (You love him?)" she asked.

"*¡Lo amo mucho!*" I confessed.

As soon as I arrived in Ecuador, I gave up any pretense of being a vegetarian. Within a few weeks I was happily eating guinea pigs, chicken feet, and whatever else was put in front of me. Now our dinner conversations often included discussions of when *Juan* was coming to get me and what *mi mama* would serve when he arrived. I voted for her delicious corn tamale *humitas,* with a roasted *cuy*—guinea pig—on the side. I didn't actually think John was coming, but it was fun to play along. I couldn't let on to the Peace Corps training staff that I was in love with my recruiter, fearing it might have negative consequences for both of us. But it was a relief to be able to take off the brave, happy mask at home with my family.

"¡Eva, Eva, Juan llamó por el teléfono!" The entire family greeted me when I returned from a day of classes at the training center.

John called? I thought. *Impossible.* Not anticipating that I'd even have access to a telephone, we had planned to keep in touch only through letters. Remembering that his host family in Burkina Faso had slept on mud floors, I had only recently fessed up to the fact that my family had beds and electricity. I didn't want John to think that my Peace Corps experience was any less Third World than his, so I hadn't told him that my family also had a telephone. I knew he wouldn't call me anyway, because he wanted me to focus on the Peace Corps experience and not be distracted by him.

But some English-speaking man had called from America. He spoke no Spanish and my family spoke no English. Still, they were sure that it was John calling to tell me of his plans to rescue me. My mother pointed out the fattest guinea pig in the pen that all Ecuadorians kept outside the kitchen. "That's the one I'll cook for Juan!" she announced proudly.

Although I knew better, even I got caught up in my family's fantasy that it was John who had called. That he would call back to proclaim that he just couldn't live without me and that I should come home. So when the reporter from my hometown newspaper called back that night to get a few quotes for a story he was writing about me, I was devastated all over again. Of course, John missed me, he told me that in every letter he wrote. But he was also sure that I was doing the right thing by being in the Peace Corps.

During the three months I lived with my host family, I literally had to climb the roof in order to be alone. Only the wealthiest people in Ecuador lived in completely finished houses. My family's house, like most in Tumbaco, sported the beginnings of a second floor waiting to be finished when money allowed. Hiding among the bare cinder blocks and exposed rebar I could finally be by myself. I would escape up there to try to gather my thoughts and make sense of the new sensations that threatened to overwhelm me. It was from up there that I saw women bent over huge basins washing their clothes and their children; clothing draped over bushes like an odd, mismatched harvest, drying in the equatorial sun; half-naked children mingling with dogs and chickens in the dirt roads.

How different it all was from the life of push-button ease and antiseptic technology that I had left behind. It struck me then, for the first time, that life in America was the aberration. The life that played out below me—barefoot and soily, among animals, in a forced intimacy with the earth—this was how most of the people on this planet lived. With its stark existence and uncomfortable realities, this was the world that I was going to have to learn to be at home in if I wanted to survive the Peace Corps. I wasn't even sure I could do that. And since this was the world that John longed to return to someday, I wondered if this would be the life that I'd be signing up for if I stayed with him.

Our three-month training was designed to teach us Spanish, technical skills, and make us more or less self-sufficient once we got dispatched to our volunteer sites. So in addition to our classes, we trainees were put in charge of a barn full of baby chicks, guinea pigs, and a rather sickly cow. I enjoyed helping to raise the chicks and guinea pigs. But later on, when it was time to eat them, I was appalled to learn that I was expected to help butcher them.

"I'm going to be an Urban Youth Worker," I emphasized. "Urban. That means I'll be near a supermarket, right?" Thankfully, there were enough 4-H types among The Misters to do the killing for all of us. Although I'm still not convinced that grasping it by the neck and swinging it around lasso style is the recommended method of butchering a chicken.

The cow wasn't meant for eating, and the animal husbandry trainees tried desperately to nurse it back to health. One morning my Spanish teacher asked me to tell her, using the passive voice, what I had noticed on my way to class. *"Le vaca ha sido enterrado* (The cow has been buried)," I told her, causing her to burst into tears. While the cow hadn't improved, my Spanish apparently had.

Like many developing nations in the 1980s, Ecuador was experiencing a large urbanization of its population. People were leaving the villages and moving to the cities in search of a better life. An increase in the numbers of children living on the streets always came along with an increase in urbanization. Some of these kids were runaways, others had parents who could no longer afford to feed them. Some of these kids stole, begged, or shined shoes to get by. Many of them sniffed glue out of paper bags for the temporary relief it offered from hunger and misery.

The Ecuadorian government had few resources to address this problem, and three *gringitas* with liberal arts degrees and experience as camp counselors weren't likely to be of much help. But Jean, Mary, and I—Peace Corps Ecuador's first Urban Youth volunteers—were gamely determined to be of use. The recruits who were going to work with rural youth dug latrines and planted gardens. The animal husbandry trainees learned to emasculate bulls. Meanwhile, the three of us in the Urban Youth program hung out with shoeshine boys on the streets of Quito and were reminded over and over again of the important difference between asking *¿Hay huevos?* (Do you have eggs?) and *¿Tienes huevos?* (Do you have testicles?). We didn't know what we'd be doing once we got to our sites, but it seemed that knowing how to behead chickens and curse like Spanish sailors was going to be crucial.

Midway through training, the three of us were sent to a mountain village to get a taste of Ecuadorian rural life. After a few days with no water or electricity and meals that consisted largely of salted fish and quinoa, we were anxious to return to "civilization." We decided not to wait for the next day's milk truck—the only way in or out of this remote village—and basically slid down the side of the mountain on our butts. Halfway down, as we were clinging to tree trunks for dear life, it became painfully apparent that, unless you were a billy goat, this was not a good way to get down from the Andes. But getting back up—and eating yet another meal of salted fish—seemed even less possible. At least we'd be able to find beer at the bottom, we convinced ourselves. If we survived.

With a combination of stupidity, gravity, and sheer luck, we made it back to Tumbaco. Jean limped to my house the next day. "Okay, this is definitely not the sort of thing I'd ask of someone back in the states," she said as she pulled me into my bedroom. "But you have got to do something about my ass!" She dropped her pants and showed me her blister-covered bottom. I pulled out my Peace Corps–issued medical kit and—using antibiotic ointment and Band-Aids—cemented our friendship forever.

I loved training and didn't want it to end. When it did, I knew that I would have to fly on my own—in a strange world, in a foreign language, without a safety net, and without John. But three months after my queasy arrival in Quito, I was a newly minted Peace Corps volunteer. My knees quaked as I got off the bus in my new home: Santo Domingo de los Colorados, a town that the veteran Peace Corps volunteers referred to as "the Armpit of Ecuador." Situated right where the Andes slope down to meet the coastal plain, Santo Domingo, named for the colorful Colorado Indians who lived there, was the third-largest city in Ecuador. We would see the Colorados in the market, their hair greased into bowl shapes on their heads and painted with red *achiote,* the coloring that most Ecuadorians put on their food. Both the men and the women wore skirts and ringed their naked torsos in black paint. The women also wore bras—but not blouses—when the Mormons came to town and told them not to go bare-breasted. The Colorados were the most interesting part of what was, essentially, a dull and ugly town.

Ecuador is one of the most ecologically varied and beautiful countries in the world. Within its relatively compact borders are the majestically snowcapped Andes Mountains, lush and tropical Amazon jungle, still-unspoiled beaches, the pristine Galápagos Islands, and nearly every imaginable ecosystem that exists. Somehow, I managed to get sent to the bus station between it all.

Anyone traveling by road up into the mountains or down to the beaches passed through Santo Domingo. All buses stopped there to refuel and exchange passengers and were immediately inundated by

hawkers, arms flailing and goods thrust in through every open window. There were women offering bananas in a dozen variations: fried,
baked, sweet, and with slabs of salty cheese; girls selling tasteless *allul-
las,* which as far as I could tell were rocks disguised as some sort of
bread; boys selling everything from chewing gum to razors. Like
crumbs in the tropics, any bus that stopped there was soon covered
with an army of human ants. The fact that all roads converged there
seemed to be Santo Domingo's entire raison d'être. The city started at
the bus station, then spread like a fungus up to El Centro, the circu-
lar town common that boasted not much more than a statue of a Colorado Indian stuck in the center. From there it spilled onto a huge
stone and dirt walkway that ran the entire length of the city. The
pedestrian mall bustled day and night with commerce: women hawking food, clothes, and household goods down the center; men and entire families running the chockablock shops on either side. Here you
could find cheap clothes made in China and wool sweaters woven in
the sierras, fresh fruits and vegetables, tins of imported sardines and
the cheap aluminum pots to cook them in. Somewhere in that may-
hem was anything you could ever need. The trick, of course, was finding it.

Within a block or two of El Centro you could get almost any
food, from pizza and hamburger to the traditional meals that you ordered by asking for *almuerzo* (lunch) or *merienda* (supper) and then
got whatever they were serving. Because the town had seen its fair
share of foreigners over the years, most notably a huge influx of Mor-
mon missionaries, Santo Domingo even had an ice-cream parlor. But
the entire town had only one hotel and it was questionable, which I
thought was an indication of the fact that visitors didn't tend to stick
around long. To get to Santo Domingo you left behind the beautiful
Andean vistas, and though you could smell the salt in the air, you were
nowhere near the ocean. Boasting neither natural nor cultural attrac-
tions, the bus station and the market basically were the high points of
town. I was never sure how or why a city sprung up there. I figured

someone just got off a bus and started selling stuff and soon thousands of people followed suit.

Like most of the other volunteers in Ecuador, I had hoped for a placement in the pure, exotic air of the sierras, as the Andes Mountains were known locally, or on *la costa*, Ecuador's many miles of coastline. I was sure I'd look cool in a woolen poncho riding my horse up to some remote mountaintop village. Or I could learn to slow down to beach speed, take afternoon siestas in my hammock, lulled by the ocean waves. Instead I got the buggy, muddy, hot swamp in the middle. I was sorely disappointed. But like Charlie Brown's sad little Christmas tree, I felt like Santo Domingo just might need me. And yet I had no idea if I was up to the task.

Dear John,

All of the The Misters got together last weekend. We've been at our sites for a month now and it seems like everyone is in a slump. Most of us haven't found work yet, and all of us would give anything for a cold beer and a warm shower (and not the other way around) for a change! I'm going to meet with the Padre from the local Catholic church who runs a shelter for homeless boys here in town. There must be something useful for me to do there. And now I'm the new volunteer representative on the Women in Development Committee. So hopefully that will keep me busy, too.

I'm the only one from my training group that got sent to the heart of the "armpit," although my friend, Donna, got sent to a village not too far from here and she comes here to get her mail. But there's a whole crew of PCVs here already. There's Jane, who's been here a year, and she's living with Carl, who's extending for his third year. Then there's Lisa and Bird, who both teach and live right in the center of town. And Keith, who was the newest volunteer in town until I got here.

So I'm not lonely, although I miss you tremendously. But I think I'm getting the hang of this. I guess I'm a lot tougher than I thought.

I'll keep you posted,
Eve

P.S. Please send toilet paper, Handi Wipes, and hair conditioner.

Chapter Five

In All of Its Third-World Glory

"You know the hardest thing about being a Peace Corps volunteer?" Jane asked when I washed up on her doorstep a few days after arriving in Santo Domingo.

"The constant diarrhea?" I asked.

"Oh, you'll get used to that," she assured me. "Either that or you'll just start eating all those bananas they sell on every street corner." Jane knew the ropes. "No, the hardest part of the Peace Corps is just finding a role for yourself. You get out to your site with some pretty lofty goals. And then you find out that what you thought you would do is not what the community wants you to do. Or that the agency where the Peace Corps sent you just wanted a token *gringo* and never had any work for you in the first place. Or you can't speak enough Spanish to be useful anyway. Be prepared. It can be really frustrating."

"I know, I know all about it. I have to be patient, not have any expectations, don't expect too much help from Peace Corps staff," I recited the good volunteer litany that John had drilled into my head. "And go out and look for my own opportunities."

"Ah," Jane looked at me admiringly. "You'll do well, little Evita. Your recruiter did a good job!"

"Yeah, my recruiter did a great job!" I wailed. "And now I can't live without him!" Jane laughed. I couldn't keep the charade up all through training and it was now common knowledge, at least among the volunteers, that I was the fool who had fallen in love with her recruiter.

When I arrived in Santo Domingo, I had been assigned to work with a strange woman in cat-eye glasses who claimed to run a home for orphans. For the three days I stayed at her house, she fed me nothing but bowls of sweet, milky coffee and the only orphans I saw were the two scabby ones who slept on the roof of her house and seemed to be her indentured servants. I excused myself one morning after coffee, took my bags, and made my way to Jane's house, which she shared with her boyfriend, Carl, a fellow volunteer. Peace Corps staff wasn't particularly thrilled about volunteers shacking up, but we were adults, after all, and there was not a lot they could do to stop it.

With Jane's help, I found a perfect apartment just a kilometer or two from the center of town. Which just goes to show that "perfect" is a highly subjective word. A moldy, second-floor walk-up with cold water and hot cockroaches would not exactly be considered perfect by most standards. But in Santo Domingo, the indoor plumbing and electricity made it a real find. The bathroom boasted a flush toilet and a shower. The kitchen had a sink with running water and a counter on which I could put the two-burner camping stove the Peace Corps supplied. The living room/dining area even had a little balcony that afforded me a view of the neighborhood. Sure, it wasn't much to look at, just a crisscross of dirt roads lined with one- and two-story cinder block houses, all sprouting the ever-hopeful rebar on the top. But the balcony gave me a place to hang my hammock.

"Don't worry," *los dueños,* or the landlords, said over me to Jane. We were the same age, but because of her better Spanish, they seemed to think she was my guardian. "She will be like our very own *hija.* We will always be right here." They pointed to their own ground-floor apartment, which one had to walk past to reach the outdoor staircase that led to my apartment. "We will take good care of her."

I bought a bed, a picnic table, some pots and pans, and a set of dishes with my Peace Corps–allocated moving-in allowance. The Peace Corps provided me with a mosquito net, a bicycle, and a small refrigerator. A volunteer on her way home left me a sewing machine and two colorful sling-back chairs. I hadn't made much progress in the Suzy Homemaker department, despite the fact that, days before I left for Ecuador, I had finally finished sewing the quilt that I had toted around in a picnic basket for a year. But I bought some cheap material in the market and made curtains for the windows and sheets for the bed. They weren't much to look at—especially up close—but who was looking, anyway? Whenever Jane, Lisa, Bird, or Keith came by it was usually for potluck meals, drinking warm beer, and venting. Carl, who was the most well-adjusted volunteer among us and never complained, made me a tiny barbecue grill for my balcony, and not being able to afford any meat, we cooked bananas on it.

It took a few weeks and most of my moving-in allowance, but I turned my simple, mold-infested apartment into a cozy nest in the jungle. For the first time in my life, I was living completely on my own—and liking it. While I still didn't have a day job, I was feeling somewhat useful. Jane let me tag along with her to the health clinic where she worked, and Lisa and Bird introduced me around the school where they taught. Some evenings we'd all cook together at Bird's apartment, hoping to be entertained by her pet parrot (for which she was nicknamed). But most nights I'd go home and entertain the endless stream of neighborhood kids whose parents sent them over to *acompañarme* anytime they thought I was alone.

We would bake chocolate chip cookies in a *campo* oven made with a huge pot on the stovetop, and read children's books or do craft projects with supplies that my mother sent. When I was finally alone, I'd sit at my picnic table, under a naked lightbulb, listening to the nightly broadcast of Voice of America on my shortwave radio, and writing letters home. I missed John like crazy. But no one was more surprised than I was that I was actually beginning to feel at home.

I might have been perfectly content to play with the neighborhood kids, hang in my hammock, and drink Peace Corps–subsidized beers for the next two years. But my Peace Corps program manager, an Ecuadorian woman named Mercedes, seemed to think that volunteers ought to be doing more than that. Hearing that things hadn't worked out for me and the cat-eye woman, Mercedes came down to Santo Domingo, determined to find me a suitable place to work.

Like a reluctant daughter meeting her mother's handpicked suitors, I trailed along as Mercedes made my introduction at every quasi social service agency and do-gooder organization in town. Mercedes, being originally from a well-established Santo Domingo family, commanded great respect from everyone. It also didn't hurt that one of her former volunteers was now married to the mayor of Santo Domingo. The mayor, or *alcalde,* was a surprisingly young and friendly guy, with a wooden leg and a soft spot for Peace Corps volunteers. But it was his wife who most impressed me. Here I was thinking I was getting a handle on expat life because I had finally made it through a week without mistakenly ordering the ubiquitous cow intestine *almuerzo*— yet again—while this *gringa* was fluently raising two bicultural children and serving as First Lady of Santo Domingo.

"Of course," she confided while we sat in her luxurious home in an upscale suburb far closer to Quito than Santo Domingo, "I only go back to the armpit these days when it is absolutely necessary."

With the help of Mercedes and her connections I soon found work in El Hogar del Niño Trabajador, a church-run shelter for homeless boys. Well, maybe "work" is not the most accurate word for what I did there. The young Colombian *hermano* who ran the day-to-day operations brought me through the two long bunk rooms and introduced me to the nearly two dozen boys in his charge.

"This is Señorita Eva, a volunteer from the United States." Like the troops being inspected, the boys, who ranged in age from five to fifteen, stood at the foot of their neatly made beds, intoned their names, shook my hand, and said *"Con mucho gusto."* The two haggard women who did all the housework seemed pleased to meet me, too, and I hoped they harbored no illusions about my helping with the laundry or the cooking.

For the first weeks I "worked" there, I didn't quite know what to do. I'd come in the morning and the boys would all be off at school.

I'd chat with the *hermano,* trying to get a sense of what he expected from me. "Maybe you could teach us English," he offered. I really didn't see how learning English was going to help these homeless boys, but we'd all gather in the dining pavilion when the boys came home from school and I'd teach them a few words in English. Eventually I moved on to teaching first aid and basic health courses. I used small grants from the Peace Corps to purchase a first aid kit for the shelter and toothbrushes and toothpaste for all the boys.

Mostly, I played games with the boys—inadvertently teaching them an odd version of baseball in which three strikes and the pitcher was out. That's what you get from learning baseball from a girl who knew nothing about sports. I wasn't very useful and didn't even feel I deserved the lunch that the ladies insisted I eat with them every day. But it gave me somewhere to be and a perch from which to look for that opportunity to do good that John was so fond of talking about. As I was beginning to settle into something that felt like the life of a Peace Corps volunteer, John wrote that he was coming for a visit.

"Will you be using some of your vacation time when your boyfriend is here?" Mercedes asked me when I told her the news during one of her visits.

"Well, actually, he's planning on staying until he starts graduate school in September. He'll be here for the whole summer."

"Just where exactly will he be staying?" she asked, surveying my one-bedroom apartment.

"Here," I said meekly.

"Oh, Eva, that is not a good idea. You have to think about your reputation." Mercedes was used to Americans, but she was still a middle-aged Ecuadorian woman at heart. "Why don't I ask Padre if he can arrange for a place for your boyfriend to stay in town?"

"That won't be necessary, Mercedes. He can stay here." She might have been my program manager, but I was a nearly twenty-five-year-old woman. And my boyfriend was not coming all the way from America to sleep with a priest!

"Well, if you are not using your leave time, you are going to have to work. This boyfriend of yours has to respect the rules of the Peace Corps."

"This boyfriend of mine was in the Peace Corps, Mercedes. For three years," I added, knowing that she'd understand that meant he'd been such an outstanding volunteer that his program manager had deemed him worthy of an extension. "He's the reason I'm here."

She looked at me for a moment. "Okay, but you must be very sensitive, Eva. Sleeping around will get you a reputation here, and that can get you into trouble." I thought of the woman across the road who had three children by three different men and the lady who did my laundry who was raising four kids on her own, neither of whom were treated any differently from any of the other overworked housewives I knew. But I suspected the whole reputation thing was tied up with being a *gringa*. And *gringas,* as anyone who watched American movies knew, were loose.

"Mercedes, I am not going to have any other men sleep over. John's the only one."

"Okay," she said. "If he's the only one and you are sure of it, then let me handle it."

A few days later I returned home to find that another program manager who was passing through Santo Domingo had left a bicycle with my *dueños.*

"It must be a mistake," I told them. "The Peace Corps already gave me a bicycle."

"Oh, this is one for your *esposo,*" they told me excitedly. "Why didn't you tell us your husband was coming?" And within days everyone in town was asking when my husband would be arriving from America. *Now this was a fantasy I could go along with.*

John's flight was scheduled to arrive in Guayaquil at four o'clock in the morning. Female volunteers were told not to travel alone at night, not to walk in unknown places alone at night, and not to check into motels alone at night. But I was a fool in love and determined to see John the moment he arrived, so I got on a bus in the afternoon for the eight-hour bus ride to Guayaquil. Arriving at the deserted

Guayaquil bus station close to midnight, I took a deep breath and reminded myself that this was no different than arriving at Penn Station, alone, late at night, not knowing a soul. Of course, I knew better than to arrive in Penn Station, alone, late at night, and not knowing a soul.

I did my best to look bigger and braver than I was and strode out to find a taxi and a cheap motel. Luckily, Ecuador's second-largest city turned out to be a smaller and steamier version of downtown New York City, with plenty of activity, even at night. It wasn't too hard to find a taxi with a driver who was eager to help a lone *gringita*. He took me to a decent and cheap motel and promised to come back to take me to the airport in a few hours. I repeatedly reminded the guy at the front desk to wake me at three. But between the excitement and my nervousness I hardly closed my eyes. All the awful things that were supposed to befall a woman alone in a fleabag motel in a strange city didn't happen. The front desk guy politely knocked on my door at three and the waiting taxi driver whisked me to the airport in plenty of time to see John's beaming face as he emerged from customs. I flung myself at him shamelessly and we kissed for a long time.

The sun was just rising as we made our way back to the city, and I got my first real view of Guayaquil, the coastal capital, in all of its decrepit, Third-World glory. Gleaming skyscrapers towering over cement hovels, slick fast-food joints next to smoky vending carts, horses and donkeys meandering between city buses, men carrying briefcases and women in high heels jostling barefoot *campesinos* hunched under heavy loads. With its warm, wet breath creeping down our necks, Guayaquil struck me as Santo Domingo on steroids. But walking hand-in-hand with John, I couldn't have cared less what was going on around me.

As soon as we got back to my site, John went to work. He found the hardware section that I had never noticed in the market and painted my apartment. He befriended the local carpenter and borrowed tools to build what must have been the only sofa bed in the entire country. He made friends with all the young men in the neighborhood and was asked to join their basketball team. Soon the same guys who had previously only leered at me on the street now politely came to the gate and asked for my husband. He charmed the *dueños* by offering his services and being up to any task that needed doing. In short, he proved himself to be a better Peace Corps volunteer than I was. And no one even seemed to notice that he spoke practically no Spanish at all.

Dear Jean,

First, let me ask you a few questions that only a fellow Volunteer could answer: If the rice you've stored in your kitchen begins hatching and you find little crawly things on your dinner plate, can you go ahead and eat them and consider it a legitimate source of protein? And does the aggressive white mold that keeps coming out of my living room wall count as a dependent and do you think the Peace Corps should increase my living allowance?

Well, here I am in my own little piece of the jungle—toiling away, sweating, scratching, and being eaten alive by my multitude of tiny (and not so tiny) housemates. When I was ten years old, I had an ant farm. Now, I live in one. But I'm so deliriously happy now that John's here that I hardly notice all that other bothersome stuff. I can't wait to bring him to Quito so you can meet him.

I'll keep you posted,
Evita

Chapter Six

❦

One Good Leg Between the Two of Us

In addition to all of his obvious charms, John also came with hidden ones—traveler's checks! He certainly hadn't gotten rich working as a Peace Corps recruiter, but he'd saved up a few hundred dollars before he quit to go to grad school, which converted to an awful lot of Ecuadorian sucres. After living on a meager "living allowance" for nearly six months, it felt like a small fortune. He wined and dined me at Santo Domingo's only fancy restaurant and took me to a low-budget island paradise, just a canoe ride off the Ecuadorian coast of Esmeraldas.

Muisne's island "resort" amounted to a row of wooden shacks on the beach. Not much larger than a cabana, ours was crammed with a double bed, a toilet, and a cold shower. But it had a rickety porch where we'd sit and watch the sunset and the fishermen. When they'd return with their catches in their dugout canoes, we'd amble down the beach to the only cantina on the island and, under palm frond umbrellas, eat shrimp and fish ceviche and fried plantain *chifles,* and wash it all down with tall, slightly cool Pilsners. We'd swim in the ocean, take rambling walks around the island, or just go back to bed until it was time for the next ceviche. We spent our evenings in the bar, or alternately, in bed.

On the third or fourth day of this lovely routine, we walked barefoot in the hot sun around the whole island. John had his pants rolled up, and his fair skin, from his shins to the tops of his feet, was burned to a bright red crisp. Hurrying back to the shack, we saw what looked like an inflated plastic bag, surrounded by long streaks of blue, splayed out on the beach.

"Must be a dead jellyfish," John said as we both stepped closer for a better look. Searing pain shot through my foot and intensified as it spread to my ankle and then to my entire leg. "Oh, shit! Oh fuck! Oh fuck, this hurts!" I looked down and realized that I had stepped on a tentacle.

"It's dead. How could a sting from a dead jellyfish hurt?" John asked.

"I don't fucking know," I screamed. "But I am in serious pain." John grabbed me around the waist and we hobbled back to the shack and took turns with the only remedy we could find for his third-degree sunburn and my poisonous pain: taking turns soaking our legs in a bucket of cold water.

By evening, we were both still in pain, but I had stopped writhing and no longer feared imminent death. We limped over to the cantina for the only other remedy we could think of: medicinal beer drinking. We asked a local fisherman for advice on treating jellyfish stings.

"You stepped on that big blue one that was on the beach today?" he asked. "You're not supposed to step on that! That's a Portuguese man-of-war," he informed us. "A warning to stay out of the water. Those things can kill you!" Well, at least I knew why it hurt so damn much.

The next day the tops of John's feet were covered with angry red blisters and my leg still pulsed with pain. But the quaint little island of Muisne had no pharmacy, no place to cash traveler's checks, and we were out of cash. We scraped up just enough sucres to pay for our canoe ride back to Esmeraldas. With only one good leg between us, we limped to a bank, cashed another one of John's checks, and caught the next bus to Santo Domingo.

Despite the less-than-romantic ending to our trip, the whole thing had felt—at least to me—like a sort of honeymoon. After all, everyone in Ecuador already thought we were married. And though there hadn't been a wedding—or even a proposal—I began to lull myself into the fantasy that our relationship had progressed to the next stage. So being jolted back to reality at the end of the summer was all the worse.

"What do you mean you're going home?" I whined when John started making plans for his return trip. "Why don't you just stay here with me?" I knew I was being irrational. John had school—and a life—to get back to. But who ever said love—or I—was rational?

"Eve, this is your Peace Corps experience. Not mine."

"Yeah, but you are so much better at it than I am. Remember the extension cord?" A few weeks earlier I had been reduced to tears in the middle of the market when, even with my nearly flawless Spanish, I couldn't get anyone to sell me an extension cord. John sent me home, sobbing, and returned an hour later, extension cord in hand.

"You'll get it. It takes time. You're doing fine."

"But I don't want you to go!" I knew I sounded like a pathetic six-year-old. But truer words were never spoken.

"I have to start school next month. And I told you when I came that I could only stay for the summer."

What followed was a two-week rerun of the conversations we'd had before I'd left for Ecuador. Me pushing shamelessly for a commitment John wasn't ready to make. John offering nothing but his annoying faith that if we were meant to be, it would all work out. He returned to the States at the end of August and I was devastated all over again. I threw myself into my work at the shelter, determined more than ever to become a model volunteer and find that elusive opportunity that would make this whole experience—the missing John, the diarrhea, and the mold that was threatening to take over my apartment—seem worthwhile. That opportunity came shortly after John left, in the voice of a homesick eight-year-old boy.

Dear John,

Well, you're back in New York by now. And I'm still here. Your basketball team misses you. The boys at el hogar all miss you. Even the dueños are asking for you (I think they need something fixed in their apartment). But no one misses you more than I do. Hey, the foldout couch you built me has been great. Jean came down from Quito and spent a few days. And Donna came in to town to get her mail last Friday and didn't leave until Monday.

The whole gang here sends their holas. They're all trying to keep me busy, to keep me from missing you. But I miss you.

I'll keep you posted,
Eve

Chapter Seven

Take Me Home

"I miss my family, Señorita Eva," Orlando said to me in between innings of their odd version of two-base baseball at the shelter. "Can you take me home?"

"Well, where is home?" I asked.

"En las sierras," he said. This wasn't a whole lot to go on since the Andes ran like a spine down much of the country.

"Well, how did you end up in Santo Domingo?" I asked.

"My village is not so far from Quito and my oldest brother went there and found work, and I thought I should do that too. But I couldn't find my brother in Quito and I just wanted to go home. But I got the wrong bus and I ended up here with no way to get home. But you can help me get home, Señorita Eva, can't you?"

I often had a reason to make the three-hour trip to Quito: to see Mercedes, or the nurse, get money, advice, or a gamma globulin shot, use the washer and dryer and hang out in the volunteers' lounge. So on my next trip to Quito, I took Orlando along.

Although I looked forward to getting to Quito, I hated the steep and twisting bus ride into the Andes. Training had filled our heads with stories of volunteers who had died in vehicles that had plunged down the mountains. I always chatted with the driver, inhaling like a sort of human Breathalyzer, before boarding a bus. But no one had, as yet, devised a quick test to assess if a driver had a death wish. Orlando and I took a seat up front, where at least I could keep an eye on the driver. I don't know why I thought being among the first to know that our driver was psychotic or asleep was a good idea, but it made me feel better.

As if the steep, curving roads weren't nauseating enough, bus drivers tended to make a sport of taking each narrow switchback as fast and as close to the edge as possible. Over the *cumbia* music that always blasted out of the radio we heard several cries of *"¡funda!"* from distraught passengers. With each cry, the driver would produce a paper bag from a stash that all the drivers carried, and in a drill that was familiar to most Ecuadorian bus travelers, the bag was frantically passed, hand over hand, until it reached its destination. This didn't always work, and more times than I care to remember, I got off the bus shaking other people's vomit from my shoes.

"Please, señorita, enjoy the view of our lovely countryside," an Ecuadorian gentleman had said on my last trip from Quito, offering to trade seats. I tried to convince him that I really didn't need to see the road dropping off beneath us as we were spiraling down from such dizzying heights. But he insisted that I trade my aisle seat for his window seat. I hated the view, but was grateful an hour or so later, when the kid sitting just on the other side of the aisle projectile-vomited all over the kind gentleman in my erstwhile seat.

Three vomit bags into this trip, we pulled into the main bus station in Quito. Rows and rows of buses were loading and unloading passengers. A jumble of people—businessmen in pressed suits, women in colorful Andean woven cloth with babies tied to their backs, ragged children begging for money—passed back and forth between the rows. The names of destinations were painted in bright colors across the tops of the fringed windshields. Orlando looked around, desperately trying to find the bus that would take him home.

"That one goes to Pichincha. And that one goes to Ibarra," I said, reading off the names labeled across the tops of the buses. "That one goes toward Mitad del Mundo. Is your house near the equator?" I asked, hoping that one of these names would sound familiar to Orlando. It was just dawning on me that following a lost eight-year-old around a foreign country might not have been the brightest thing I'd ever done.

"Otavalo . . . *sí*, that one," Orlando said, grabbing my hand and pulling me through the crowd to what he thought was the right bus. The bus wound its way out of the teeming city, past comfortable-looking suburbs and then into the rugged mountain landscape. Orlando's face was glued to the window the whole time. I nervously checked my watch and tried to figure out how I was going to get us back to Quito before dark if we got hopelessly lost. At least in Quito we could spend the night at Jean's apartment or in one of the cheap but clean hostels that the volunteers frequented.

"Look!" Orlando suddenly squealed. "It's the church with the broken roof! And there is the farm with the llamas! This is it, señorita!" Orlando pulled me out of my seat. "This is where we get off the bus!"

Once off the bus, we got a ride in the back of a pickup truck to the farm nearest Orlando's home. After the driver let us off, we walked for another half mile.

"My uncle lives down there," Orlando said, pointing down a muddy path. My confidence increased. "And here is the school where my oldest brother went," he said, sprinting down a dirt road and leaping over a low, moss-covered stone embankment. He bounded up two rickety stairs to a small, wooden house and came out a moment later wrapped in an ancient woman's embrace. Two small boys with smudged faces peered out from behind the old woman's skirt.

"*Mi abuela,*" Orlando sighed.

Orlando's grandmother welcomed us as if God had come down from heaven onto their land. Orlando's younger brothers, wearing muddy rubber boots and torn sweaters, practically vibrated with excitement. Abuela hugged Orlando and cried. She hugged me and cried as the brothers danced around all of us. She apologized as she fed us watery potato soup. It was nothing like the rich, cheesy *locro* that my host mother used to serve me. But it tasted delicious. The brothers stared in awe as I ate. Abuela stroked Orlando's face and my hands as the little boys rifled through my backpack.

"*Gracias, gracias, señorita,*" Abuela repeated over and over. When I got up to leave, she handed me a plastic bag full of small, dirty potatoes. "To thank you for bringing our boy back," she said. "I only wish we had more."

"*Gracias a usted,*" I intoned and hugged the bag of potatoes to my chest. Orlando and his family escorted me to the nearest farm and arranged a ride for me back to the bus station. On the bus ride back to Quito I gazed at the bag of potatoes on my lap and was elated. *Could this be what I do?* I wondered. *Could this be that opportunity that John talked about?* I had my answer when I returned to El Hogar del Niño Trabajador a few days later, and was greeted with a chorus of "Take me home, señorita! Take *me* home!"

The young *hermano* pulled me into his office. "Eva, can you take them home? Not all of them, of course. Some of them came from bad situations and really shouldn't go back to their families. But the ones who just got lost. Could you take them home? And the ones who want to visit their families, could you take them?"

So I became a social worker of sorts, digging into the boys' histories, trying to find out where they had come from and whether or not it was a good idea to try to reunite them with their families. I heard horror stories of abuse and dysfunction, angry stories of boys running away from home, and wrenching stories of parents who simply couldn't afford another mouth to feed. But the saddest stories came from the boys, one as young as five, who had simply gotten lost in a big, unfamiliar city that just didn't have the infrastructure or resources to reunite lost children with their transient parents.

I came away from these sessions with a broken heart and a list of boys who I thought I could help. Mercedes not only approved of the project, she offered to help me find overnight accommodations with her friends and family all over the country. The Peace Corps agreed to pay my bus fares and the church agreed to pay for the boys and thus

I became Peace Corps Ecuador's Peter Pan, traveling in the company of lost boys.

"I ran away from my home in Esmeraldas," nine-year-old Linder told me. "My mother is *muy, muy pobricita,*" he said, emphasizing the poor part. "So I came here to find work. But I would like to tell her that I'm okay."

"Hey, I know how to get to Esmeraldas," I said, remembering the lovely trip John and I had taken there over the summer. I had hardly noticed at the time, since I was too busy mooning at John, but now I recalled the clumps of glue-sniffing boys on the streets and the broken-down barrios we had passed on our way in and out of that city.

"And us too! We are from Esmeraldas too!" chimed a pair of recently arrived brothers when I announced that I would take Linder home next. "We ran away from home. But now we want to go back," the older one said, and the younger one nodded enthusiastically.

The four of us boarded a bus early one morning for the long trip to the coast. I had packed a change of clothes and my toiletries along with my standard Peace Corps survival kit. Eight months in the Peace Corps had taught me never to leave home without a bandana, which can be used as a tourniquet, sling, compress, washcloth, and most commonly as a shield against the noxious fumes of burning tires or teargas (I had already stumbled into several political protests); a book, because, no doubt, you will be stuck waiting somewhere for something; and a bottle of filtered water, because even if you're dying of thirst, you really don't want to drink the tap water. The boys each brought the toothbrush I had given them and nothing else.

"So, *mis hijos,* how do you feel about going to see your parents?" I asked once we were settled on the bus. I thought it would be helpful to get the boys to talk about their feelings. The three usually loud and rambunctious boys stared at me blankly. Perhaps my very American let's-just-talk-about-it approach wasn't going to work here. We rode on in silence.

We arrived in downtown Esmeraldas in the early afternoon and switched to a "monkey bus," open on all sides and splashed with brightly colored beach scenes and painted with slogans. Men and boys often climbed an attached ladder and rode on the top of the bus, nestled in with huge bunches of lashed plantains and bananas. Women never rode on top, from what I could tell. But when the boys climbed the ladder, I followed them, sensing this could be my only chance. The boys seemed to be having a great time, laughing and yelling as the muggy air slapped at their faces. I wedged myself between some bananas, held on to the tiny little handrail for dear life, and wondered why anyone would choose to do something so stupid.

We rode out of the city this way for what seemed like a very long time. As soon as the ocean came into view, we climbed down and switched buses again. Thankfully, this one was fully enclosed. We rode for miles along roads that paralleled the beach. "This is where we get off," the brothers announced among nothing but beach and palm trees, and I immediately had warm memories of my trip to the coast with John.

We turned into a stand of palm trees, and a collection of what looked like wooden shipping crates on stilts came into view. *Oh, cute little beach cabanas! I wish John were here!* A naked toddler sat out front of one of these, idly banging rocks together. "Mama, we're home," the elder brother yelled through the doorway that gaped open like a broken mouth. A drawn woman poked her head out, stared briefly at me, and nodded at the boys. She stepped through the door and scooped the toddler onto her hip, shooing the flies that had congregated around his runny nose.

"Thanks for bringing us home, señorita," the boys said. They followed their silent mother into the shack while my romantic notions about life at the beach evaporated.

Linder and I walked back the way we had come, got on a bus, and went back to the center of the city.

"Linder, Señora Mercedes has arranged a place for us to stay tonight. Should we go there now and then go to your house tomorrow?" The sun was high in the sky, but I had no idea how far we were from Linder's house, and I didn't want to get stuck in some unknown part of Esmeraldas after dark.

"No, no, señorita, my house is close. We can walk from here." Linder took my hand and led me through a maze of streets strewn with garbage and beggars reclining on the broken pavement, into a neighborhood teeming with barefoot children and through an alley that reeked of urine and feces. *How had John and I missed this on our vacation?* At the end of the alley was a three-story building that sagged more than it stood. I wondered if they condemned buildings—or even had building codes—in Ecuador. I thought of the fine white dust that powdered my apartment after each heavy rain that Carl said could be asbestos, which Ecuadorians used for roofing material. Linder bounded through the building's front door, but I stood rigid in the doorway. Breathing something that might or might not be asbestos was one thing, having a building collapse on top of me was quite another.

"Venga, señorita." Linder took my hand and pulled me up a dark staircase. *"Mi casa,"* he said as he knocked on a door at the top of the stairs. When the door opened, a huge figure obscured any light that might have come from the other side of the doorway. Linder immediately began crying, and just before I could grab him and run back down the stairs, he fell against the enormous creature. *"Mi mama,"* he gasped between sobs.

The woman bent down and swept Linder up into her huge arms and shuffled back through the door. I took a deep breath and followed them in.

"I am Eva," I said by way of introduction. "Linder has been staying with us at El Hogar de los Niños Trabajador, which is run by the Catholic Church in Santo Domingo," I said as we stood awkwardly in a tiny room strewn with food debris. This was the kitchen, I assumed, because it had a sink and a counter, but none of the other telltale signs of a kitchen. With Linder still sobbing in her arms, the woman led me into an adjoining room, cramped with a bed, a table, and a sagging couch. There was only one other door in the apartment, which I assumed led to the toilet, but perhaps it didn't and that would explain the smell in the alley.

"Please, señorita, sit down," she said, motioning toward the couch. I perched myself on the very edge of the couch, thinking it didn't look much sturdier than the building. I hoped this wasn't going to take very long.

"Here is some information for you about our shelter." I handed her the one-page information sheet that I had written in very basic Spanish.

"Linder is a good boy," I said. "He is welcome to stay with us." He hugged his mother tighter.

"He goes to school every day," I added. "And after school, he works in our workshop and the boys make things that we sell to tourists. See." I held up the slatted bamboo bag that the boys had made me. I wished now that I had encouraged each of the boys to bring one for their mothers. But I had never even thought about their mothers before.

The big woman smiled and whispered something into Linder's ear. Linder nodded but continued to sob.

"Señorita Eva?" Linder crawled down from his mother's arms and stood beside me. "Can I stay here with *mi mama* tonight, instead of going with you?" As long as the building didn't fall down around him, I didn't think any harm would come from letting Linder stay. Besides, I didn't think there was any way I could have pried him from his mother if I'd wanted to. So we agreed on a meeting time and place for the next day.

I took a deep, grateful breath as soon as I was outside. I didn't even mind the smell. As Linder walked me back to where I could get a taxi, I wondered if I would ever see him again. Having seen where he came from, I was certain that he was better off at the shelter, materially at least. The filthy neighborhood, the dilapidated building, the cramped, dirty apartment—how could that be good for a child? But what did we have that could compare to a mother's arms around a small boy?

I was relieved the next morning to see Linder waiting for me at our agreed upon meeting place.

"*Gracias, señorita,* for bringing our boy home. I am Linder's uncle," said a man standing next to Linder. "We are happy to know that Linder is well and we know that he is good with you." He handed Linder a small brown paper bag as they said good-bye. "It's not much, but the family collected a few things for Linder to have with him. He's a good boy, our Linder," he said, tousling the boy's short brown ringlets.

"*Si, señor,*" I agreed. "Our Linder is a very good boy." I hugged Linder as we walked to the bus station. Linder seemed far more relaxed on the bus ride back to Santo Domingo than he and the other boys had been going down. He proudly showed me the contents of his paper bag, which included some photos, a white shirt, and the toothbrush I had given him. After a few hours, he used the bag as a pillow and slept against the window. I watched him and felt once again as if I had found the thing I was meant to do.

By the time thirteen-year-old Antonio came to *El Hogar* two months later, I had begun to do an intake questionnaire with each boy who arrived.

"Well, I would like to tell my mother that I am okay," Antonio answered when I asked if he wanted to go home. "But I don't want to stay there. And you will come with me, won't you, señorita? I live not far from here."

Antonio's nervousness was contagious as we took the short bus ride to where he lived the next afternoon. I took some comfort in the fact that we got off the bus right where I'd get off to visit Jane and Carl. But we walked down a dirt road going in the opposite direction of their house. We climbed the stairs and knocked on a door to a house that was raised up on bamboo stilts.

Antonio's mother opened the door and ushered us inside. "Antonio! You are all right!" She smiled at her son, but there was a twitchy expression on her face that made me think of a frightened bird. Just as his mother embraced Antonio, a tall, broad man came in from outside. I could smell beer escaping from his pores when he stood close to me and grunted.

"Well, your Antonio is a good boy," I said cheerily, trying to convince myself that all was well. "We are very happy to have him stay with us. We are just down the road and you are welcome to come visit anytime."

"Well, that sounds good," Mama said with a tense smile. "Doesn't that sound good, Papa?"

"Antonio needs to come outside with me!" the man bellowed. "He needs to come outside with me right now!"

"Now, Papa, this good señorita has come with Antonio to visit us. You don't have to go outside with him now."

"Antonio needs to go outside with me now to have his hair washed!" Papa insisted. Antonio shrugged and calmly followed his father outside. "You stay!" the father yelled at me as he left.

"Well, señorita, are you from America? Where did you learn such good Spanish?" As we sat there and made forced small talk, I realized that I had no idea what I had gotten myself into.

After a painful few minutes Antonio came back into the house with his black hair soaking wet and plastered to his head. "Papa says I can go back with you now."

"That's good. Isn't that good, señorita?" Mama asked nervously.

"Yes, that is good." I was convinced of that. "Antonio, maybe we should go now."

As Antonio and I were saying good-bye to his mother, Papa came stomping into the house, a dull butcher's knife in his hand.

"What would you do, señorita, if I tried to keep my son from leaving with you?" He wiped both sides of the knife blade across his pants.

"Well, señor, it is my job to protect all the boys in our care." I tried to look brave and harmless all at the same time. "And I would certainly do whatever I could to protect Antonio as well." Even to my own ears, it sounded ludicrous. I knew I had absolutely no way to protect Antonio or any of the boys. Or myself for that matter. "So, I guess we should be going now?"

"Yes, yes, they should be leaving, right Papa?" Papa grunted, but the hand holding the knife relaxed just a bit. Antonio and I backed out the door and ran back to the main road. I looked across the road to the dirt path that led to Carl and Jane's. I wanted to keep running to the safety of their house.

But Antonio and I got on the bus and rode back to the shelter in silence. Antonio said good night and hurried to the long bunk room that he shared with ten other boys. I quickly greeted the women who were bustling around the kitchen, but I needed to process what had just happened—preferably in English and over a beer. I declined their invitation for supper, and walked toward the center of town, hoping I'd find one of the other volunteers.

The post office was smack in the middle of town, right near the ice-cream parlor and hamburger joint—all the usual *gringo* hangouts. But I didn't see anyone, so I went into the post office to pick up my mail. A note was stuck to the outside of my mailbox. *"Eve, come over as soon as you can. Lisa."* I remember thinking that her day couldn't have been as bad as mine. I wondered if she had any beer in her house. I grabbed my *Newsweek* and my small pile of mail and hurried the few blocks to Lisa's house. Lisa was outside when I walked up the road. There was an odd, serious expression on her face.

"Hola, chica," I said, looking closely at her. I could see she had been crying. "I just got your note. What's up?"

"Eve . . . ." Lisa hesitated, looking down at the ground. Then she looked me in the eye and blurted, "I was raped."

Dear Jean,
    Okay, I get it: Life in the Third World sucks.
People are poor and desperate and awful things happen
all the time. I can now walk past an entire family

living in a cardboard and plastic shack beside an open sewer pit and not flinch. I can now survive on nothing but rice and rice and rice with an occasional chicken foot thrown in. I get it. Do we get to go home now? I'm sure you heard about Lisa already. All the volunteers down here are pretty freaked out. What are you hearing up in Quito?

I just found out that the Peace Corps is sending me to a Women in Development conference in Guatemala next week. (I'm not sure what they're hoping I'll get out of it, but I'm hoping for a hot shower!) I'll be coming to Quito on Monday and flying to Guatemala on Tuesday. We'll talk then.

I'll keep you posted,
Eve

Chapter Eight

Falling Apart Where No One
Knows Your Name

When I first walked into the plush hotel lobby with the Ecuadorian dirt still under my fingernails, I was sure someone had made a huge mistake. *This is way more luxury than the Peace Corps allows.* But I checked in anyway, hoping I wouldn't get busted for the crime of actually being comfortable while being in the Peace Corps.

After the initial shock of Lisa's rape a few weeks before, I fell into the support role for several of the volunteers left behind. Lisa was quickly medically evacuated, "medevaced" as we called it, back to Peace Corps headquarters in Washington, D.C., where she could get the care and support she needed. But there was no one around to help the rest of us process the fears and anxieties that often surface after a rape. Because of my experience as a rape counselor, I became the designated "hand-holder" for everyone else.

Propped up in the wickedly luxurious bed my first night in Antigua, I heard a rumbling and watched the window blinds shimmy. I thought it was an earthquake and ran to the doorway and stood there, like I'd always seen in the movies. A confused bellhop came by and convinced me that it was nothing more than a burp from Antigua's semi-active volcano, and I should go back inside. But all night long, I was full of anxiety and waited for the earth to shake, for the volcano to blow, for the other shoe to drop.

The next three days, alone in that hotel, were hell. I tried to go to the conference on the first day, but I couldn't make sense of anything. All I could feel was panic. All I could hear were my own racing thoughts. *I am totally alone. I am totally vulnerable.* I spent the rest of the time lying beside the pool, telling myself to calm down and trying desperately to stop my mind from racing. Each night, I would lie in the bathtub with the water up over my ears, hoping that would muffle the cacophony of my own panicked thoughts. I felt like I was on a plane that was about to crash and could do nothing to stop it. I was falling apart in a country where no one even knew my name.

I had heard the stories of volunteers going crazy, volunteers committing suicide. The nurses had warned us to watch out for—and to come to them with—any symptoms of emotional stress. So in a rare moment of clarity, I packed my bags, checked out of the hotel, and headed for Guatemala's Peace Corps office to get help. I wedged myself, along with half the population of Antigua, onto a bus headed for the capital. Like a baby being rocked, I was lulled by the rhythmic movements of the bus as it jerked and contracted its way down through the lush green mountainside—so that being pushed back out onto the hard, gritty streets was as painful as being born. I briefly considered not moving at all and simply melting into the sidewalk as the city swirled around me. But a *gringita* turning into a puddle on a busy street in Guatemala City was not likely to go unnoticed. Not wanting to add embarrassment to my already fraying mental state, I kept moving.

At the Peace Corps office, I tried to explain, without seeming crazy, that I thought I was going crazy. I was certainly not the first volunteer in the world to walk into a Peace Corps medical office and unravel, and talking to the nurse calmed me down somewhat. That, and the tranquilizers she gave me. She booked me on a flight back to Ecuador the next day and got two Guatemalan volunteers to look after me until I got on the plane. We did what most Peace Corps volunteers do when they get together—we went drinking. The next morning, tranquilized and hungover, I was poured onto the plane by the Guatemalans. Back in Ecuador, our own nurse was certain that I wasn't going crazy. "After all," she told me confidently, "you've always been so together before."

She arranged for me to see a counselor, who told me to draw pictures of each of my family members as animals. Her request seemed odd to me, but no odder than losing my mind in Guatemala for no apparent reason, so I went along. I desperately needed to believe that this had been an isolated incident, and if drawing my dad as a dog was going to keep it from happening again, then I'd play along. I went back to Santo Domingo, praying that I'd calm down and life could go back to the way it had been.

But life didn't get back to normal. By keeping busy during the day I was able to hold the panic at bay, but just barely. The neighborhood kids had fallen out of the habit of constant *acompañarment* while John was visiting over the summer. Now, alone in my apartment at night, the panic attacks returned. And each one seemed worse than the one that came before.

There was a definite "tough it out" mentality among Peace Corps volunteers. We liked to think of ourselves as kind of like the Marines— without the guns, the uniforms, or the strict code of conduct, of course. I decided to tough it out by moving in with Jane and Carl. But a Peace Corps volunteer who requires babysitting by other Peace Corps volunteers is not such a useful thing. And after a few more consults with the Peace Corps nurse, it was decided that I should be medevaced.

My last few weeks in Ecuador are mostly blurry for me. But I have a crystal clear recollection of Jane helping me pack for the trip to Washington, D.C. She folded up my underpants, gingerly as if they might break. They were red and pink and blue, and Jane folded them in half and then in half again, so that they were tiny little red and pink and blue squares, no longer recognizable as underwear. And I remember thinking that I could smuggle thousands of them into America that way.

I arrived in D.C. on a frosty night in early December, stunned and cold. Living on the equator for the past ten months, I seemed to have forgotten about winter and about the need for a coat. A Peace Corps van picked me up at the airport and took me not to the padded cell I had anticipated, but to a very nice hotel. I nervously checked out the suite I was assigned to. The carpeting, plush furniture, and hot water in the bathroom were almost enough to make me panic. I had clear and painful memories of what had happened the last time I stayed in a place like this.

"Hi," came a voice from the bedroom. And out padded a slight woman with dark hair. "I'm your roommate. Leah—Sierra Leone—Fungus." The medevaced volunteers' version of name, rank, and serial number, I guess.

"Eve—Ecuador," was all I said, not quite sure I wanted to be known as "Eve—Ecuador—Just going crazy." But I felt better knowing I had a roommate. I had two, in fact. Lori—Nevis—Dislocated knee slept on the pullout couch.

The next morning, Lori took me to the volunteers' lounge of Peace Corps headquarters. "Here's your first stop." She pointed to a large box of coats, hats, gloves, and scarves. "And there's your second." She pointed to a long counter partitioned into at least a half-dozen sections each with its own chair beneath it and telephone on top. "WATS lines," she said. "You can call anywhere in the states for free." I hunted through the box until I found a coat and gloves that fit. I passed the phone bank and went to find the Peace Corps nurse who was assigned to my case. It was a bit weird being back in America without John—or anyone in my family—even knowing about it. But I just didn't have my head together enough to know what to say to them. I wasn't exactly anxious to report to anyone that I was losing my mind. Especially not John. Even if I could call for free.

I kept wondering what the medical staff knew about me. I suspected that the nurse back in Ecuador had sent an official, high-security telex to Washington to let them know I was bonkers. But no one seemed to be pointing at me and snickering. The nurse, a man with kind eyes, listened attentively as I recounted the last few weeks.

"First let's get you a physical and a full lab workup. There could be a physical cause for what you've been feeling."

"You mean I could be sick and not just crazy?" I wanted to hug this guy.

"Either way, I don't think you're crazy. But there are lots of ill-nesses that could make you feel psychologically unstable."

My mood was lighter as I went off to the doctor, hoping he'd find something serious enough to explain my panic attacks and nearly per-manent sense of dread, but not so serious that my name would end up on the memorial plaque of dead Peace Corps volunteers that I'd no-ticed on my way in. I decided to hold off calling John until I could tell him the good news that I was actually sick. But the physical and the lab tests revealed nothing. And I was even more depressed the next day, sitting in the volunteers' lounge.

"Yeah, something I inhaled while butchering the chickens," I overheard one volunteer say into a phone.

"Just another week on antibiotics and I should be good to go," said another.

I eyeballed all the volunteers in the room. *Damn,* I thought, *why can't I have tuberculosis?*

"You know, Eve, the Peace Corps is rough on a lot of volunteers," my nurse gently told me when I returned to his office. "You're living in some pretty hard situations, dealing with all kinds of harsh things. A lot of volunteers find it hard to take. You know, it might be a good idea to go talk to one of our social workers." I got the sense he thought he might have to talk me into this.

"Can you get me an appointment today?" I asked.

"I'll get you the next available appointment," he said. "You might be with us for a little while." He handed me a piece of paper. "Go downstairs to Returned Volunteer Services and they'll give you a cou-ple of weeks' per diem. You'll need some money." Cushy digs, free health care, and spending money to boot! It might have been a spa va-cation, except for my racing thoughts and the fact that now I was walking the two miles to and from Peace Corps headquarters because being in the metro was setting off panic attacks.

"Do you think I'll be able to get back in forty days?" I asked. Forty days is the longest a volunteer is allowed to be on medevac before being automatically separated from the Peace Corps. Not that I even knew if I wanted to go back to Ecuador.

"Let's talk about that after you've had a few visits with the social worker," the nurse said. Which was good, because at the moment, I was horribly confused. I wanted to go back to my life in Santo Domingo, which was finally falling into place. I also wanted to be with John, who was in America. I was petrified of going back to Ecuador and being plagued by anxiety, and equally frightened of staying in America and losing John because in addition to disappointing him, I was now crazy.

For the next two weeks, I existed, with the other medevacs, in a kind of Peace Corps no-man's-land. We didn't work, but we did bathe—in hot water, no less. Could we even be considered Peace Corps volunteers anymore? We were Americans who took sightseeing tours of supermarkets, oohing and aahing our way up and down the aisles after our months of deprivation. The only thing I bought, however, were several tubes of sparkly bubble gum flavored toothpaste, because I thought the boys at the shelter would get a kick out of it.

We had all been totally immersed in our host culture and now were in various stages of shock at being suddenly thrust back into America. We'd seek out tiny ethnic eateries, desperate for the food of our host countries or at least the chance to get amoebas. Anything to make us feel like we were still in the Peace Corps. At night, we'd all huddle around the hotel heating vents like tropical refugees. The others talked about their reasons for being there—a torn ligament, a uterine cyst, a mysterious fungus. I remained silent about my own shroud of anxiety and coveted their physical ailments. I actually found myself envious of a woman with a brain tumor.

After I'd been in Washington for three days, I finally called John—

and both my parents. Because I didn't have a convenient—but not too frightening—physical ailment to blame this all on, and I didn't want to fess up to losing my mind, I told them that my blood pressure was high. True enough, since with everything else that was going on, it was really high at the moment. But I told them not to worry, and not to think about coming down to D.C. I'd keep them posted.

Three times a week I dragged myself, like a cold, wet blanket, into the social worker's office and tried to make sense of the panic that had taken over my life. For that one hour, I felt something other than crazy. It wasn't quite sanity, it just wasn't panic. I checked out the other clients on their way out when I went in or on their way in when I went out. I did a mental once-over but could never convince myself that any of them looked worse off than me.

"Eve," the social worker began after several sessions, "from what you've told me, it seems like the beginnings of your anxiety can be traced back to your friend's rape. So I have to ask you, have you ever been raped?"

"No," I answered, quite clear that I hadn't been. "But I did work at a rape crisis center before I joined the Peace Corps."

"Well, why did you choose that work? Had you had some personal experience in that area?"

"No," I said. "Although I always thought it was odd, the sense of connections I had with the kids who told me about being molested. Their stories always felt so familiar to me—like déjà vu. It was kind of odd."

"Well, were you ever molested? Maybe when you were a child?"

"Molested? No." I was silent for a few moments. "Molested? No. Well, what do you mean?"

"I mean, Eve, did anyone ever do anything to you, sexually or physically, that you didn't want them to? Did anyone ever touch you in a way that you didn't want them to?"

"No. Well, there was a guy who lived down the street and I used to babysit for his kids from the time I was thirteen until I went away to college. And, yeah, he was inappropriate all the time. I mean, he used to ask me to sit on his lap when he drove me home. And he'd push me up against the wall and kiss me on my way in or out of his house. And . . . Jesus Christ!" I stopped.

It was the first time I had ever openly acknowledged what had happened. But the moment I said it, it was as familiar to me as dust. It was like I had unearthed an old photograph of myself and remembered everything about the moment that the picture was snapped. Just this one brief conversation, and the years of buried memories came flooding back.

"I think you're going to need to work with a therapist around this issue for a while," my counselor told me a few sessions later when I asked if she thought I should go back to Ecuador. "I suspect it will take a lot more than the time you have left on medevac."

"So that's it? This is how it all ends?" I asked later as the nurse unceremoniously signed the papers that medically separated me from the Peace Corps. Part of me was devastated—I was abandoning my boys and losing my newfound identity. I'd never get to say my goodbyes, never see my cozy little apartment again. But part of me was relieved—now I'd get to go home to comfort and, hopefully, to John.

"I have a feeling this isn't the end for you," the nurse said. "I don't know if it will be with the Peace Corps, but I have the feeling you'll get back overseas again."

But I didn't think I'd ever have the courage to go back. At that moment, it took all the courage I had to go downstairs and call John and tell him I was coming home.

Answering machine, beep:
Hi, John. It's Eve. I'm coming home. My train gets into Penn Station at four ten this afternoon. Will you meet me?

Chapter Nine

These Eggs Aren't Getting Any Fresher

I headed back to New York a mess. Sure, I was relieved that I wasn't actually going crazy. But I felt like a failure for not being able to "stick it out" in the Peace Corps and like an idiot for not recognizing the sexual abuse in my past. I was afraid of the reactions of friends back home once they realized that I hadn't been gone for two years. Heck, some of them might want their Swiss Army knives, Imodium, and water bottles back. But John's reaction was the one that meant the most to me. And the one I was most afraid of. I carried my bags and my uncertainty off the train in New York City and there he was.

"It's good to see you," John said, scooping me into a hug.

"Can I stay with you until I figure out what I'm going to do next?" I asked.

"Of course. You can stay with me until you get settled." I noticed that he hadn't said, *You can stay with me until we're both old and gray and our teeth fall out and our ears are hairy,* which, of course, was what I was hoping for.

"Aren't you embarrassed to be with me? I'm a Peace Corps failure!"

"Oh, Eve. You're not a failure. You went and you did some good and you got something out of it. No one expects you to stick it out no matter what. It's not an endurance contest. You are definitely not a failure."

I didn't believe a word he said, but I gladly took up residence, once again, under his African blanket. This was the best part of coming home. In fact, it was the only good part. As soon as I got home, I started therapy to try to stop the anxiety attacks. This meant dealing with the memories of childhood sexual abuse that had resurfaced. This is painful work under the best of circumstances. And I was not in the best of circumstances.

In training they warned us about the difficulty of adjusting to life back in the States. I had laughed at that absurd notion back then. But now, as the rest of the world zipped purposefully around me, I had no idea what to do, where to go, or how to get there. Reverse culture shock hit me like an avalanche and I responded like a fart in a blizzard. I was lost without the things that had framed my life in Ecuador: my newfound sense of purpose at *El Hogar;* the Voice of America radio broadcaster reminding me every Monday night to take my malaria pill; the weekly arrival in my mailbox of the latest issue of *Newsweek,* which I would read from cover to cover before using it as toilet paper; weekends with Donna sleeping on my couch; writing detailed letters home each evening to document and make sense of my day; going to bed when the stars were clear above my balcony and waking up when the neighbor's annoying rooster started to crow. I had nothing now to help me make order of this strange world. And unlike Ecuador, it was a world with too much to do and too many choices.

"Soup, soup, soup," I whimpered. I was sweating and shaking in the supermarket. "I just want some soup."

"You're in the soup aisle," a clerk said, pointing at the shelves full of soup all around me.

"Too many choices!" I croaked. "I just want soup!"

At the checkout counter the cashier asked, "How do you want to pay for this?"

"Um, dollars?" I said, wondering if maybe they accepted sucres.

"I mean cash or debit card," she said impatiently.

"Cash," I said, still unclear about the whole debit card thing. When I'd left, people were just beginning to use debit cards to withdraw money from the handful of automatic teller machines, mostly in Manhattan. Now it seemed like you could get money out of walls on every street corner and debit cards were beginning to take the place of cash in people's wallets.

"Maybe we should start looking for an apartment for you," John said after I'd been staying with him for a few weeks.

"Can't I just stay here?" As far as I was concerned, I had fulfilled my part of the bargain. I'd gone into the Peace Corps. Now wasn't it time for John to love me forever?

"Here?" he asked, spreading his arms to fill most of the width of his tiny bedroom. "You really can't stay here very long." Nice guy that he was, his roommates had stuck him with the tiniest bedroom in the apartment.

"Why not?" I panicked at the thought of living alone. I needn't have panicked; I couldn't possibly afford my own apartment on my meager Peace Corps readjustment allowance.

"Listen, Eve. I love you. But I never said we should live together. I'm not ready to commit to that."

"But what about that time on the Long Island Expressway? Remember when our helmets were stolen and you said we'd tell our grandchildren about this? Our grandchildren. What about that?"

"That?" He seemed surprised. "I meant I'd tell my grandchildren and you'd tell yours. I didn't mean they'd be the same grandchildren."

I had been sure since the day we'd met that John and I were meant to be together. I'd gone to live in a Third-World swamp so that John would be sure of it too. And now, for the first time, it dawned on me that I could be wrong. I was devastated. I was dizzy. I was having a hard time breathing.

"Evie, don't be a cling-on," my mother said. "It'll scare him." She was right, of course. But I was jobless, homeless, and a mess. The only thing I could think to do was to cling to John for dear life. "You've got to give John his space," my mother advised. "He'll come around."

So I found a room in an apartment two miles away from John's and, just as important, one mile from my therapist. There was a bodega on the corner where I could get *platanos* and guavas, and a Latin American restaurant where I could order *almuerzo* and not have to make any choices. I found a job as a health educator, although the sum total of my experience in that area consisted of putting tampons in soda bottles. But the fact that I spoke Spanish seemed to be qualification enough for the job in the heavily Hispanic neighborhood.

On the long subway rides to and from work, I'd keep my head buried in my latest self-help book, hoping to ward off anxiety attacks and appear more like a normal person. But without the certainty of John in my life, everything else felt as bleak as the subway tunnels we crept through. From where I sat, the future looked about as fuzzy as the platforms that whizzed by. I was giving John his space—not calling him every day, not expecting to see him all weekend, every weekend—but it was nearly killing me.

"Hey, let's get you a cat," my mother suggested when I was at my lowest. It was spring of 1989 and all eyes were glued to the grainy video coming from half a world away, as college students were staring down tanks in China. My mother found me an adorable, long-haired peaches-and-cream-colored kitten. I named her Beijing, in honor of the uprising, since "Tiananmen Square" didn't exactly roll off the tongue. And while Beijing didn't quite make up for not having John with me 24/7, she did help.

With a little time and a lot of therapy, I managed to regain my balance while not completely sabotaging my relationship with John. I was no longer a "cling-on," and he did stick around. For that, my mother dubbed him "Saint John." I still would have preferred to be living with him. Let's face it, I wanted to be halfway to happily ever after already. But having John halfway across town beat not having him at all.

John was studying at Columbia University's School of International and Public Affairs, and once again, I found myself surrounded by people who'd been in Ouagadougou during the coup. Sure, now I could say "I'm an RPCV" like I was flashing my entry card into their secret club, but then whomever I was talking to would say something like "Oh, I was Togo, 1980 to '82; Sara here was Zimbabwe, '84 to '86; and James was Micronesia, '72 to '75. You?" And as soon as I said

"Ecuador, 1988," the whole gig was up. Everyone knew that your Peace Corps passport should be stamped for no less than two years. So there I'd be, like the awkward girl at the Girl Scout jamboree. All uniform, no merit badges.

"It's all in your head, Eve," John assured me. "Don't worry about it." I worried anyway, but found it reassuring that John still loved me regardless of what was going on in my head.

I enjoyed working as a health educator, even though the doctor I worked for had a well-earned reputation as a brilliant lunatic. I decided to get a graduate degree in public health, hoping to expand my career options. Unfortunately, my job at Columbia Presbyterian Hospital did not come with free tuition to Columbia's School of Public Health. But in addition to studying at Columbia, John was working in their admissions office. His job came with free tuition for employees and their immediate families.

"Will you marry me, John?" I asked, only half joking.

"I really don't think free tuition is a good enough reason to get married, Eve. Besides, I know it's kind of old-fashioned, but if there's going to be a proposal around here, I'd like to be the one to do it."

He was not so old-fashioned, however, that he was opposed to moving in together. By June our relationship was back on steady footing, and John's lease was running out. We found a lovely garden apartment with a bedroom that opened onto a small yard surrounded by rosebushes. Much to John's parents' dismay, their son, who was supposed to be the priest, was now the first member of the family to live in sin. A real *shonda*, his parents might have said if they spoke a word of Yiddish. My parents, who were each already working toward their third marriages, had no qualms about John and me shacking up.

"So, will you marry me now?" I asked again, after we'd been living together two months. I wanted to make his parents happy, and besides, school was starting in a few weeks.

"Let's just live together for a while longer," he said. "We'll see how that goes."

Well, John wasn't exactly cooperating, but everything else in my life was falling quite nicely into place. I started a master's program at Hunter College's (considerably cheaper than Columbia's) school of public health. I found a new health education job at a hospital in Brooklyn. John and I both worked full-time, attended classes in the evenings, and came home to a purring Beijing in our little rose garden love shack each night.

"Will you marry me now?" I asked when we'd been living together about a year. It was beginning to be a regular habit. By the third rejection, you'd think I'd catch on.

"You know, I just don't think we should talk about marriage until we've been together long enough."

"Well, what exactly defines long enough?" I asked. I thought it was a rhetorical question.

"Five years," he said as if it was a rule that every guy knew. *Maybe it was.*

I quickly did the math. It had been a year and a half since I'd been back. We'd been dating for nine months by the time I went to Ecuador, then another nine months while I was there. That totaled three years, but I was hoping to get extra credit for the time in Ecuador on account of how miserable I'd been without him. I thought I deserved it, like combat pay. Anyway, for me it certainly seemed like we'd been together long enough to talk about marriage. But, of course, I had known from the day we'd met that we were destined to be together. So every day after that was superfluous as far as I was concerned.

At least, as my mother might say, I had my career to fall back on. After a few months at my new job, I was recruited to pilot a new adolescent HIV prevention program for an AIDS prevention center at SUNY Health Sciences Center in Brooklyn. It was 1990 and AIDS was sweeping through New York City. I developed a program that trained at-risk youth to become peer educators, using music, theater, and after-school activities to grab their attention. It quickly became a model for reaching inner-city youth, and I wrote curricula, trained trainers, and consulted with the New York City Board of Education,

Board of Health, and other agencies. I taught a course at the SUNY medical school on my HIV prevention techniques, presented my work at conferences, wrote a chapter for a textbook, and was even appointed to an American Medical Association panel on HIV and adolescents. All of this while sailing through public health school with straight As and not even once getting arrested for sitting in at anyone's office.

I was meeting all kinds of fascinating people who were working in the field of HIV/AIDS. Among them was Susan, who worked with me at the AIDS prevention center and had recently finished her MPH at Columbia University. Susan's exuberance and her ever-ready sense of humor—even in the midst of sometimes depressing work—made her a lot of fun to be with. The two of us soon became regular lunch partners and Susan quickly became one of my best friends.

Everything was more than falling into place; it was coming pretty easily. At twenty-eight, I was certainly on track for having it all. Except, of course, for the husband part. Oh, I knew I had the right guy. But he just wasn't falling into the husband place. It was then that I resorted to the age-old strategy of women nearing thirty everywhere.

"Look, buddy, these eggs aren't getting any fresher," I said, or something equally romantic. "I want to get married soon so I can have kids by the time I'm thirty-five." Coming from the big, happy family that he did, I knew John wanted to have kids. "I'm giving you a year to make up your mind."

"Are you giving me an ultimatum?" he asked, rather calmly. "Because, I have to tell you, I won't respond well to an ultimatum."

"Well, then let's just say you have a year to figure out if I am the woman you want to spend the rest of your life with." It seemed reasonable enough to me. But so did stamping my feet and whining, *Just marry me already, will ya!* I resolved not to say anything more about it—for a year.

Over the next few months there was no indication that John was moving any closer to popping the question, although everyone around us seemed to be getting married. John's best friend, Andy, had gotten married—in a double wedding, no less—soon after I'd returned home. That spring, Andy hoisted me up on his shoulders and I caught the bouquet at the wedding of another of their college friends.

"Great," I said to Andy as he put me down. "I've got the bouquet, but not the guy."

Andy grinned at me. "Don't worry, Eve. John is not marrying anybody *but* you." I was slightly comforted by that, but not much, considering Andy was drunk at the time.

But married or not, our little family grew. (No, not that way! Not that *that* hadn't crossed my mind.)

In October of that year, my brother found a stray kitten that looked like a short-haired version of Beijing. I gave it to John as a birthday present. Naturally, we named him Berlin, for the wall that had recently come down. So by New York City standards, our family of four was now complete. Not much more than two adults and two cats could fit into our apartment, anyway.

But the clock on my ultimatum—as well as my uterus—was ticking away, although no one seemed to hear it but me. I stuck to my resolve and didn't bring it up, as long as you don't count things said while drunk or in the throes of passion. John never mentioned the ultimatum or marriage. But June rolled around again, and with it, another wedding season. Driving from the ceremony to the reception of another friend, John pulled the car over on the side of the road. He turned to me and stared.

"What?" I asked.

"Nothing," he said. "You're just really, really beautiful."

"I knew you'd like me in this dress," I said. The retro red dress had a snug bodice, flared skirt, and open back. And though my mom had recently turned my hair orange with a bottle of Sun-In, I still thought that if I stood over a subway grate and a huge gush of air hit me just right, (and if you were in dire need of glasses) I'd look just like Marilyn Monroe.

"Not just the dress," he said, taking my hand. "You are really beautiful."

He pulled the car back onto the road without saying anything more. But at that moment, I knew: This was a guy worth waiting for.

"The ultimatum is lifted," I whispered into John's ear as we danced at the reception that evening. I would wait forever if I had to. *Damn it!*

A few weeks later, on a hot and humid Friday evening, I was sitting and watching Beijing and Berlin chase each other around the roses in our backyard. I was desperately trying to catch a breeze and vaguely wondering where'd we go for dinner when John got home. It was way too hot to cook in our unair-conditioned apartment.

John snuck up behind me and tapped me on the shoulder. "These are for you," he said, handing me a dozen long-stemmed red roses.

"Wow," I said. I knew from the baby's breath, the green tissue paper, and the heart-shaped "I Love You" balloon attached to it that he'd actually gone to a florist. "Not even from the corner bodega!"

"See? I can learn," he answered.

"What's the occasion?" I asked. I racked my brain. It was a month away from my birthday. I'd always considered our anniversary to be our first date, which was in April. I'd been doing well at work, but nothing special had happened recently. *Oh my God, has he done something bad?* I thought.

Then, right there on our back patio, John got down on one knee. "Will you marry me?" he asked.

"You're kidding!" I said. "You don't mean that."

"No, I mean it. I love you and I want to spend the rest of my life with you."

"Well, well," I kind of sputtered. "What about the five-year rule?"

"I just needed to figure it out in my own time. You were right all along. You are the woman I was meant to be with. You. So will you marry me?" *Well, it sure took you long enough!* I wanted to say.

"Yes, yes, yes!" is what I said.

And then I called my mother.

Part
Two

Chapter Ten

🍃

Oh, God . . . We're Going to Uganda

Ah . . . the Russian Tea Room. Okay, I'll admit it. The Russian Tea Room probably wasn't what John had in mind for an "international experience." But exotic yet perfectly safe, it was exactly what I had in mind. Besides, the food was delicious and the booze was plentiful. Best of all, when I walked out the door, I was still in America.

"So, where do we go next?" he asked as we waltzed out of the Russian Tea Room after celebrating my graduation from public health school.

"We look for jobs overseas?" I asked my beloved. I hoped that his urge to be of service to a world in need was something I might catch, like mono. While I did, indeed, feel an urge to go back overseas, it was compelled by something other than pure altruism. I had failed to live up to the unwritten stick-it-out rule of the Peace Corps: When the going gets tough, the tough down a few more beers and keep slogging through the mud or the dust as the case may be. Nearly three years of therapy had helped me understand that I'd gone to Ecuador with psychological baggage and left under extenuating circumstances. But I still wanted to know if I had what it takes to survive overseas. And deep down inside, I feared that I really didn't.

Master's degrees in hand, we pounded the international pavement looking for work. John applied for positions in economic development, small business, and anything remotely related to Africa. I applied for jobs in HIV/AIDS, public health, and anything that required

Spanish fluency. Secretly, I was terrified of the prospect that one of us might get an offer. But international job searches are usually long and complicated, so the chances of actually having to go overseas felt bless-edly remote. Besides, I didn't think anyone was really going to hire me. The sum total of my international experience, after all, was one aborted stint in the Peace Corps. John, with three years experience in Africa and an Ivy League master's degree that had required him to do field research in developing countries, was another story. And after a few months of looking, he was offered a two-year contract with CARE as a manager of a savings and loan project in Arua, Uganda.

"Hmmm . . ." Susan looked over the information packet that CARE had sent us. "It says here that northern Uganda is a bit run down on account of the civil wars that have been going on there for the last twenty years." She paused. "Oh look, it says it has a golf course and tennis courts left over from the colonial days. Doesn't sound all bad."

"Well, it won't exactly be New York City. But we knew that, Susan."

"Wow, no running water," she said, reading further. "Ah, bathing is highly overrated, anyway. At least you'll get three hours of electric-ity every night."

"Yeah, I'm thinking about bringing our TV and VCR. You'll send me tapes of *Murphy Brown* and *Mad About You,* won't you?"

"Oh, I'll send you great care packages. But it says there's a bar in the town where all the workers from the nearby refugee camps hang out. Now that's where you'll want to be spending your nights." Susan looked at me. "I know John wants this. But is this really what you want?"

"I don't know. What girl wouldn't want this?" I laughed. "Okay, it doesn't sound great. But John raves about Africa. He swears I'll love it. And Uganda is supposed to be really beautiful. You know—the Pearl of Africa and all. CARE is offering us a great deal. We'll have a house, a car, all the benefits—even extra pay and R and R because Arua is considered a hardship post."

"A hardship post? That's where you want to go? Really?"

"Well, it's the AIDS capital of the world. The epidemic is so wide-spread that USAID—that's the United States Agency for International Development—has a whole slew of people over there just working on AIDS projects. That's gotta be a good thing."

"That's not a good thing, Eve."

"Well, maybe it means I've hit the career jackpot." I shrugged. "Who knows? In a year, maybe you'll want to move there, too."

A few days later, I told my friend Jean about it. "Do you really think this is a good idea?" she asked.

"No worse an idea than sliding down the Andes on our asses!" Jean had moved to New York and become a social worker after finishing the Peace Corps.

"I'm serious," she said. "Do you really think you're ready for this?"

"I've got to be ready for this. I have no other choice."

Jean looked me in the eyes and, as usual, saw right through me. "You have plenty of choices, Eve. You're the only person who seems to think you have to go live in the jungle in order to prove yourself. No one is making you do this."

"I'm making me. I have to do this, Jean. You know how it is. No, you don't know how it is." I was thinking of how I had left Ecuador, with no closure and no good-byes, just lots of tiny undies hastily stuffed into my suitcase. "You made it. You COS'ed. I never did."

"COS'ing? Is this really what all this is about?" Jean asked.

Close of service—"COS" in Peace Corps speak. The final conference. Those last halcyon days as a Peace Corps volunteer. It was during this conference that you filled out your papers, collected your readjustment allowance, and bid a bittersweet farewell to all things Peace Corps. Then you boldly headed off for your final fling—trekking through India and Nepal, backpacking through Africa, cruising the Galápagos—on your way to reentry into the real world, where the cold beer flowed like mother's milk and your family and friends welcomed you like a conquering hero. At least that's how I'd imagined it.

"Geez, Eve. You didn't COS," Jean continued. "So what? You think you have to stick it out for two miserable years in some jungle outpost to prove yourself? There are plenty of people who never even go into the Peace Corps, much less COS, Eve. It's not like you can't get on with your life."

But in my strange world, that's exactly how it was. I was tired of feeling like a fraud among the *fou-fou*-eating, henna-footed jet-setters. I so wanted to be a full-fledged member of their pack, with the merit badges and all. And I needed to know, once and for all, if I had what it takes to stick it out overseas.

"Would this be a good career move for John?" my mom asked when I told her about the job in Uganda.

"Oh, you know him. He doesn't think in terms of career moves. He simply wants to be where he can be of most use."

"Ah, Saint John," she said. "Such a comfort to have a live organ donor in the family."

"Mom!"

"Well, who else can I count on if I ever need a kidney?" she said, and I knew she was right. Left to my own devices, I knew I would never be as good a person as John. I planned on going out with all the kidneys I came in with. But when I'd married him, I had hitched my wagon to his good star. And for all my misgivings, I knew that I'd follow him to the ends of the earth. And now, apparently, I was going to get my chance.

"Yes, I was in therapy for three years," I shouted through the pay phone from a rest stop on the Massachusetts Turnpike. "It was very helpful. I feel much better now. What? Why was I in therapy?" A bus belched to a stop behind me. "Um, well, when I was in the Peace Corps, a friend of mine was raped and it triggered my own repressed memories of childhood sexual abuse." A stream of passengers dribbled by on their way to the restrooms. "I had severe anxiety attacks and was medically evacuated." I wondered if three good years of therapy could be undone in one ridiculous moment.

The psychologist and I had been playing phone tag for a week. After months of interviews and negotiations about John's contract, there was one last hurdle to clear before going to Uganda: I had to prove my emotional stability. John was a safe bet to survive two years in a rural African outpost. After all, he had sailed through two years in the Peace Corps and happily signed on for a third. But in international work it's often a case of "love me, love my dog." And I was the dog. Since CARE would be footing the bill for both of us, they wanted some sort of guarantee that the dog could handle it.

An eighteen-wheeler blew by. "Excuse me, I missed that," I said to the invisible man on the other end of the line. "No. I haven't had an anxiety attack in about two years." I felt exposed saying all this on the side of a highway to a faceless stranger. But I desperately needed this guy to believe that I was okay enough to go to Uganda. And I desperately wanted to believe it, too.

"Do I think I'm ready to try living overseas again?" I repeated his last question and squelched the urge to say, *Why the hell else would I be standing in a truck stop having this bizarre conversation?* Instead I answered, "Yes, I'm definitely ready. I've had three years of therapy. I'm married now, so I'll have support if I need it. I can handle it."

"I'm sorry you had to do that," John said when I got back to the car. He wrapped me in his arms and kissed the top of my head.

"The guy said he'd sign off on my medical clearance." I looked up at him. "We're going to Uganda."

"We're going to Uganda!" John shouted and hugged me tighter.

Oh, God, I thought, uncertain if the pounding in my chest was excitement or the beginnings of an anxiety attack. *We're going to Uganda.*

We finished our trip through Massachusetts, bidding farewell to John's family and friends. Back in New York, I gave a month's notice at my job and prepared for two years in a rural Ugandan outpost by going to Pottery Barn to buy a cappuccino machine. Best to come prepared, I thought. I also picked up a new set of dishes—plates painted with the word "Plate," and bowls painted with the word "Bowl." I thought these would be nice conversation starters among our new, largely illiterate, neighbors.

Once we ascertained that the cats could, indeed, come with us, I took them to the vet for a checkup. I was concerned about Beijing. I'd recently noticed her banging into walls and even once saw her fall off the edge of the bathtub as she tried to drink out of the leaky bath faucet.

"I'm concerned about her balance," I told the vet. "Maybe she has an inner ear problem."

The vet checked her out and looked at her eyes for a long time. Then he called in his associate, who also looked at her eyes for a long time.

"Your cat does not have an inner ear problem," the doctor announced. "Your cat has an eye problem. The problem is she has absolutely no blood vessels in her eyes."

"Oh, well, what do we do about that?" I asked.

"We can't do anything about that. She's blind. Your cat is totally blind."

"What? Beijing is not blind. I've seen her chase butterflies around the yard. She's not blind."

"Well, she hasn't always been blind. But she's definitely blind now. Look." He shone a penlight into her big, blank eyes. "See, there are no blood vessels in there. None. I've really never seen anything quite like it. But an organ that receives no blood doesn't function."

"Beijing is blind?" I repeated. "Blind?"

"That would explain why she's been bumping into things. And falling off the edge of the tub," he said.

"I guess that explains why she started drinking water out of the tap. She could hear that. Maybe she can't find her water bowl! Oh, my poor baby." I hugged her soft, fluffy body to my chest.

"Well, what do you do for a blind cat? Get her a Seeing Eye dog?" I asked.

"Don't worry. She's fine. Other than the blindness, she's perfectly healthy. And cats can be pretty adaptive," he said. "I suspect she's doing just fine. Whatever you do, though, don't rearrange the furniture in your house."

Okay, I thought. *No rearranging the furniture. Just rearranging the continent.*

In addition to the cats, the cappuccino machine, plates that said "Plate," and bowls that said "Bowl," a television and a VCR, I inexplicably packed a dozen wool sweaters, to go to a country that's on the equator. For his part, John prepared for our journey by buying scissors and reading up on how to cut his own hair.

As we made our final preparations CARE repeatedly assured us that reports of sporadic guerrilla activity in Arua were largely overblown. However, our departure was delayed by a month when the CARE country director was shot by armed bandits while visiting Arua. I think he was attempting to show everyone what a nice, safe place it really was.

> Dear Susan,
>
> Okay, so I was all big and brave until you and Brad left us at the airport. And then I just bawled like a baby. What the hell am I getting into? It took me all the way to our layover in Nairobi before the reality of the situation hit me: We're going to Africa! Okay, by then we were already in Africa. But that's when I finally started to get excited.
>
> Sometimes I wonder, though, how will I survive two years without you and Jean? I really don't know. I mean, missing John was one thing, but can a woman really stay sane for two years with only her

husband for support? Oh, no, now John is jealous! Listen, it's okay for you to have lunch with other gals, now that I won't be around the hospital anymore. Just don't tell them all your deep, dark secrets. Okay?

Well, it's a good thing Jean is getting married. I swore to her that I'd come back to be in her wedding. So at least we know I'll be coming home in May. That's only forty weeks away. Surely I can hang on for that long. Can't I?

I'll keep you posted,
Eve

Chapter Eleven

A Lovely Little Corner of Hell

Idi Amin and AIDS. That was the sum total of what I knew about Uganda before we arrived there in August of 1993. And then, of course, there were all the hellish reports that most Americans heard about Africa from the news: famines, droughts, refugees, and civil wars. So I was not feeling particularly reassured as our plane made its approach into Entebbe International Airport.

"Out your windows you can see Lake Victoria," our pilot said. We circled low over a huge body of water interrupting the lush landscape below. The lake was dotted with tiny green islands, some of which were ringed by white, sandy beaches. "It is the biggest lake in Africa. The second biggest lake in the world."

"Huh. It's a lot greener—and wetter—than I thought," I said as I looked out the tiny window.

"See, I told you, Africa is gorgeous," John said, grabbing my hand as we bumped down onto a runway lined with gently swaying palm trees.

"Is that what I think it is?" I pointed through the palm fronds to a rather dilapidated compact building. Rusted metal letters that seemed to be trying to spell out "Entebbe" hung off at odd angles, the whole building looking as if it had been strafed by bullets. "And that?" I pointed through the palm trees to the rusting hulk of an airplane on an adjacent runway. "Is that what I think it is?"

Okay, I actually knew a few more things about Uganda. In preparation for our journey, we had watched any and all movies that took place there. *Raid on Entebbe* was about the 1976 Israeli army raid that freed a planeload of Jewish travelers being held hostage, with President Idi Amin's blessing, at Entebbe Airport. Our plane doubled back, taxiing past the hijacking relics, and came to a stop near a wide, two-story building with yellow columns out front and no noticeable bullet holes.

Okay, just breathe, I told myself as the plane came to a full stop.

"Ready?" John asked.

"Hmm-hmm," I breathed as we got up and began shuffling toward the exit. *In through the nose and out through the mouth,* I reminded myself. *There is nothing to panic about. I will not have an anxiety attack today. I will not have an anxiety attack now. Well, certainly not before even setting foot on African soil!*

I stepped off the plane and into air that felt like a warm bath. I took another deep breath and got my first whiff of Africa: a mixture of melting tarmac, perfumed flowers, and just a hint of BO. It reminded me of summers at my grandparents' bungalow colony in the Catskills. Smelly but soothing.

As we entered the sparse white customs hall at Entebbe International Airport, I realized for the first time that practically everyone around us—the pilots, the baggage handlers, the customs officials, and the overwhelming majority of our fellow passengers—were black. I wondered if I would be treated differently, discriminated against because of this. My question was quickly answered as John and I were almost immediately summoned from the back of the milling crowd.

"Please, please, come," a guard said, motioning us toward a counter. "We do not like to make our guests wait."

At the counter, a uniformed man took a cursory glance at our passports and visas and banged his stamp down hard. "*Karibu.* Welcome to Uganda," he said, smiling.

"*Karibu,* Mr. Waite John! *Karibu,* Mrs. Brown Eve! *Karibuni!* You are welcome!" Someone was yelling our names backward and waving frantically at us as soon as we came through customs and into the main hall of the airport. A man next to him smiled broadly and held up a sign marked "CARE."

"I guess that's us," John said, grabbing my hand.

"Well, hallo there. I am Ogora Adam. Your deputy project manager." A very dark-skinned man about our age vigorously shook John's hand. Then he turned to me. "You must be Eve! I am Adam!" He laughed and offered me the same vigorous handshake, which involved most of my lower arm. Adam was black. Not brown like a lot of the African Americans I knew. Adam was blue-black, making his brilliant white smile practically glow.

"*Karibuni* to you both. Welcome. Welcome to Uganda," he said in an accent that seemed half British and half mouth-full-of-rocks. "I hope you will enjoy our country. Adam and Eve. Adam and Eve," he repeated, laughing. "Oh, I love it. This is going to be what? This is going to be great!" Based on what I'd heard about Uganda, I couldn't quite figure out why this guy was so happy. I thought maybe the parasites had gotten to his brain.

"Sir, madam." The older man holding the CARE sign offered his hand to each of us and bowed slightly. "I am Alex. I welcome you to Uganda and I will be happy to collect your things and drive you to CARE headquarters in Kampala." Alex's skin was lighter than Adam's, but he spoke in the same, thick accent. He reached for my carry-on bags.

"Yes, we should go to where the baggage will be coming out," Adam said, leading the way.

"You will have much more, I assume."

"Actually, most of our things were shipped freight. So we don't have that much stuff with us now," John explained.

"But there are the cats," I added, slightly embarrassed.

"You brought cats?" Adam asked.

"Cats?" Alex echoed.

"Our pets," I stammered, suddenly aware of how ridiculous it must look to bring house cats to Africa. "They're part of our family. We couldn't just leave them."

"No, of course not," Adam said. "Let us go find out where we can meet your cats."

"Oh, what big, beautiful cats," Adam exclaimed when we had located our pets in their travel crates. "No wonder you could not leave them behind."

"Do you have names for them?" Alex asked, putting his fingers into their crates.

"This is Beijing. She's a female," I said. "And the boy here is Berlin."

"Oh, what wonderful names!" Adam said. "Maybe soon you will have one named Kampala! Or Arua!"

"Well, only if some major world event happens there. I got Beijing during the Tiananmen Square massacre," I said, reaching in to give her a reassuring pat.

"And Berlin? Did you get him when the Berlin Wall came down in 1989?" Adam asked.

"Yes. Exactly." I was thrilled that our new friend kept up with world events. Like a lot of Americans, I had just assumed that Ugandans didn't have access to world news.

"Ah, when they have babies, madam, I would very much like to have one," said Alex. On a continent where ten percent of all children died before their fifth birthday because of lack of access to basic medical care, I couldn't possibly confess to having had our cats surgically sterilized.

"I'll let you know if that happens," I said.

Alex loaded our baggage and our cats into a Land Rover with the CARE logo painted on the doors.

"Madam," Alex said as he graciously opened the back door for me.

"John." Adam held open the other door. Then Adam and Alex got in up front and Alex settled in behind the steering wheel on the right side of the vehicle, which was the wrong side of the vehicle as far as I was concerned.

"You have seen our beautiful what?" Adam asked as Alex eased us out of the airport parking lot. I began searching for the correct answer, when he continued. "You have now seen our beautiful new airport. And I assume you also saw what is left of the old one."

"Yeah, I wondered about that," I said.

"And you know about the what?" Adam asked.

What is with the "whats"? I wondered.

"The hijacking and the Israeli raid on the Entebbe Airport," Adam said, answering his own question.

"Yes, we know about all that." I was glad we'd done some research—even if it amounted to watching movies—because if Adam was any indication, there *were* going to be quizzes.

"Well, in rescuing their people, the Israeli army destroyed what? They destroyed some Ugandan airplanes during that raid. We have a shiny new airport, but no money to take down the old one or remove the old airplanes that were destroyed in the raid. So they remain there, like a what?" Adam asked, but this time I just waited. "Like a museum."

I watched in quiet horror as Alex swung us onto the wrong side of a very nicely paved road. I thought that cultural sensitivity might require that I keep mum about someone's speech quirks, but I wasn't sure what it said about screaming when your host drives down the wrong side of a highway. But the vans and four-wheel-drive vehicles around us, advertising Missionary Aviation Fellowship, Save the Children, Mulago Hospital, and Lake Victoria Hotel from their flanks, were all driving on the left-hand side of the road too. None of their passengers seemed to be screaming, and as they say, "When in Rome." Or Africa, as the case may be. I must have skipped over the part in the CARE packet that said they drove on the wrong side of the road over here.

So I didn't scream, I just looked out the window and counted bridesmaids. At least, I thought all the women in elaborate dresses with flared waists and puffy sleeves were bridesmaids. Who would wear that kind of thing of her own accord? *A little formal for shopping,*

I thought, as I watched them pick over papayas, mangoes, bananas, and pineapples piled up at the side of the road. *The rubber flip-flops are a practical touch.*

"Adam," I asked, "are those women buying fruit for a wedding?"

"Excuse me?" he replied.

"Those women," I said, pointing to yet another group of shiny polyester-clad women at yet another thatched-roof fruit stand. "Why are they dressed like that?"

"Oh, those are *gomesis*. That is traditional Bugandan dress for women. My father is a tailor. He can make you one if you would like one."

"You'll look great in that, Eve," John said.

"Here in Uganda we have forty-eight different what? We have forty-eight different tribes. Buganda is the biggest tribe and many of them live around Kampala. Up in Arua, we have the Lugbara tribe. You and John will now be Lugbara!" Adam laughed. "Which is kin to my tribe, Achole. We are also from the north, in Gulu. My wife and children are still there. But they will join us soon in Arua."

"Do Lugbara women wear *gomesis*?" John asked.

"Ah, what the women in Arua wear you will soon find out," he said, laughing.

"Is it like Burkina Faso?" John asked. "Do they wrap themselves in *pagnes* on the bottom and not much on top?"

"Ah, yes, in the villages, they do!" Adam said. "But here we call them *kitenges*. Those are the very pretty pieces of cloth you will see all the women wrapped in. Eve, I am sure you will be wrapping yourself in a *kitenge* in no time!"

So this was going to be my new wardrobe choice: topless or polyester bridesmaid? I spent the next few minutes pondering which option I preferred.

We passed by several hotels with manicured lawns and gardens and then far more small shacks with corrugated tin roofs. Branches sporting clusters of red, purple, orange, and yellow flowers covered the sides of every building, arched over every gate, and sprouted out of cracks of red dirt in the sidewalk, making even the most ramshackle hovel look tropical and exotic.

"What are those beautiful bushes that are growing everywhere?" I asked.

"Oh, that one is bougainvillea," Alex said, pointing to the flowering branches that seemed to cover everything. "And that one with the big flower"—he pointed to the small bushes sporting plate-sized pink and red blooms—"that one is hibiscus."

"They are gorgeous. I didn't know Uganda would be so beautiful."

"Oh, madam." Alex sat up straighter in the driver's seat. "This is Uganda. Put a stick in the ground and it will bloom!"

"You have heard of what?" Adam asked. "You have heard of the Pearl of Africa. There is a reason the British called this place the Pearl of Africa! Uganda really has many wonderful things. But, unfortunately, people tend to hear only about the bad things."

"You have heard of what?" Adam continued. "You have heard of Idi Amin." Alex shook his head gravely and let out a tiny sound like air escaping from a tire.

"Of course we've heard about Idi Amin," John and I both said.

"Of course, you have. The whole world has heard of our Idi Amin. Crazy man," Adam laughed. "But before and after him we had what? We had Milton Obote. I bet you have not heard of him." And for the remaining forty-minute drive to Kampala, Adam kept up a steady stream of political and historical questions and answers about Uganda and East Africa. I was thoroughly impressed with his vast storehouse of knowledge, but far too jet-lagged to take in much of it. I enjoyed listening to his rich accent, though, and began to relax when I figured out that we weren't really expected to fill in the "whats."

As we got closer to the city, the fruit stands were replaced by wooden storefronts stacked tightly against one another, all covered in the same reddish brown mud that crept up between cracks in the sidewalk. An animal carcass hung from the awning of one shop, a pile of grease-covered car parts in front of another, soda and beer cases spilled out the door of the next. People milled about in front of them all. Variations of this same scene went on for miles. We bumped along surrounded by cars, motorcycles, four-wheel-drive vehicles, filthy white vans, and bicycles all crammed with passengers, until we finally crawled to a stop at a huge traffic circle.

"Welcome to Kampala," Alex announced as we inched our way clockwise around the circle. The mix of people, vehicles, and vendors didn't look so much like a capital city as a flea market gone mad. We turned onto one of the roads that fanned out in front of us and in the distance I saw several large, modern buildings that seemed to grow out of the smaller mishmash of one- and two-story structures made of wood and cement. We passed through a block full of sturdy cement shops, some with awnings painted with names like "Patel" and "Choudhury."

"You've heard what?" Adam asked. *I've heard I'm going to die of malaria and parasites, among other things.* But I don't think that's what he was looking for. "You've heard that East Africa has many resident Indians, yes?"

"Yes!" John and I both chirped, thanks to the fact that our pre-departure movie education had also included watching *Mississippi Masala.* "Idi Amin had expelled them all in 1976. But many are coming back now," Adam said. He waved his arms at some of the brightly painted buildings and I noticed for the first time a fair number of Indians—women in saris and men in crisp Nehru-collared shirts—in the mix of brown and black faces on the street. "They are good business people and own many of the shops in Uganda."

I took a closer look at the array of shops. *Who knows?* I thought. *Maybe they will have decaf cappuccino after all!*

"What are those?" I asked, pointing hopefully to several Western-looking stores with plate glass windows and signs that read "Duty Free!"

"Kampala has several duty-free shops," Adam said.

"Like at airports?" John asked.

"Yes, just like at airports."

"What can you get there?" I asked, vowing to stock up.

"You can get anything you want there, Eve. Alcohol, chocolates, perfume, cigars, electronics. All kinds of fancy things." *Okay,* I thought. *Now we're talking.*

"Yes, nice, isn't it?" Adam seemed as happy as I did. "I can't get anything there, though. You have to have a foreign passport to shop there." He laughed, although I couldn't for the life of me figure out why that was funny.

"But don't get too used to it," Adam said. "There are no duty-free shops in Arua." He swept his arm out the window and laughed once more. "In fact, there is not much of any of this in Arua."

"Okay, what the heck are those?" I asked, pointing to three pre-historic birdlike creatures towering over a pile of garbage. They looked like something out of a Flintstones cartoon.

"That is a marabou stork," Alex said. "Ugly, eh?"

"Scary is more like it." I couldn't stop staring—bald, scabby heads, sharp, pelicanlike beaks, huge black wings, and big white bellies, all balancing precariously on top of long, twiggy legs.

"*Hakuna matata.* That is Swahili for 'no worries,' Eve. They like garbage and dead things, but not people." Adam laughed. "Of course, the national bird of Uganda is the what?" *Ooh, I knew that one, having read it somewhere in that huge information packet from CARE.*

"What is the crested crane, Alex?" I shouted.

"Yes, the crested crane," Adam said. "But I am Adam. He is Alex." Adam pointed to Alex.

"I know you're Adam. I'm Eve!" I was getting punchy. "It's a joke. From a television game show in America," I explained.

"Ah. *Jeopardy!*" Adam shouted.

"You watch American television?" John asked.

"No, of course not. And you will not be watching television—

even African television—in Arua, either. But I read newspapers from all over. And I listen to the radio every day. You would be surprised by what you can learn listening to BBC and Voice of America."

Alex deposited the cats and our luggage at a hotel and took John and me to CARE headquarters, where we were introduced to the CARE country director, an American named Stan.

"Welcome to the CARE family." Stan had a slight drawl and a hearty handshake, especially for a man who had recently been shot. His laid-back manner as he introduced us around struck me as more cowboy than country director. But I suppose being in the Third World is a bit like being out on the range: Both will roughen you up around the edges if you stay long enough.

The alarm bells in my internal clock were going off. I hadn't slept in two days, and what I wanted more than anything was to get horizontal. I was hoping it would be in a bed and soon. But it wasn't looking promising as we were whisked to some expat staff member's home nestled in one of Kampala's many hills. Inside the large, airy house were an impressive spread of food and an equally impressive assortment of alcohol. Outside on a lovely patio lit with mosquito coils and blue bug zappers, I was introduced to and promptly forgot about fifty people. CARE staff members and their families ate, drank, talked, and laughed. They were Ugandan, Kenyan, Filipino, Canadian, British, and American, all unfailingly kind and welcoming.

"Do you know Elizabeth Marum?" I asked all the Americans, hoping someone could lead me to the USAID woman who, in my mind at least, was going to save me from unemployment. She was the HIV/AIDS connection, according to the folks I'd spoken to back in the States. And I held fast to the hope that she would find me a job on one of her AIDS projects.

Several of John's fellow staff members extended dinner invitations to us. Each took great pains to explain which of Kampala's twenty hills he or she lived on, as if it meant anything at all to us. The spouses all volunteered to take me shopping. There was a lot I still had to learn about expat life, but clearly eating, drinking, and shopping were top priorities.

Finally, someone must have noticed that our eyes were glazed over, and John and I were reunited with an antsy Beijing and Berlin in the hotel room. A sweet-smelling breeze and the chattering of strange birds wafted in through the open window as we collapsed into bed. I could swear I heard the screech of wild monkeys, which was hardly likely considering we were closer to the Sheraton than the jungle. I drifted off to sleep with visions of bridesmaids, prehistoric penguins on stilts, and plane carcasses dancing in my head. And I thought sleepily, *What a lovely little corner of hell.*

Dear Mom,

   Here we are, safe, sound, and surprisingly comfortable in Kampala. One week down . . . only 103 more to go! Uganda so far is nothing like I expected. It's not awful at all. People have phones, flush toilets, and even toilet paper. And colonialism may be dead, but all the trappings of it are still here. So while most Ugandans are poor and live simply, anyone with any shillings to spare (and that includes us self-sacrificing development workers) lives in a fancy house with a housekeeper and has a fancy car with a driver. So, really, a Jewish American Princess might be able to live out her fantasy in Africa, after all, although I still haven't found the mall yet.

   John is already settling in at CARE. He's so adaptable, it's nauseating sometimes. But I'm moody and culture shocked enough for the two of us. My birthday was quiet, but not depressing. John sent a beautiful bouquet of roses and carnations (yes, Kampala has a florist that delivers!). The folks at CARE gave me a birthday card and I got a card in the mail from one of my former medical students (see, mail here works just fine). I did not get a card from the woman who birthed me, however. We had dinner and a birthday cake at the CARE assistant director's house.

And quietly, my ovaries turned one year older . . .

I'll keep you posted,
Eve

Chapter Twelve

Home Sweet—or at Least No Cow Dung Here—Home

"You are welcome," a young man in a blue uniform said as he opened the gate. "Shoo, shoo," he barked at the goats that grazed just outside the gate. They squealed and ambled a few feet away.

"Hello, James," Stan called out the window to the young man as he drove into the square compound. He pulled the vehicle up to a long, one-story cement building that was bright yellow and had matching verandahs on either end. The compound was tidy, its neatly trimmed grass punctuated with a few trees. The requisite bougainvillea grew up and flopped over the six-foot-high fence.

"Look at that," I said, nudging John and pointing to a long skinny sign hanging over the double garages that served as the seam between the two Siamese-twin houses. Blue letters on a white background spelled out "J. Waite & E. J. Brown" with an arrow pointing to the house on the left and "CARE Guesthouse," with an arrow pointing to its mirror image on the right. "You think they knew we were coming?"

"James, I'd like you to meet John Waite, our new Savings and Credit project manager, and his wife, Eve Brown," Stan drawled.

"Welcome," James said, shaking each of our hands. "I am James. My family lives in the boys' quarters." He pointed to a small house at the back of the compound. "Thank you for coming to Uganda. May I bring your things into the house?"

"Please," Stan said, and James began unloading the back of the vehicle.

"Boys' quarters?" I said.

"In colonial times, everyone had servants—or 'boys.' That's where they used to house them," Stan explained.

"Oh, too bad you're here already," called a white woman in sturdy shoes and a no-nonsense dress from the porch on our side of the house. "I was hoping to have enough time to get another layer of cow dung onto your house before you arrived!"

I stood there, staring. *Where, exactly, does the cow dung go?*

"Oh, I'm just kidding. I'm Pauline, Terry's wife," she said, shaking our hands.

"I'm Terry. Welcome to Arua," said a white-haired man standing next to her. We already knew from our orientation in Kampala that Terry was John's boss and head of the CARE Arua office. We'd heard that Terry's development days began back in the Queen's colonial service in Rhodesia. He looked every inch the part in his khaki shorts and kneesocks; a safari hat sat jauntily atop his frosty-bearded head. Based on how long they had been around the development world, I assumed they were close to our parents' age. But there was no mistaking these two for a pair of rocking-chair grandparents.

"This is your house," Pauline said. She opened the double door from the verandah and ushered us into an airy living room with a huge rattan mat that covered the painted cement floor.

"Wow! Nice furniture," John said. He ran his hands along the wood coffee table that sat between a simple but sturdy couch and two chairs. It had taken some effort on my part to convince him not to ship the coffee table that he'd made in the seventh grade and had been dragging around the world with him ever since.

"Wow! Furniture" was all I could manage. It was all much nicer than I'd expected. Okay, anything with walls would have been nicer than I'd expected.

"We've set you up with the basics," Pauline said. "But if you find you need anything else, or want to switch out the furniture, you can take anything you need from the guesthouse next door. It's all pretty much the same, but help yourself."

"Oh, soft couch," John said, testing the cushions that rested on the simple wood frame. This from the guy who'd once lived with a dead mouse under the couch cushions. I seemed to have been the only one who had noticed the smell—and the rigor mortis lump.

"You have a nice big kitchen," Pauline said, leading us through a doorway off the dining area that held a rectangular table surrounded by blocky wooden chairs. "Your refrigerator and stove run on propane. You'll want to be sure to let James or someone at the office know when you're running low. Here's your water filter." She pointed to something that looked like a cross between a large thermos and a small drum sitting next to the sink. "You'll want to refill it with boiled water every night."

I wondered if I should be taking notes.

"You've got a small hot water heater. You won't get a lot of hot water," she said, nodding at a white enamel box that sat on the windowsill and had a small pipe running into the sink below. "But if you turn it on every night when the power comes on, you should have enough for your house girl to do the dishes in the morning."

Er, house girl? Now I *knew* I should be taking notes.

"Here's your storage pantry," Pauline said as she swept across the room and opened a door as if she were presenting the grand prize on *The Price Is Right.* I didn't dare ask what I might be storing in there.

"Now I'll show you the private quarters." Pauline led us out of the kitchen and through a doorway on the opposite side of the dining area. "Bedroom, bedroom, bedroom," she said, motioning to three open doorways off the long hallway.

"Wow, three bedrooms!" John exclaimed.

"Wow, beds!" I exclaimed.

"You'll want to be sure to sleep under your mosquito nets every night. Lots of malaria around here," Terry said. "There are two kinds of malaria, you know. The kind that can kill you, but once it's treated it's gone. And then there's the kind that won't kill you, but it lives forever in your blood. Lucky us. In Arua we have both!"

"We've already started taking our Paludrine," I said, proud that I was already on top of my prophylaxis.

"And we got shots for yellow fever and cholera, and took two of the three doses of our typhoid pills," John reported. "We accidentally left the third in our friend's refrigerator. Should we worry about that?"

"I wouldn't," Stan said. "Why'd you take all those in the first place?" he asked.

"Well, that's what it said in the packet you sent us," John said.

"Oh?" he said.

Hadn't he read the packet? "You mean they don't have all those diseases here?" I asked.

"No, they got 'em, all right. I guess I just don't worry about that too much. The medical care here is really quite good. I didn't even have to be medevaced when I got shot. They patched me right up in Kampala." *And, silly me, I was busy worrying about piddly little diseases like cholera and typhoid.* Maybe CARE should have updated the welcome packet. Instead of vaccinations, perhaps we should have been told to get bulletproof vests.

"Well, here is the bathroom." Pauline pointed to a room with a sink and a tub with a shower.

"Um, where's the toilet?"

"Oh . . . outside," Terry said, smiling.

Call me prissy, but I had been hoping for indoor plumbing.

"Terry, you'll scare her off!" Pauline slapped him lightly on the arm. "There actually is one outside, but that's for the *askaris,* the guards that work around the yard. You'll have them in and out of your compound, working in your yard and in the guesthouse next door. Your toilet is right here." She led us to a small room right next to the bathroom. I felt infinitely better. The whole house looked very civilized. No cow dung anywhere.

"Well, we'll leave you two to get settled. Stan, I've got the guest-house all set up for you. We'll expect you all for dinner tonight at our house," Pauline said.

"Gin-tonics at sundown?" Stan asked.

"Of course. It's medicinal, y'know!" Terry said. "The quinine in the tonic water helps prevent malaria."

"Really?" I asked.

"Well, I wouldn't count on it. But it's a good excuse to drink."

"Oh, bring along your tennies," Pauline said. "We've got a bad-minton court."

"Tennies?" John asked.

"That's sneakers for us Americans," Stan said.

"Well, it's certainly very kind of you to have us to dinner so soon," John said.

"That's what we do around here," Terry said.

"It all comes around. You'll feed us when we've been on the road," Pauline added. "You'll see."

An hour later, Stan walked us down a dirt road and across a field to Terry and Pauline's house. A tall, skinny man, wearing the same blue uniform as James, stopped hacking at the grass with a machete and opened the gate.

"Good evening, sir. Welcome."

"Good evening, Solomon. I'd like you to meet our new arrivals. This is John Waite and his wife, Eve."

"Ah, welcome," he said. I tried not to stare at the row of perfectly straight scars that decorated his forehead from the bottom of his hair-line to the tops of his eyebrows.

"All the CARE compounds have *askaris*," Stan said as we followed the long, palm-tree-lined driveway into a lush, green yard. "You'll have James during the day and Nasser at night. And occasionally Solomon, here, or Busiya—he's usually next door at Hatchard's house—or one of the other guys from the office will fill in on days off. You'll like these guys. James over at your house is young, but he's great."

"Just in time for a game," Terry said, coming down from the verandah as we reached the makeshift badminton court laid out behind the house.

"Just in time to watch," Stan said. "But maybe these two want to join you for doubles."

"I had Solomon rechalk the lines today. So we can play a proper game, if you guys know how," Pauline said, joining Terry on the court.

Boys' quarters, house girls, badminton . . . Who knew that postcolonial Africa was so much like, er, colonial Africa?

"Well, I'm certainly game for anything," John said.

"I guess I am too," I said with a shrug. *What's next,* I wondered, *Robert Redford buzzing overhead in his open cockpit plane?*

Stan sunk into a cushioned seat on the shaded verandah and watched as Terry and Pauline proceeded to whip our butts in a rousing game.

"Geez, what do they put in the Geritol here?" I whispered to John as we limped over to the verandah.

"Don't worry, you'll get the hang of it," Terry said. He handed out drinks after the game. "We play every evening."

We sat on the verandah, drinking as the sun sank quickly behind the green hills in the distance.

"I'll go check on supper." Pauline popped out of her chair.

"Can I help?" I asked.

"It's all done, really. I had Beatrice set up before she left. But come on in and I'll give you the tour, if you'd like. Terry's the senior staff member in Arua, so we have the big house." She led me through the beautiful wood-and-glass doors. "It certainly isn't fancy by Kampala standards," she said. "But we like it." I followed her through the living room and dining room, both with parquet floors and huge louvered windows. Her house was definitely grander than mine by any standards. "Your kitchen is bigger," she said, showing me the small, well-equipped kitchen. "But we've got what we need." I noticed her pantry was very well stocked. Very.

"Does someone sleep in there?" I asked, pointing to the sleeping bag curled up on the pantry floor.

"No! That's for making yogurt," she said, as if every Jewish girl from Brooklyn knows it takes a sleeping bag to make yogurt. "Once you figure out where you're going to get your milk, I'll give you some starter so you can make your own."

Okay, so I had no idea what she was talking about. But something about the way she said it told me I was not going to be getting my milk—or my yogurt—from a corner bodega.

"Here are our private quarters." She opened a door to a hallway across from the dining room. "Three bedrooms, like yours, but I use the little one as an office. And go ahead, look into our bedroom," she said, pointing me to the large room at the end of the hall.

"Wow," I said. "Nice built-in dressers. That's neat."

"No, look behind you, through that door."

"Oh, wow! A master bathroom!"

"Yes, an en suite bath. In Africa!"

Yup, it was definitely nicer than our house . . . or our apartment in Brooklyn for that matter.

"Here," she said, continuing the tour down another hallway, "Terry has his shop." I poked my head into a room loaded with hand tools, wood, and projects in various stages of completion. "And there are Solomon's quarters," she said, pointing further down the long hallway.

"Is that what I think it is?" I said breathlessly.

"Oh, the washing machine?" Pauline shrugged.

"You have a washing machine?" I stared at the most gorgeous thing I'd seen in a week.

"Well, we have one. But we certainly don't use it."

Can I use it? I wanted to ask. The fact that I was coveting my neighbor's modern appliance after only one week in Africa was probably not a great sign.

"Why don't you use it?" I asked, and Pauline looked at me as if I didn't know a thing about living in the bush. Which was fair, since, let's face it, I didn't.

"Well, we'd have to fill it by hand, for one thing. There certainly are no water hookups in this house. And it would take more water than we could spare. And then we'd have to either run it when we get power at night or turn on the generator."

I still didn't see the problem.

"Anyway, Beatrice does all the washing by hand."

"Who is this Beatrice? She sounds handy."

"Beatrice. Our house girl."

"Is she really a girl?" I asked. "Shouldn't she be in school?"

"Oh, Beatrice is a perfectly grown-up woman with children of her own. It's what they call housekeepers around here. I didn't make it up. Beatrice has been helping me get your place set up. I can send her over to work with you until you get your own house girl."

Okay, I thought. *I am going to have to get this lady straightened out.* I might have been incompetent. I might have been undomestic. But I didn't need to hire people to do my household chores. Besides, the whole servant thing was kind of creeping me out.

"Terry," Pauline said as he walked into the house with John and Stan. "Why don't you put on some dinner music?"

Terry thumbed through a collection of record albums next to the stereo on the sideboard in the dining room. "How about the Carpenters?" he suggested. *Thus answering the age-old question of who still listens to the Carpenters? Apparently, people who've been, quite literally, living in a jungle for a long while.* I wondered if I should break it to them that Karen was dead.

Dear Jean,

Before I can give you my first impressions of Arua, I have to fill you in on the adventure of just getting here.

So, let's see, first I wake up with a case of . . . how shall we say it . . . Idi Amin's revenge? Development workers' tummy? The tourist trots? Well, you get the picture. But Stan, the CARE country director, who's driving us up to our new home says, "Hakuna matata, we can stop whenever you need to go to the bathroom." I'm a bit relieved, thinking, "Thank God this country has public restrooms." And as we're driving I'm keeping my eyes peeled for one of those universally recognized restroom signs or maybe a discreet pit latrine somewhere. But pretty soon, I get it. He meant we can literally stop whenever you need to go, and, well, you just go. It's like the whole country is one big latrine. I don't know . . . is that a good or a bad thing? (Note to self: when traveling in Uganda, always wear a skirt. It makes going to the bathroom by the side of the road much more discreet.)

So we drove for eight hours, getting tossed around on these dirt roads, dipping and bouncing around on these unavoidable crater-sized potholes and getting completely coated in thick red dirt. The whole route is lined with mud-and-thatch villages, barefoot women carrying loads of wood on their heads and babies on their backs, and dust-covered children who wave to us ceaselessly. (John and I both have sore arms from waving back the entire time. Stan doesn't bother to wave back. I don't know if that's because he's been here so long or because his arm still hurts from being shot in it the last time he drove up to Arua.)

We drove through bombed-out shells of villages and battered army tanks rusting by the side of the road. Then we drove through nothing and I mean great, long stretches of NOTHING. Then we came to the monkeys and the baboons—which dragged around their bright blue bottoms like they owned the road, and let's face it, they do. Then we came to the Nile River, which we crossed on a "ferry." A rather flimsy-looking metal raft, which was all there was between our Land Rover and all those hippos and crocodiles.

Then we got to the other side of the Nile and we drove some more. We drove until just about a minute before I was sure we were going to fall off the edge of the earth. Then we came upon a green, flowering oasis. Ahhh . . . Arua, our new home.

I'll keep you posted,
Eve

P.S. A note about tampons. You can find Tampax in Kampala but not in Arua, and no sign of my preferred o.b.'s anywhere. So I've got it all figured out, and based on what I brought with me, I have rationed myself to fourteen tampons a month. One cycle down: fourteen tampons exactly! So far, so good.

Chapter Thirteen

Two Kinds of AIDS

"Are you ready for your first what?" Adam asked, smiling and laughing, as he always seemed to be. He was staying next door in the CARE guesthouse until his wife and children joined him in Arua. "Are you ready for your first safari?"

"I thought safari is when you go to see wild animals," I said.

"Well, we are going on safari to see what? To see banks and economic development projects in the south."

Oh, I thought. *This is so what? This is so backward.* "They have banks here? Real actual banks with windows and tellers?" I was amazed.

"Yes, of course," Adam said.

"And lights?" Based on what I'd seen so far in Arua, I found that very hard to believe.

"Yes, Eve, real banks with lights and everything." Adam laughed. "Remember all of Uganda is not like Arua."

"Well, it sounds like a backward kind of safari. You know, instead of leaving the comforts of the modern world for a glimpse of the wild, we'd be leaving the wild for a glimpse of modern life."

"You don't have to go, Eve," John chimed in. "It'll just be for a week, and you've hardly had a chance to get settled in Arua. We haven't even finished unpacking yet."

"Stay all alone up here while you two go traipsing off to parts of the country with paved roads and electricity? I don't think so."

So we went on our first "safari," which I soon figured out is the exotic word for driving on roads so bad that you piss blood for a week afterward. And while the goal was seeing modern life rather than wildlife, we saw both. To get to Kampala, or the rest of developed Uganda, you had to cross the Nile River in Murchison Falls National Park. With so many animals in the park you could barely cross the road without hitting a blue-assed baboon, or cross the Nile River without hitting a hippopotamus.

Our first stop was in Kampala, where the staff at CARE headquarters had planned our itinerary and supplied us with a driver. While there, I put in a call to Elizabeth Marum, the contact I was counting on to get me a job.

"I'd love to meet you," she said in a singsong voice, in which I detected a mild Midwestern accent. "But I'm heading out of town for a few days to visit some of our projects. Can I call you when I get back?"

"Um, I'll be back in Arua by then."

"Arua? You're going to Arua?"

"Yeah, I was hoping you might know of some AIDS projects up there."

"Arua? Well, USAID doesn't have any projects in Arua. In fact, I can't even travel north of Murchison Falls. It's against embassy regulations for official Americans to travel there. It's considered too unstable. What are you doing in Arua?"

"That's where we're posted. My husband works for CARE."

"Arua?" she asked again, and the long pause that followed was not particularly reassuring. "Well, why don't you call me before you come down to Kampala next time? We can meet then."

"Um, yeah, there are no phones in Arua." This was going to be trickier than I'd anticipated.

"Listen, just send a radio message down to the CARE office before your next trip and have them call my office to let me know you are coming." Clearly, Dr. Marum knew how things worked around here. "If we're around, we'll have you and your husband over for dinner." She then proceeded to tell me which hill in Kampala they lived on.

Once on safari, we were greeted with glee wherever we went. This may have been simply because John and I were *mzungus,* the African term for Caucasians. Being white in Uganda had a certain similarity to being a celebrity in America. People seemed to fawn over us—and expect things from us—wherever we went. Of course, part of this might simply have been that in a country with little public transport and few privately owned vehicles, seeing our CARE-emblazoned Land Rover meant the possibility of a ride. Whatever it was, we were invariably fussed over, given tea and peanuts, or groundnuts as they are called in Uganda, and asked to sign the ubiquitous Visitors Book.

But after three days I grew bored by these meetings. John and Adam could—and did—talk happily for days about microlending and marginal economies. But much as I tried to look interested, after a half dozen of these meetings, even the thrill of electric lights was wearing off and I was bored. So while the boys were at yet another meeting at yet another bank, I decided to take a walk around the lovely town of Kyotera.

Kyotera, a small dusty town famous for absolutely nothing, is located in the Rakai district, famous for . . . well, AIDS. Uganda has the dubious distinction of being the epicenter of the AIDS pandemic in the 1980s and '90s. Within Uganda, the Rakai district led the nation in all things AIDS-related. The first known case of HIV in Uganda was identified there, and the district was still first in HIV prevalence and number of AIDS orphans.

But regardless of its unpleasant fame, it seemed no different from any of the other backwater Ugandan towns we'd visited. The dusty main road housed a hodgepodge of shops. I walked past one with dozens of tinny black bicycles, each one a carbon copy of the next, overflowing onto the red dirt outside. Inside the bicycle shop there were, of course, rows and rows of toilet paper. Maybe it was just me, but I still thought bicycles and toilet paper made strange bedfellows.

But apparently in Uganda they go together like tires and tuna fish. It was all very entertaining, but frustrating as hell if you needed, say, car parts and didn't know to look in the shop that sells soda.

Further up the road was a long row of tiny "lockup" shops. These were literally holes in the wall that were stacked floor to ceiling with goods. Browsing was impossible in these cramped spaces, and this sucked all the joy out of shopping for me. But there was no need to browse since my tour of Uganda had already taught me that all lockup shops carried pretty much the same items: huge cans of cooking oil donated by USAID, gritty toilet paper, and a few canned goods from Kenya. You asked for what you needed and made your purchase through a window carved into the outside wall. A corrugated tin sheet of metal was hinged to the top of this window and would be propped up by a stick if the store was open or hanging down if the store was "locked up."

As I approached the row of shops, I could hear the already familiar hawking and bartering sounds of the open-air market, which I knew would be just behind the row of lockup shops. Ugandan towns are pretty standard this way. And I knew too what they would be selling: starchy, tasteless *matoke*—the basis of all Ugandan meals—as well as sweet potatoes, papaya, pineapple, and bananas. So far I had managed to avoid shopping in these chaotic markets. We ate out while we were on the road, and because I hadn't fully set up house yet in Arua, we'd been frequent guests of Pauline and Terry's. But I knew I'd have to master the market sooner or later.

It quickly became apparent that Kyotera did not enjoy its fair share of *mzungus*, and I felt glaringly obvious as I walked up the road. No one was yelling *"Ife mani sende!"* (Give me money!) like they did all the time in Arua, but at least a dozen pairs of sleepy eyes were glued to me. I wished that I had wrapped a *kitenge* over my skirt to blend in more with the women around me. But who was I kidding? Nothing could make me blend in with the women around me. Glad to have an excuse to stop somewhere, I entered the open doorway below a sign proclaiming "Dr. Rashid's Center on AIDS Research."

I strained my eyes looking for evidence of a scientific establishment, or at least someone in a white coat. Instead, what I saw was a shop identical to the others that snugly surrounded it: a narrow cement room, its cracked floor swept impossibly clean, its whitewashed walls tired and peeling. A young woman unbent herself from the plastic pail in which she was washing her clothes.

"You are welcome," she said in that most characteristically polite Ugandan manner. "How can I help you?"

"I'm looking for Dr. Rashid's Center on AIDS Research," I told her. "I saw the sign from the road."

"You have come to Dr. Rashid's Center on AIDS Research," she answered in a voice brimming with officiousness. "And I am a staff member." I tried to mask my surprise. She ushered me inside and offered me a seat on a wooden bench. "Excuse me, please, while I get the Visitors Book."

I sat and waited, enjoying the coolness of the concrete wall on my back as I leaned against it. Taped to the opposite wall was a display that I assumed was meant to impress visitors with its officialness. It contained one unframed certificate testifying that Dr. Rashid was a member in good standing of the Ugandan Society of Traditional Healers, and two letters from the Ministry of Health. One letter stated that while Dr. Rashid was not a trained medical doctor, he could perform certain "basic, noninvasive medical procedures." The other letter stated that Dr. Rashid's experimental treatments on AIDS patients were highly questionable and that he should be closely monitored by the local medical authorities.

My hostess returned and I signed the Visitors Book, stating the obligatory date, name, address, and reason for my visit. While she took far too long to read the few words that I had written, she gladly allowed me to browse among the wooden shelves holding clear bottles of liquids in vivid shades of reds and greens, and muddy browns and yellows. I read their labels: "Red Liquid—for malaria, anemia, and cancer" and "Green Liquid—for fatigue, loss of appetite, tuberculosis, and AIDS."

I must have laughed out loud because the woman rushed over to give testimony that these liquids did indeed do as their labels proclaimed. "I myself am an AIDS victim," she declared. "My husband and child died of AIDS eight years ago and I had been near death myself from the disease. But now I am completely healthy!" Her bouncy enthusiasm underscored her renewed health.

I asked her about her miraculous recovery.

"Well, I have been taking treatment from Dr. Rashid's Center on AIDS Research and now I am very nearly healed!"

"Really?" I asked incredulously.

"Oh, yes," she assured me.

"And have you had an HIV antibody test recently?" I asked, trying to steer her toward reality.

"Well, yes," she answered sadly. "And, of course, I am still positive." I was relieved that she seemed to recognize that Dr. Rashid's magic liquids did not cure her AIDS.

"But," she continued brightly, "that is only because I am still having sex with my boyfriend, and he is positive, too. But Dr. Rashid says that if we could just stop having sex for two years, then we would surely both be HIV-negative again."

"Do you really believe that?" I asked. "Because in all the years I've been working with people with AIDS, and in all the articles I've read, and from all the medical professionals I've spoken to, I've never—" I stopped myself. As an educator, I thought she needed to know the facts, but I also wondered whether I had a right to stanch her hope.

"Well," she said with a smile, "we know what you Europeans think. But that is because you do not believe in our traditional cures, and you have to believe in them or they will not work. Dr. Rashid has cured hundreds of people. I am one of them."

"Is Dr. Rashid here?" I inquired. "I'd love to talk to him and learn more about his cures."

"Dr. Rashid cannot be here. He spends too much of his time traveling to other parts and teaching people about his cures."

"Too bad. I'd really love to meet him. I'm hoping to do some

AIDS education work in Arua. Maybe I will have a chance to meet him up there someday."

"Arua?!" I was already getting used to the alarm I got from most Ugandans when they learned we would be living in the West Nile. "Black people live up there!"

"Er, yes, that seems to be so. Black people live all over Uganda," I informed her, although I had assumed this was common knowledge.

"No, down here, we are brown-black. Up in the West Nile, they are black-black. And they are not civilized up there. You should be very careful that you yourself do not get AIDS."

I had an African American friend in New York who loved to tell me that only whites could be racist, insisting that black people couldn't be. I couldn't wait to tell her about this.

"Well, since I won't be having sex with anyone but my husband and he won't be having sex with anyone but me, and neither one of us is HIV-positive, I don't see how I can get AIDS even by living in Arua." I'll admit I needn't have given the details of my sex life to this rather questionable stranger. But I was a little shaken from the unexpected racism. Or was it shadism?

"Here in Uganda we have two kinds of AIDS. There is the one you can get from sex. This is the kind that Dr. Rashid can cure. But there is also the kind that you get from being cursed. They have much of that kind of AIDS in the West Nile. And that kind can never be cured!"

I really couldn't think of anything to say. So I thanked her, wished her continued good health, and said good-bye. And on the slow walk back, I felt a creeping sense of uneasiness take hold. *What if everything I know about AIDS prevention is useless here?* Suddenly, two years in Arua began to look like a very, very long time.

Dear Susan,

Just want to get a letter off in the mail before we head back to Arua. I spent the day in Kampala shopping while John was at more meetings. Good news about Kampala: Decaf is available . . . as is Baileys Irish Cream and Lindt chocolates and wine from France, Germany, Australia, and occasionally California, and beer from Germany and America, and canned tuna and all kinds of things. So while we are a bit deprived in Arua, one trip to Kampala—where we buy everything we can fit in our Pajero (that's our huge, jeeplike SUV)—and we're set.

Did some meeting and greeting at Save the Children. They are hoping to set up some projects in Arua eventually, but have nothing there now. I also met with some folks at UNICEF again. They're talking about having me consult on one of their projects. And maybe next time I'm in Kampala I'll finally get to meet with the woman from USAID. Keep your fingers crossed that something will pan out for me.

I was chatting with Alex, the CARE driver who was toting me around this morning. I asked him if he has any children. Seventeen children, he tells me, by six different wives! This is all going to seem normal to me one day, isn't it?

So these days Kampala feels downright luxurious to me. And it is, really. There's a Sheraton Hotel with two bars, four restaurants, and an amazing health club. There's a fancy "golf club" and several members-only social/recreational facilities that have tennis, squash, swimming, etc. Soon Alex is coming back to take me to the American Club, where I'll swim, eat, and sunbathe! I know, rough life, right?

Don't get me wrong—you know I love being spoiled. But it is a weird mix of deprivation and luxury here. And all this subservience, politeness, and deference to white people, well, it's making my skin crawl. I wonder, is this going to seem normal to me one day, too?

Okay, gotta shop.

I'll keep you posted,
Eve

🍃

Chapter Fourteen

The Birth of a Domestic Bush Goddess

As soon as we returned from safari, Terry got John oriented in his new job, and Pauline attempted to make a respectable bush wife out of me. This was no easy task considering the nondomestic raw material she had been given to work with. I had always lacked whatever it was that enables people to separate egg whites or iron a shirt without burning the coffee table. Even under the best of circumstances—and we are talking electricity and running water here—I had yet to grasp that sorting laundry meant by color not by thickness. In New York I had learned to accommodate my domestic disabilities, by eating out a lot and buying clothes that didn't need ironing. But that strategy was going to require some rethinking in the bush.

"Here's where you'll want to buy your beer and soda," Pauline said as she gently eased her muddy Land Rover to a stop in front of a tired-looking shop. I wondered if I'd ever be able to maneuver our stick-shift Pajero through the mud, crowds, and crater-sized potholes as deftly as Pauline just had. "They won't sell you full bottles without empty ones. So Terry and I are giving you a crate each of empty soda and beer bottles. Be sure you pass them on when you leave." *Ah . . . empty beer bottles, the gift that keeps on giving.*

"This shop sells soap from Kenya," Pauline said as she pointed to a small lockup shop. "All the other ones sell the local lye soap your house girl will want to use even though it'll burn holes in all your clothing."

I followed Pauline through an alley teeming with women balancing huge loads on their heads and lined with half-limbed lepers and other beggars. I couldn't help staring at the outstretched hands and handless limbs. "Should I give them money?" I asked.

"Sure, if you want to. But you should know you will be asked for money—and favors—all the time here. To everyone here, you are rich. And they won't stop asking." I'd never been rich before. I distributed a handful of ten-shilling notes among the group to a chorus of "thank you madam" and thought I would quite enjoy my newfound wealth.

We emerged from the alley onto a broken cement walkway that was lined on both sides by women who stood in little stalls behind stacks of tomatoes, onions, potatoes, cabbages, and okra, all calling out an inventory of their wares. Further down along the walkway, women sat on colorful straw mats amid pineapples, papayas, and mangoes, or on plastic sheets covered with bunches of bananas. Each row of vendors backed up to a covered area where older women sat and cooked over smoky fires or wove the colorful straw mats and baskets that hung from the corrugated tin roof. Beyond the covered areas were more rows of women hawking grains, rice, and plastic dishes. The perimeter was ringed with lockup shops.

The merchants on either side of me vied for my attention by waving and shouting at me. I prayed that I wouldn't lose Pauline in the crowd as she zipped ahead of me, striding across boards that served as bridges over deep ruts filled with murky water. I stopped praying once I realized how impossible it would be to lose sight of a white person in this sea of black people. I followed lamely behind as Pauline squeezed onions, hefted cabbages, and sniffed pineapples. I watched in absolute amazement as she kept a straight face while bargaining down the already ridiculously low price of tomatoes.

We stopped in front of a group of ancient-looking women surrounded by baskets, chattering away indecipherably amongst themselves.

"Dried beans, groundnuts, and termites," Pauline said, pointing to several of the baskets. "Do you need any?"

"Well, I suppose we could use some groundnuts and beans." But I somehow doubted that I'd ever have a need for termites. I pointed to what I wanted and all the other women smiled and slapped my chosen saleswoman on the back.

"Give her a couple of bags," Pauline reminded me, and I pulled out two of the stash of plastic bags that I had stuffed into my woven shopping bag before I left the house. I paid for my two-hundred shillings' worth of beans and groundnuts with a thousand-shilling note. The old woman I bought them from laughed as she tucked the bill into the beans in one bowl and retrieved the change from within the beans of another bowl.

We walked past a row of young women selling something in old soda bottles and what looked like heavy, golden water balloons. "Hello, Madam Pauline," they called out.

"Hello, ladies," she called back.

"What are they selling?" I asked.

"Oh, that's cooking oil. Donated by your government, as a matter of fact. Look." She pointed to the five-gallon red-white-and-blue cans that said "U.S. Food Aid."

"Now, Eve," Pauline said as she led me to a row of wooden stalls on the outside of the market. "Look at that stall. And that one over there. And that one." She pointed to the three small huts that served as butcher shops. "What do you see?"

"Ummm . . . well, there's a cow hanging upside down from a hook. At least, I think it's a cow. It's hard to tell when they're all skinned like that. Yes, it must be beef because there's the cow's head propped up on the counter."

"But what do you see hanging around the meat?" Pauline prodded me.

"About a billion very black people shouting and waving their arms?"

"No, no. The flies, Eve, the flies. See the flies? See how they're all over that carcass over there. And this one." Pauline pointed her arm at various stalls. "But that one over there, his doesn't have any flies on it. Would you say that's the one we want to buy meat from?"

"I would say that I am seriously considering vegetarianism."

"Sure you are, Eve." Pauline raised her eyebrows at me. "And when you're done with that, which one would you buy meat from?"

"I guess, the one without all the flies." I so wanted to give Pauline the right answer. She was generous and kind and my only friend. But she was so competent it was intimidating. I had already failed a pop quiz about my water filter earlier that day. When Pauline had asked if I was using steel wool or a soft cloth to clean the candles inside the filter, I knew I was in trouble. Because aside from the fact that I did not know whether I should be scouring or gently wiping the ceramic candles, up until that moment I hadn't known that my water filter had candles—ceramic or otherwise—much less that I was supposed to be cleaning them.

"No, no, Eve," Pauline said. "All the other meat has flies on it. Now how do you suppose this fellow keeps the flies off his meat?" She continued talking even as she led me through the chattering horde of humanity inching toward the front of the meat vendor's stall. Seemingly oblivious to the dead animal bits all around her, she poked her head behind the counter and reached over it with one arm.

"See, there it is!" She pointed to a bright yellow can of insecticide. "The ones with no flies on them have all been sprayed with Doom!

"You know," Pauline continued as she led me away from the meat vendors, "on Tuesdays and Fridays they have fresh fish at the market. You have to get here right when the fishermen come. It sells out pretty fast. I usually send Beatrice or Solomon to get it for me. It can get a bit hectic here on those days." *Hectic? What did she consider the bedlam going on around us now?*

John and I lived on a mostly vegetarian diet for a long time. Even while repeating the mantra "Flies on meat are a good thing," I couldn't quite work up the courage to buy meat from the bazaar. And I didn't dare attempt to go to the market on fresh-fish days.

Still, I knew I had it easier than most of my neighbors. I had a propane-powered stove and refrigerator, while most of them still cooked over a wood fire. People out in the village had no electricity whatsoever and even those of us in town were limited to three hours of electricity a day. We had a generator discreetly hidden away in our yard—for urgent uses like when I needed crushed ice to make piña coladas. But the first time I did that, the embarrassingly loud motor shattered the otherwise quiet afternoon, practically broadcasting the fact that the white lady was making boat drinks in her blender. From then on, I made do, like everyone else, with power from 7:00 p.m. until 10:00 p.m.—as long as there wasn't a war, a political crisis, or a thunderstorm.

But the truth is, I probably could not have survived long without those little luxuries. In Ecuador, I knew of a few Peace Corps volunteers who'd "gone native"—eschewing Western comforts and luxuries to live like the locals. I've always thought that was admirable, and nuts. And though I may have learned to live more simply than many Americans, I doubt I would have survived long without at least the possibility of a flush toilet, a shower, a video, and some cheese now and then.

Pauline, who was the undisputed Martha Stewart of jungle living, valiantly tried to pass her good-living tips on to me. But I was hopeless, rarely getting past the "firsts." "First you fillet the fish," she'd tell me. Or "First you pluck the chicken." Or "First you pasteurize the milk."

John, whose idea of haute cuisine is tuna-noodle casserole, ate whatever I served him—which was mostly some variation on the noodles, potatoes, and vegetable theme—and never complained. I couldn't even master rice, because first you had to clean the stones out of the rice by tossing and catching it in a woven funnel-shaped thing that looks enough like a sun hat that, let's just say a *mzungu* could easily embarrass herself. I watched local women do this task quickly and gracefully. But whenever I tried it, I ended up with half the rice on the floor, rocks in our supper, and something that looked an awful lot like a hat on my head.

I knew from the Peace Corps that a person could survive for months on a diet of potatoes and beer. But I was already sushi and latte deprived and getting cranky. Luckily, gin-tonics and badminton at Terry and Pauline's was an almost nightly ritual. And if we stuck around long enough, with sad, hungry, puppy-dog eyes, Pauline would usually invite us to stay for dinner. Like manna in the wilderness, somehow that woman whipped up gourmet meals of perfectly cooked fish, chicken stews, curries, rice pilaf (hold the rocks), bread warm from the oven, and the most decadent chocolate cake. So while I could see that, in theory, it was possible to eat well up here, deep in my heart I knew that I lacked the gene to make that happen.

"The catchment tank is nearly empty. Did you forget to turn on your water mains?" Pauline asked while making one of her daily sweeps through the compound, ensuring that all was shipshape at the guesthouse and probably hoping that things were in some sort of shape at my house.

"Forget? No." *Not know a damn thing about water mains? Yes.* I made a mental note to remember that the big metal tank in the yard was for storing water.

"Eve, when are you going to hire yourself a house girl?"

"I'm not."

Pauline gave me a benevolent smile. It was the kind of smile usually reserved for a three-year-old who announces that her best friend is coming for tea—from Mars. "Everyone here has help."

It did seem like household help was the norm in Uganda, and not just among expats. In fact, every place I'd seen so far—from fancy gated estates to circles of mud huts—had staff. There was always the requisite *askari* to man the gate and to constantly slash the grass—which, like everything in Uganda, was constantly growing—with a thick metal machete, known locally as a *panga*. Then there was always a house girl (who was always called a "house girl" even if she was a grown woman), a nanny to look after the kids, and sometimes even another nanny to look after the house girl's kids. Those who could afford it hired people. But even families with no money seemed to have a plethora of indentured relatives who filled the jobs.

"I think I can manage to clean my own house." True, Pauline and Beatrice had spent the past two days helping me unpack and finally get settled into my house. But I was already coming to the bleak realization that I was probably never going to find work here. I was making contact after contact both here and every time we hit the road. I got lots of offers of tea and groundnuts, but no offers of work. "What else am I going to do all day but take care of the house? Besides, we've got enough help around here already." James lived with his wife, two kids, and younger brother in the "boys' quarters" behind our house. Every night when James got off duty, Nasser relieved him and spent the night on my front porch.

"How are you doing washing your laundry by hand? And ironing *everything* to kill the mango fly eggs?" Pauline's emphasis on "everything" made me a bit nervous since I hadn't ironed *anything* in years. I didn't dare ask about the mango fly eggs. Besides, I was doing fine in the laundry department because I'd hired James's wife to do it. "And how much water do you figure you can carry from a borehole?" she continued, and I vowed to find out what, exactly, a borehole was and where I might find one. "And how do you like scrubbing floors on your hands and knees every day? Because if you don't, mind you, you'll have all kinds of creatures in your house. You'll hire a house girl," she said, flashing me that smile again, and now I knew I was the delusional three-year-old waiting for the spaceship to arrive.

"Oh, no I won't." I was happy enough to have the *askaris* in the yard, slashing the grass with their *pangas*, looking out for snakes, and protecting me from the onslaught of curious kids and whining goats that spent most of every day outside my gate. The *askaris* even ran errands and answered my endless questions. But I felt inadequate enough as it was, with no job prospects and all my obvious shortcomings as a bush wife. I was little more than an oddity for the neighbors—and the goats—to stare at all day. The last thing I wanted was someone else looking over my shoulder and making me feel even more useless.

"It's not a bad thing," she said, rolling her eyes at me. "It's hardly white slavery!"

"Don't you mean black slavery?" I asked.

"You know what I mean. Anyway, you'll be giving someone a very good job. Trust me, whatever you pay will be more than a woman could earn anywhere else. And with much better conditions. You'll have people lining up for the job. Just let me know if you want me to help you find someone."

I stuck to my guns, and broom, playing Suzy Homemaker on the African frontier for a few more weeks. Really, there wasn't much else for me to do. Sure, I could hire someone and then sit around watching soaps on television and eating bonbons all day. But there were no soaps—or anything else—on television in Arua. And no bonbons either.

But in September, when Beatrice found a nest of black mambo snakes while mopping behind a dresser in Pauline and Terry's house, I cried uncle ("house girl," actually). Keeping house and making meals from unidentifiable scratch was pushing the limits of my domestic envelope as it was. I knew enough to admit that removing killer snakes was beyond my skill set. Unfortunately, I proved to be just as inept at hiring household help as I was at most of the other domestic tasks. I mean what, exactly, does one ask of an applicant for this type of job? "When did you first realize you enjoyed cleaning other people's toilets?"

So, basically, I just hired the first woman who applied. I didn't know a thing about hiring help, but I knew a few things about recognizing AIDS. And the first woman who applied was clearly in the advanced stages of AIDS. Now this might have deterred some people from hiring Aisha, but I wasn't going to let a little bit of AIDS—or a lot—stop me. Besides, I reasoned, hadn't I come to Uganda hoping to help people with AIDS? Well, this might be as close as I got.

So I'd hired a house girl and done something to help someone with AIDS. Feeling rather pleased with myself, I turned my attention to finding something useful to do.

Dear Mom,

I had practically the whole United Nations over here for dinner on Rosh Hashanah. Not a Jew in the bunch. (I think I'm the only one in the whole country.) But Pauline, bless her heart, found me an apple to dip in honey that I bought from the one-eyed old man who brought it to my gate (I had to pick a few bee parts out, first). And John Hatchard, the crazy Brit who also works for CARE, snatched some sacrificial wine from the local Catholic church. Anyway, I'm explaining to everyone about how Rosh Hashanah is the Jewish New Year and Hatchard's wife, Anna (she's Ugandan), says to me, "There are only three religions in the world: Catholic, Protestant, and Muslim. So which are the Jews?" Oy vey!

No, I am not exactly the bush hostess with the mostess, but at least I had help. We now have Aisha, our "house girl!" I guess it's true what you've always said about me: Scratch below my hairy legs and armpits and there is a Jewish American Princess hidden inside.

Oops. I think Berlin just discovered that James's family keeps chickens in our yard. He's cowering behind the kitchen door looking rather frightened. The chickens cluck like crazy and everyone's damn goats bellow all day long. I swear, it's enough to turn a vegetarian into a carnivore.

Poor Beijing has taken to peeing in odd places. The bottom of our closet on John's dirty socks seems to be her favorite place. She even pooped on a rug once. Well, I'd chalk it up to her being in a big new house

and being blind, maybe she can't find the litter box,
but she seems to find the bottom of our closet—and
John's socks—pretty consistently. We think that she
didn't like the wood shavings that we were using in her
litter box. (Guess what? No cat litter in Uganda!)
We've switched to sand (which there is plenty of
around here) and things have gotten better.

I'll keep you posted,
Eve

Chapter Fifteen

🌿

The Voice of the Mzungu,
or Food, Glorious Food

"*Ife mani sende. Ife mani sende.*" The chorus of begging children followed us as we walked down the road to the CARE office. "Hey, you, *mzungu, ife mani sende.*"

"Oh, isn't that nice," John said, waving enthusiastically at the children. "The kids all greeting us like that."

"Honey, they're asking us for money!"

"Well, it's nice that they're talking to us," he said to me. "*Mingoni,*" John yelled to the children. "*Mingoni,*" he greeted the women who passed us with huge loads of bananas on their heads.

"*Goni yo,*" each one of them answered and, then, holding on to their bananas, doubled over with squeals of laughter.

"They seem really impressed with your language skills," I told him. We'd started taking Lugbara lessons as soon as we arrived in Arua. I usually have an easy time picking up new languages, but Lugbara was driving me crazy.

"Lugbara is not a written language," our tutor told me whenever I asked how to write something so I could review it later. It apparently was not a language that had rules or bothersome syntax either.

In addition to learning how to handle the ubiquitous demands for money, I had managed to learn enough to make my way through the market. And John managed to learn how to say "hello."

What John lacked in language-acquisition skills he more than made up for with his ability to assimilate. With more than six feet of pale skin and a bright red beard, John was easily the whitest man in Africa. Yet, he believed that no one actually noticed this. Wherever he went, he behaved as if he belonged and people treated him as if he did. Not me. I knew I was the short, white center of attention wherever I went. But being the limelight-loving Leo that I was (and harboring the secret belief that I was Marilyn Monroe's reincarnation since I was born the day after she died), I usually didn't mind the attention.

Still, I was afraid that I'd be a distraction at the nutrition class in the village of Nicu, where I was headed with two of John's colleagues. Our safari down south had taught me that you could not be a *mzungu* fly on the wall. Wherever we went, John and I had received a gracious welcome, an obvious seat of honor up front, and a request to say a few words on the topic at hand. This was kind of fun at first, making us feel appreciated. But it got pretty tiresome once we figured out that they weren't asking us to speak because they thought we had something intelligent to say. It was simply about the color of our skin.

But since this was a health presentation to a women's club, I thought that maybe I could add something useful to the discussion. At least I hoped that I wouldn't be too disruptive. Besides, now that Aisha was cleaning my house, sort of, in between coughing jags and intense fatigue, I needed something to do.

The women's club meeting was scheduled to begin at 10:00 a.m. But John's colleagues, Susan and Patience, assured me that these things never begin on time. I had already noticed that in Uganda, nothing begins on time. At 10:00 a.m., we got into the CARE Land Cruiser and began the eleven-kilometer drive. The distance was short but the condition of the dirt road, even on this clear and dry morning, ensured at least a half-hour trip. Looking through the window at the anthills and acacia trees, I wouldn't have been surprised to see a giraffe or a lioness grazing in the distance.

I was amazed that my fellow travelers seemed to be carrying on a conversation. I was hard-pressed to make out anything with the jolting and banging of the vehicle over the holes, dips, and rocks in the road. Over the road noises, I couldn't tell if they were speaking heavily accented English—which they might have spoken for my benefit—or their native Lugbara. So I concentrated on the view: compounds of thatched-roofed huts, called *paillotes,* rimmed with brilliant flowers. A barefoot and bare-breasted procession of women wearing brightly colored skirts, carrying enormous loads of wood, charcoal, and fruit on their heads, most with babies wrapped tightly to their backs. Young girls with bright yellow plastic jerry cans or clay bowls on their heads and water splashing onto their shoulders. I looked ahead at the goats, chickens, and cows that wandered onto the road—like they wandered everywhere in Arua—hoping my unerring watchfulness would somehow keep them out of our path.

At 10:40 a.m. we rolled into the center of Nicu, which was basically a well-worn intersection of two dirt roads with a few covered stalls selling sugarcane. We passed the village meeting place, an arching ficus tree whose broad leafy branches provided a cool, shaded area in the surrounding grass. It was empty except for two grazing goats and the playful squeals of the young girls filling their jerry cans at the nearby hand-pumped well, or borehole. We parked our vehicle and got out.

"Now, how will everyone know it's time for class?" I asked Susan and Patience.

"We will just wait here. They will notice us." And sure enough, within minutes it seemed like the entire village stopped what they were doing and began to gather under the ficus tree.

Someone brought a small wooden bench out of a market stall for Susan, Patience, and me to sit on. The villagers began to seat themselves on the ground, forming a circle around us—women and infants on one side, men on the other side. While the adults slowly assembled, a small group of children gathered quickly behind our bench. They jostled and pushed each other to get close to us.

"How are you?" a small, high-pitched voice chirped in the very formal, stilted English that Ugandans used.

"I am fine," I answered. "How are you?" The entire group of children fell into a mass of giggles.

"I am fine. How are you?" chimed a second, bolder voice.

"I am fine," I dutifully replied. "How are you?"

"I am fine. How are you?" a third voice followed.

Getting a little bored with your game is what I wanted to say. "I am fine. How are you?" is what I did say. And in this way, the game continued until each child had gotten to ask the question and had received an answer.

When Susan and Patience felt that enough adults had gathered, they began the session. I was still struck by the irony of a man standing up and introducing himself as the chair of the women's group, although I'd already seen that kind of thing several times. But it was common for men to hold most of the positions of authority in rural Uganda, even though, from what I could tell, women did the bulk of the work.

The assembled group stood and sang the national anthem and bowed their heads while an elder intoned a prayer. The formality of the whole thing struck me as odd, seeing as how I was sitting among bare-breasted women under a tree in the dirt. Susan, Patience, and I duly rose as the chairman introduced each of us. Finally, Susan began, in seamless Lugbara, to explain the basic concepts of nutrition.

Despite Patience's translation into English, I quickly became bored. Susan talked about the different food groups and I checked my watch. Since the topic was food, I thought about what I would make for lunch. Even with my comparatively luxurious kitchen, meal preparation was still a major preoccupation for me. I could have asked Aisha to prepare our food, I suppose. After all, I knew I didn't have to worry about contracting HIV in this way. But I was starting to get concerned about catching tuberculosis, which I was now pretty sure she also had.

In addition to John and me, I was now making lunch for Aisha and anyone else who was working in our compound at lunchtime. I usually made supper for the two of us, and often, Adam, who was still staying in the guesthouse, still waiting for his family to arrive from Gulu. He had been waiting for close to two months, but waiting seemed to be a way of life for Ugandans. And it seemed fairly common for a husband to be off working in one part of the country, while the wife stayed with the children elsewhere. With his great sense of humor and wealth of stories about Uganda, I never minded having Adam over for dinner. Plus, he was always willing to try everything I cooked—even if it wasn't the Ugandan staple dish, *matoke*. "You had better take a photo of this, Eve," he told me one night when he was helping John clean up after supper. "I do not think you will see many Ugandan men washing dishes."

So I was doing a lot of cooking and shopping. Because we were so far from any major towns and because there was no refrigeration in any of the shops in Arua, our diet was pretty much made up of what was grown locally. So far that had meant a lot of tomatoes. On any given day, at least a dozen women hawked improbably high piles of bright red tomatoes. I'd asked around for green ones so I could experiment with making fried green tomatoes (someone had sent us the movie) and word spread. Now several of the tomato ladies proudly kept aside a pile of green ones just for me and I felt compelled to buy them all, and thus we also ate a lot of green tomato experiments.

When we had first arrived I'd been thrilled to see all the mangoes. They were piled high in the market stalls and dripping from trees in our yard. We greedily ate them tart and green early in the season, and sweet and soft later on. We also cooked them into sauces, made mango mousse and ice cream with a hand-cranked ice-cream churner that got passed among the expats. Then we made huge vats of mango chutney and ate that on everything. Then we got bored with mangoes.

Of course, there were the old reliable potatoes, rice (without stones, now that I had Aisha to clean it), okra, and the ubiquitous, starchy *matoke*, which looked like a large, dark banana. It was deceivingly difficult to prepare. You had to score and then peel the tough skin in an arduous operation guaranteed to turn your fingers black. Then you had to boil it, mash it, and serve it covered in sauce to give it flavor. Its main appeal, as far as I could tell, was that it expanded to fill your stomach. It certainly didn't have much taste.

As Susan continued her lecture, I perked up when I heard Lugbara words that I recognized: *au gbe:* egg; *nyanya:* tomato; *osu:* beans; *lesu:* milk. But I was relieved when Susan finally finished her lecture. I was hungry and anxious to get home to lunch. But we wouldn't be leaving just yet. After the lecture came time for questions and answers, and as I had already learned in Uganda, there were always lots of questions.

The typical way of teaching in Uganda is pretty standard. Teachers lecture and students listen. The strict hierarchy of Ugandan society and its almost cloying politeness rule out the possibility of open exchange in a classroom setting. So the question-and-answer period, which provides the only opportunity for discussion, tends to go on forever.

"To which food group do grasshoppers belong?" asked one woman. I scratched my head but couldn't remember learning that in public health school.

"Grasshoppers are protein," Susan explained. "But you must be careful not to eat the poisonous ones that leave the holes in your laundry." And right then and there, I vowed never to eat those Darth Vader–looking grasshoppers that swirled around and then landed on my clothesline.

"Why do fried termites upset my stomach?" asked an old woman. Now I was pretty sure I could hazard a guess, but I let Susan answer.

"Even too much of a good thing can give you an upset stomach," Susan warned. And everyone nodded as if they had all had more than their fill of the treat they called "African Buffalo." Everyone but me, it seemed.

Then, when it seemed that all questions had been answered, came one from an ancient gentleman on my left. I was quite surprised when he stood up and addressed me.

"Madam," it was translated by the chairman, "you have been kind enough to come here today to join us. All this time you have listened to us. But we have yet to hear your voice. Would you be so kind as to let us hear the voice of the *mzungu?*"

All of his neighbors enthusiastically began nodding their heads and clapping their hands as if he had finally asked the one question that had been burning inside all of them. It was the grown-ups' version of the game the children had been playing with me earlier. They just wanted to hear the voice of the *mzungu.*

"*Mingoni,*" I said in greeting as I stood up, slightly embarrassed. Great white smiles and warm laughter spread among the group. They clapped and all started talking at once.

"They are happy to know that you speak Lugbara," Patience translated. "They want to know what else you can say in their language."

"*Ife mani sende?*" I ventured, not knowing if it was appropriate. But let's face it, it was the sentence I knew the best.

The group erupted in great waves of laughter and clapping. Not knowing much more, I continued with the only other words that I knew. "*Au gbe, nyanya,*" I told them, thinking hungrily of what I would have for lunch. "*Osu, lesu!*"

The cheering and clapping continued as I quickly exhausted my shopping list—and my vocabulary. But I smiled as I stood there speechless.

"Well," said the old man who had asked the question. "It is good to know that even for *mzungus,* food is the universal language!"

Dear Mom,

Well, I'm still not working—unless you consider baking bread and shelling peas and that sort of thing working.

Yesterday I was out in the garden with James. (I know, it's autumn where you are. But here it's eternally summer.) And as if it's not weird enough having someone to help me in the garden, I also have someone to fetch me tea! Aisha sets up a lovely table on the verandah and I invite James to join me for a cup of tea. Well, if his skin weren't brown, I'm sure he'd be blushing twelve shades of red. Apparently, *mzungu* are not supposed to invite the "help" for tea! James made himself a cup of tea but wouldn't sit down to drink it. Finally, he asked, "May I go somewhere to sit and drink my tea, madam?" ("Madam" is my new name.) I told him he could sit wherever he liked and offered him the empty chair next to mine. "Oh, no, I couldn't sit there, madam," he says. "That is Mr. John's chair!"

Did I tell you about all the expats in the neighborhood? I'm making friends! In addition to Pauline (who has taken me under her wing and is determined to help me survive here), I now have a Dutch friend named Coby. She also followed her husband here (he works for a Dutch organization) and she's also desperately looking for a job. And they have a two-year-old son. In fact, there are four expatriate families with kids here. And the three Italian M.D.'s—one is an OB/GYN—who live on our road. And the consensus is that it is perfectly safe to be pregnant here, and even to deliver in a pinch. In fact, they all say it's the best place to raise kids. So, I just wanted to let you know that John and I are thinking about it.

I'll keep you posted,
Eve

Chapter Sixteen

Scaredy Cat

The blast made us all drop our forks and made the needle on the Johnny Mathis album skip. Good food; old music: We were having dinner at Pauline and Terry's house.

"What the bloody hell was that?" yelled John Hatchard. I thought he sounded more like a Liverpool docker than a project manager. But with his Ugandan wife and his years of living in Africa, he was as much African as British now. "That nearly blew my bloody arse off!"

We all looked out the window toward where the blast had come from and saw nothing unusual.

"I'll see if I can raise anyone on the radio," Terry said, heading outside to his Land Rover. All CARE vehicles had two-way radios, our main means of communication since we had no telephones. Shortly after we'd arrived, we'd each chosen a radio handle. John was "Burkinabe"—a native of Burkina Faso—and I was "Scaredy Cat," because, well, that's how I felt much of the time.

A few minutes later he came back. "The guards at the office think it sounded like a hand grenade somewhere near the roundabout. Best for us to just stay close to home for the night."

"Got any more beer?" Hatchard asked as he continued eating.

"Hatch! You think you should drink beer if the town is being attacked?" his wife, Anna, asked.

"What else should we do? Could get bloody killed. This is Africa, my dear. Might as well have a good time."

"Shouldn't we try to find out what's going on?" John asked.

"Nothing we can do now," Terry said. "We'll sort it all out in the morning."

"How do we find out what's going on around here? Read about it in *The New Vision*?" I asked.

Hatchard snorted. "That rag comes out of Kampala. They don't give a rat's arse about what's going on up here. The only thing that newspaper's good for is wrapping fish in."

The newspaper did seem to be more interested in reporting giant rodent sightings than the instability in our region. But we had the local grapevine, which was already abuzz by the time we returned to our compound that evening.

"It seems like something happened at the White Rhino Hotel," Busiya said, putting out his cigarette and jabbing his finger in the direction of the hotel compound just a few hundred yards from our own. At least that's what I thought he said. Busiya didn't speak much English, which never stopped me from lecturing him about the hazards of smoking.

"What kind of something? Terry and Pauline's whole house shook and they're even farther from the White Rhino than we are."

"Maybe it was a bomb," Adam said.

"A bomb?" I was stunned.

"Probably just a small bomb," he added. "Probably Kony rebels. These things happen all the time where I am from." The Gulu region to the east of us was under nearly constant attack from a band of guerrillas under the leadership of rebel fighter Joseph Kony. In addition to bombings and hijackings, these rebels generally terrorized communities by reportedly hacking off the ears, noses, and lips of their victims.

"Oh, I'm sure it wasn't a bomb," John said. "Let's just go inside. I'm sure we'll find out in the morning that it was nothing."

"Yes, probably not a bomb at all," Adam said. He was smiling as he always was. "Maybe just a hand grenade."

"Adam! It's not a coincidence that my radio name is 'Scaredy Cat,' " I told him. "I worry!"

"Well, there is no point in worrying. Things happen here. That is what? That is life here. Just get on with it." It was one of Adam's favorite sayings.

The rest of the night was quiet, although that didn't stop me from tossing and turning. I tried to convince myself that it was good that Busiya was filling in for Nasser. He knew how to use his spear for more than just banging it ceremoniously on the ground to announce visitors; one night he presented me with a giant bush rat skewered cleanly on the end of it. I declined his offering and he took it home for his wife to cook for supper.

"Someone threw a hand grenade over the fence into the White Rhino Hotel," James told us the next morning.

"A *mzungu* was killed and many others were taken to hospital," James's wife added.

"Was it anyone we know?" I asked.

"No, there was a group of European tourists staying at the hotel."

I didn't know which was more shocking: A bombing around the corner from my house or the fact that there were actual tourists in Arua.

"People are saying it is the Kony rebels. That they are now attacking tourists," James said. Up until then they tended to attack villages that refused to cooperate with their campaign to destabilize the government or, inexplicably, women who rode bicycles. "And they are saying that there will be more violence to come in Arua."

People were saying all kinds of things. But the local authorities assured us that this was just another case of the sort of wanton violence that erupts occasionally in the West Nile. The tourists, unfortunately, just happened to be in the wrong place at the wrong time. Living in the wrong place all the time, as I did, that didn't really make me feel a whole lot better. I secretly hoped that some of the other expats in town would pack their bags and go home so I could follow suit. But no one did. Not Coby and Bernard. Not the four Italian families. Not the missionaries who were sprinkled all around town. And certainly not Pauline and Terry, who, I got the feeling, had lived through worse in their long overseas career.

But still, I was uneasy. I didn't want to come across as too much of a scaredy cat, but was I really the only one who was unnerved by the hand grenade?

"Are you worried at all about our safety here?" I asked John.

"That was just a fluke. Things like that happen all over the world. Remember that social-work student who was murdered right down the street from our apartment in Brooklyn? We didn't leave Brooklyn because of that." He was right. But then again, he was a guy who had blithely lived through a coup in Burkina Faso.

"Bernard says if places like this were peaceful and stable, they probably wouldn't need development workers," Coby said when I brought the subject up with her.

"So you guys aren't thinking about leaving?" I asked.

"Nah," she said. And I trusted her judgment. She was a nurse and had a child to think about. She and Bernard seemed sensible enough. But then again, they had spent the past seven years in Nicaragua, which at the time was in the middle of its own civil war.

As a precaution, CARE put armed police guards in each of our compounds at night. I was definitely not thrilled about having a man with an AK-47 sleeping on my porch at night. But since it was widely believed that it was off-duty policemen who were responsible for most of the trouble around town, it was always a good idea to pay them to keep their friends away.

After that, nothing happened. And I mean nothing. That was the thing about life in Arua. Life was day after day of languid nothing much broken occasionally by some adrenaline-pumping, life-threatening crisis, which was then followed by another long stretch of rather dull nothingness until the next explosive crisis. It was hard for friends and family back home to believe that our life could actually be dull. "Are the elephants rifling through your garbage cans?" an old colleague from Brooklyn asked.

Ha! I thought. *Like we have garbage cans!*

The elephants weren't anywhere near my garbage, although every kid in the neighborhood was. When I found a group of kids playing with an empty tampon box, I made a mental note to tell Aisha to do a better job of burning my trash. Except Aisha had mysteriously stopped coming to work a week earlier. One of the Italian families was getting ready to return to Italy and recommended that I hire their house girl, Rose. Young and healthy as an ox, Rose had the added advantage of knowing how to make spaghetti sauce and pizza. So when Aisha still didn't show, I hired Rose.

Then one day I saw Aisha in the market. "I thought this would be a better job for me, madam," she said from behind a huge pile of potatoes. And I certainly agreed. It just might have been nice if she'd informed me. But Rose was doing a fine job of keeping house and even cooking. The only complaint I had, and it was minor, was that Rose had strong body odor. But in this she was not alone, as I was discovering. Rose was not the only one in town who stunk. And I took it as another reason to find something to do outside of the house.

Dear Susan,

Fill me in on the latest gossip at work. No, wait a minute, don't tell me. I already got a letter from Christine (you know her, she's the new and improved me at the AIDS prevention center). Why didn't you tell me she was doing my old job so well?? I've been gone four months and she's already written four grants, published an abstract, and snagged my old consultancy! Here I am doing absolutely nothing with myself—feeling useless and grungy to boot. My hair is a mop and my face is breaking out (and you laughed when I packed that tub of mud mask!).

I know, I know . . . I chose to leave all that behind (what the hell was I thinking??). Now I am on this new path with new challenges and there will be new achievements and successes to come, RIGHT??? I won't just sit out here in the jungle for two years twiddling my thumbs, RIGHT? This is the beginning of a whole new life for me. And success in this life can't be measured in grants and abstracts and consultancies. So how the hell will I know if I am succeeding?

Last night all the expats in town got together for a progressive dinner party. We went to a different house for each course. We had bruschetta, grappa, and tiramisu at the Italians; crisps and beer with the Brits; curry with homemade mango chutney at the Canadians (who used to live in India). It was great fun, great food, and fabulously interesting folks.

But for some reason I woke up this morning hating this place. All I could see in front of me was this endless stretch of empty days. I am networking nonstop—both here and every time we go to Kampala. But it never seems to amount to anything. I'm beginning to think I was not cut out for this life. Fabulous dinner parties are just not enough to keep me feeling fulfilled. Worse yet, all the other wives here seem to breeze right through this. They never get homesick or full of anxiety. Pauline told me that once I get used to this life, I'll never want to go home again. Meanwhile, I'm wondering if it's too early to book tickets home for Jean's wedding.

Well, I have to go eat some lunch. Then one of the other expat wives is coming to pick me up for a trip to, oh, I don't know, somewhere where you can buy green beans. Everyone is very excited about this. Should I be worried?

I'll keep you posted,
Eve

Chapter Seventeen

Notes from (Way Out in) the Field

"Welcome aboard Missionary Aviation Fellowship flight 121 to Kampala. Our flight today should be nonstop, *inshallah,* and we expect to be landing in an hour, *inshallah.* Well, an hour after we take off from Arua International Airport, which will be as soon as that family of cobs leaves the runway." I looked at my fellow passengers, both of them, and wondered why neither one was laughing. Our pilot intended the *inshallahs*—the commonly used Muslim phrase for "God willing"—to be funny, didn't he? And surely neither of them actually thought that the tin-roofed cement shed next to the dirt runway constituted an international airport. I could see that he wasn't joking about the wildlife delay.

"Once we are in the air," the pilot continued, "we will be offering our complimentary beverage service. Feel free to turn around and serve yourself a soft drink from the cool box behind you." Based on the accent, I guessed this pilot was British. I'd come to prefer the pilots who were Dutch, like Coby. She was competent and full of common sense, which I'd begun to think of as a Dutch trait. "Before we take off let's all bow our heads for a moment of prayer."

I wasn't sure if this was a good thing or not. I mean, asking for God's help when flying over the African jungle in a plane the size of a Volkswagen Beetle might very well be a wise move. But entrusting myself to a pilot who felt the need to ask for God's help before we even took off worried me. I bowed my head politely, though, as the pilot thanked Jesus for all kinds of things, but I was praying that there was a beer in that cool box for me. And I gladly added my "amen" when the pilot's list of petitions ended with a safe landing in Entebbe.

So far, Uganda had not exactly proven to be the boon to my career that I had hoped. It had been a boon to the newly established commercial enterprise of the Missionary Aviation Fellowship (MAF), since I'd spent much of the past three months flying back and forth to Kampala, chasing phantom job leads. MAF was a group of missionaries whose role had previously been limited to flying Protestant missionaries and their supplies around Uganda. An odd religious calling, I guess. But also practical, considering the awful conditions of roads to so many of the isolated places where missionaries worked. Though their planes were teeny—their jumbo jet was an eight-seater—flights weren't always full. So MAF had recently begun selling their open seats to us heathens. Tickets were relatively inexpensive and came with a shuttle ride to or from the airport on the Kampala side, as well as in-flight sodas and prayers.

So far, my quest for meaningful work resulted in little more than earning me enough frequent flyer miles on MAF to get a free flight anywhere I wanted to go. That is, if MAF gave out frequent flyer miles (they didn't) or went anywhere I wanted to go (they didn't). I zipped down to Kampala for every meeting, workshop, or conference I was invited to, handing out CVs and business cards like they were candy. Several times I was so close I thought I could almost taste a consultancy contract. Turns out I was just tasting enough tea and groundnuts to last a lifetime.

"I know what you're going through, Eve," Elizabeth Marum said when I finally met her (two months after my first attempt) at the US-AID office. "On our first tour overseas, I followed my husband, Larry, to Bangladesh. I had all this experience, a master's degree, and I was finishing up my dissertation for my Ph.D. I gave the director of Oxfam my CV and told him I was looking for work. He glanced at my CV and then asked, 'Can you type?' "

"Boy, back in the States I just assumed with my AIDS background I'd find something."

Elizabeth nodded sympathetically and gave me a big smile. "If you were in Kampala, I'm sure you would. I'd find a way to use your skills. But Arua? Now that's going to be much harder. Not much going on there. But keep doing what you're doing. Try to get your foot in the door and at least see if you can get some short-term projects."

I thought I finally had my foot in the door when UNICEF invited me to a three-day conference in November to evaluate and improve the training component of a peer education project. They couldn't hire me, of course. Like many projects in Uganda, this one was a partnership with a local agency, so UNICEF couldn't offer me a job without their agreement. But by participating in the conference, I would be introduced to all the players, and that, they assured me, would most likely lead to an offer. They could provide my room and board and a per diem of fourteen thousand shillings, roughly twenty dollars per day.

Even with the involvement of the world's foremost health promotion agency, this conference was pretty much like every other conference or workshop I had been to in Uganda so far. Speaker after long-winded speaker went on at length about their area of expertise, regardless of whether or not it had anything at all to do with the point of the conference. I began to suspect that speakers were paid by the word in Uganda, double for words that no one in the audience understood.

As usual, I was introduced with great fanfare and asked to sit up front for every session. As usual, no one asked for my input. Which might have been a good thing, because I don't know how well it would have gone over if I'd added my two cents: *Quit yakking about gender disparity and inheritance laws and just stop all the unprotected fornicating already.* By day two I was so frustrated that I considered leaving. Either that or chewing my own arm off.

I didn't leave, though. A *mzungu* couldn't just slink out quietly.

Besides, I never knew what networking opportunities might arise. And the humor and camaraderie of the participants—community educators, mostly young women, many of them living with AIDS—kept me from chewing off my own arm.

"Auntie, I have a headache," one of the participants said over lunch on day two.

"I am going back to the room to check on Margaret. She did not come to the session this morning," answered the middle-aged woman that everyone called Auntie Lucy. "I will bring you back a tablet for your head," she said, making her way across the dining hall, a big cement hall lined with long wooden tables and benches.

"Auntie," another young lady called out before the stout woman could get out the door, "I cannot find my key."

"All right," Auntie Lucy called back. "First the sick. Then we will look for your key."

"And you?" Auntie stopped in front of me as I was finishing my lunch of *matoke* covered with a watery fish sauce. "Do you need something?"

"I don't need anything, thanks," I said. "But I was wondering why everyone calls you Auntie?"

"Oh," she said with a laugh. "This is our African tradition of *Ssengas,* aunties who teach the young girls about life and sex and traditions. To prepare them for marriage. In my village, I am the *Ssenga.* So here, I am everybody's auntie. Even yours!" She let out a deep baritone laugh.

"You need something, you tell your auntie," a young woman at my table said and everyone nodded and giggled.

That evening, when we were back in our rooms getting ready for dinner, the electricity went out. I had noticed a lantern and matches in my room, which I hadn't needed because the bare bulb that hung from the ceiling shed enough light for the tiny room. Suddenly thrown into darkness, I wished I actually knew how to light the kerosene lantern.

"Auntie Lucy?" I called, walking with my lantern in the direction of the room that had been a beehive of activity for the past two days. "Can you help me light my lantern?"

"Oh, silly girl," Auntie said, but not unkindly, "how can you live in Africa and not know how to light a lantern?"

How can you people call yourselves health educators but not know that simply lecturing people won't make them change their behavior? I wanted to counter. But I had to admit that making fire trumped understanding the Health Belief Model on Maslow's hierarchy of needs, so touché. Auntie Lucy patiently instructed me in how to raise the wick just enough, but not too much, and how to replace the glass top to protect the flame.

"Come, now we will collect the others for supper," she said, taking my arm.

"Ladies, listen to your auntie," she bellowed as we made our way along the winding pathways between the low cement buildings of the nunnery that now doubled as a conference center. "Everyone bring your lantern to supper or you will not find your way back afterward." I was still surprised at how quickly it got dark in Entebbe. Night falls as swiftly as a guillotine this close to the equator.

The women emerged from their rooms, carrying their lanterns. Like a string of bobbing fireflies, we wound our way to the dining hall, which was lit by candles that the nuns had set out on the tables. As I ate supper with the other participants, everyone's tongues seemed a little looser. Maybe it was the candlelight; or the fact that the organizers and presenters had gone back to Kampala for the night.

"Are you married, Eve?" a woman on my right asked, passing me a huge bowl of *matoke*.

"Yes, I am. And you?" I answered, scooping a small amount of the sticky yellow mush onto my plate. I was hoping one of the other bowls being passed around held a less starchy starch.

"Yes, but my husband died of AIDS. Now I am the second wife of my husband's brother. So I am a widow and a wife!" I watched her ladle a greasy chicken sauce over her heaping plate of *matoke*.

"You do not care for *matoke*?" a woman across the table asked me.

"Oh, I like it," I said, ladling a fair amount of the sauce over it. In truth I found it tasteless and hard to digest, but I wasn't going to disparage the national dish.

"Did you want to marry your husband's brother?" I asked the woman next to me as I passed the sauce bowl. All the women at the table laughed.

"Here it does not usually matter what we want," someone answered and several others clucked in agreement. "It is tradition in most tribes that when a man dies, his wife or wives are inherited by her husband's brother."

"This is one of the reasons why AIDS spreads so much here," Auntie Lucy explained. "If her husband died of AIDS," she pointed to the widow/wife, "then she has it too. And when she goes with the brother of her husband, he will have it soon and give it to his other wives."

"Yes," said the widow/wife. "This is a very big problem for us." Someone passed me a bowl of boiled potatoes, which I heaped greedily on my plate.

"Ah, this one prefers potatoes!" Auntie Lucy yelled as if she had unearthed the secret of my soul. The women clucked and slapped their thighs.

"Did you wish to marry your husband?" a young woman on my right asked me.

"Yes, of course!" I said. And I heard giggles.

"Why did you choose him?" a woman sitting opposite me asked.

"I loved him. Isn't that why you get married?" I said.

"Oh, no!" several of them said in unison while others let out hearty laughs.

"Sometimes there are love matches," Auntie Lucy said.

"But not very often," added another woman.

"Me?" said a young woman on my left, "I do not want a husband. What good are they? They just bring you more work and more mouths to feed." There was a murmur of agreement.

"Well, they are good for sex!" the woman across from me announced to the thigh-slapping chuckles of several others.

"But not much else!" a woman shouted from the very end of the long table.

"Ah, besides, I have AIDS now," the young woman on my left continued. "So some men will not want to marry me now."

"Does having AIDS make it so that no one wants to marry you?" I was pleased at how open these women were to talking.

"Marry? Maybe not," chimed another woman. "Have sex with us? Sure. A lot of men here do not care."

"Here life expectancy is what?" Auntie Lucy asked.

"Forty-seven," I answered before I realized that Auntie Lucy was playing Socrates, like Adam often did.

"When you get infected with HIV, you do not just die. No, you can live with it, sometimes for some years," Auntie explained as others nodded. "So for many men, especially those who are already older, they are not so afraid of getting this disease. They think, Sure I will die soon anyway. Why should I change my ways?"

"And changing health behavior is very hard," I added, suddenly understanding the AIDS situation in Uganda much better than I ever had.

"Especially changing the sex behavior!" one woman shouted and everyone else howled with laughter.

"Do you like our breakfast?" Auntie Lucy greeted me at the door of the dining hall the next morning. "Or should I ask the cook to make you some potatoes?"

"Oh, no. I love the breakfast, thank you," I said, taking a seat on a bench. I did love Ugandan breakfasts of sugary tea and hard-boiled eggs. I noticed there was something of a scramble to sit at my table. And as we crowded around, the women were quick to pick up where we had left off the night before.

"Do you have any babies?" a young woman next to me asked.

"Not yet. Maybe soon," I said.

"How many years have you been married?" she asked.

"Two years," I said.

"Why no babies? What are you waiting for?" Auntie Lucy, who always seemed to be nearby, asked.

"Well, I wanted to have a career; you know, get my work settled before I had children."

"But what about your husband? What does he say about that?" a woman across the table asked.

"What about his mother? What does she say about that?" someone shouted from the next table. All the women laughed.

"Here your husband's mother will make him take another wife if you do not have a baby soon enough," Auntie Lucy explained.

"Well, in America, the rest of the family usually stays out of it." I couldn't imagine my mother-in-law meddling in our sex life. My mother, however, was another story. "And as for my husband, well, he wants whatever I want. I mean, he wants to have children someday. He comes from a family of five brothers," I added.

"Will one of his brothers inherit you when your husband dies?" someone yelled from across the room.

"No!" I said. "In America it wouldn't go over very well to . . . um . . . to marry your husband's brother." *Even if he is dead,* I thought. *The husband, not the brother.*

"So your husband wants you to work, not have babies?" the young woman next to me asked.

"My husband wants me to be happy," I answered.

"Your husband sounds like a very unusual man," someone said.

"Not so unusual in America," I said. "But my husband is a very good man."

"Ugandan men are not that good," my neighbor said.

"None of them?" I asked, thinking of Adam, who spoke so sweetly of his wife, Sarah, although she and their children had yet to join us in Arua. And I wondered about the many men who worked for CARE. They were all so unfailingly kind and helpful to me. Did they treat their wives differently?

"Of course not," Auntie Lucy intervened. "There are good men here. But it is not unusual for women to be mistreated. My own husband was very good to me. Now he is dead and I stay on my own. I did not wish to go to his brother. But our life is not like your life."

We all sat quietly for a few moments.

"But listen to your auntie, dear," Lucy said, interrupting the silence. "Do not wait too long to have babies." *Strange how my African auntie was beginning to sound a lot like my Jewish mother!*

"So what is your work?" a woman asked from the end of the table.

"Well, in America, I used to run an AIDS prevention program," I said, and many of the women looked surprised and clapped their hands in joy. I wondered why else they thought I was here. "But here, well, I really haven't found work. So I just keep going to workshops like this, hoping I can find a way to contribute."

"You can contribute to us," someone shouted. "This project is a good one. We have learned a great deal about HIV slash AIDS. But we do not seem to be able to change people's behaviors. Can you help us with that?"

"I thought that's why we were here. I thought that's what we were going to talk about at this workshop," I said.

"Ah, these workshops can be useless," someone said.

"Well, why did you come?" I asked.

"Well," someone said, gesturing around the dining hall, "three meals a day and per diem!" Ah, for me the measly per diem was an unexpected bonus. For them, it was sorely needed income. I was beginning to understand why these seemingly pointless conferences and workshops were so damn popular with Ugandans.

"You mean nothing will change? The program won't improve?" I asked.

"Maybe you can tell us some things to make our program better," someone said.

The workshops over the next two days remained painfully irrelevant. But the lively conversations we had at mealtimes, breaks, and informal nighttime gatherings made up for it. Regardless of what the organizers had planned, these women were interested in learning ways to improve their program. So I explained to them what I knew about adding value to health messages to increase the likelihood of health behavior change. They listened, asked questions, and took notes. And Auntie Lucy made sure there was a bowl of potatoes at my place at each meal.

"So will you be working with us again?" several women asked as the conference ended and we were preparing to leave.

"I don't think so," I told them. The organizer from UNICEF had pulled me aside at the closing ceremony and told me that his Ugandan counterpart didn't want to hire "another blond-haired, blue-eyed consultant." It had been a while since I'd looked in a mirror, but as I recalled, I was a brown-eyed brunette. But I didn't argue the point.

"Well, when we return to our village, we will remember what you taught us and we will add value to our health education message," the widow/wife told me.

"And we will remember the Health Belief Model," one of my dinner tablemates said, waving a diagram that I had made for her.

"We must help people personalize the risks," a young woman said.

"And help them understand the benefit of changing their behaviors," someone else added.

"And help them believe that they are capable of succeeding!" several of them shouted. I was too stunned to say anything. "Wow!" I finally managed. "I am so glad I could help."

"And now, you take some advice from your auntie," Lucy said, throwing her arm around my shoulder. "Do not wait too long to have a baby."

Dear Mom,

Yesterday, our new house girl couldn't come and I was having Pauline and Terry over for supper after they drove up from Kampala. No big deal, right? Wrong! I started at ten in the morning, dusting and sweeping the house (Did you say vacuum? Did you say electricity?), beating and brushing the chair cushions and rugs. By noon I was dripping sweat and hacking up the chickens for supper. Unfortunately, Domino's Pizza does NOT deliver here, so I was also making lunch for my hardworking husband who comes home for lunch every day at 1:00 (since there are no little delis, or anything else for that matter). Okay, chickens hacked to pieces, I begin shelling the peas—which is not all that easy—and I finally get the saying "like peas in a pod." Then I'm peeling and chopping carrots, potatoes, okra, and green tomatoes. Then making the buttermilk batter to fry everything in—but first I have to make the buttermilk.

Well, by 7:00 we sit down to supper and by 10:00 John and I are both back in the kitchen cleaning so as to avoid the nightly invasion of ants. By the time the lights went out, I fell into bed, exhausted. When Rose arrived this morning, I nearly kissed her smelly feet.

I'll keep you posted,
Eve

Chapter Eighteen

Getting a Life

"G'day, mate," they'd say. Or *"bonjour," "guten Tag,"* "hello," "hola." *"Jambo,"* if they really wanted to impress me with how long they'd been in Africa. As if you have to be a real old hand to know how to say "hello" in Swahili. I didn't care how they greeted me. I was beginning to resent the whole lot of them.

Arua was the last pit stop on the way north to the Sudanese refugee camps. As more and more refugees flooded into the camps, more and more aid workers passed through Arua. Suddenly, we were smack in the middle of the hopping hot spot of the development set. We were ugly with Americans working for the Red Cross, Brits with Save the Children, Indian and African bureaucrats with the United Nations High Commission for Refugees. And several times each week an unknown foreigner from the UN or a relief agency would drive across my lawn to ask if there was any room in our guesthouse.

"You have to talk to Pauline. She runs the guesthouse. You might find her in there now. Follow the sign," I'd say, pointing to the sign that clearly stated that the guesthouse was over there, and my private domain was right where this fool had parked his jeep. The sign, by the way, that hung over the garage at the end of the paved driveway.

It was pretty slim pickings for guest accommodations in Arua. If you didn't mind sleeping on a soiled mattress, using an outhouse, and weren't too worried about the recent hand grenade incident, then there was always the White Rhino Hotel. But if you preferred clean bedding, indoor plumbing, and a place that hadn't (yet) been targeted by terrorists, then the CARE guesthouse was one of the few options in town. And if it wasn't reserved for CARE's use, Pauline graciously rented out the empty rooms. Pauline was always gracious. I was becoming less and less gracious the longer I remained (a) unemployed, and (b) the perceived receptionist for those who were employed and looking for a place to stay.

So we often had an assortment of aid workers sharing our compound. And I'd get to hear their fascinating tales as they came and went or popped over for a meal or to ask about where they might pick up supplies. They were going to set up water filtration systems and document measles outbreaks in the camps. Or they were developing retraining programs for decommissioned child soldiers. Meanwhile, I was sitting on my verandah telling Mickey Mouse stories to kids who wouldn't even talk to me. Literally.

I'd started helping James's twelve-year-old brother, Georgie, with his English homework. He'd sit with me after school and we'd read a chapter from his English book and look up new words in the dictionary. Eventually, James's four-year-old son, Brian, and two-year-old daughter, Doreen, would toddle up to join us on the verandah. Brian, who adamantly refused to speak to *mzungus,* would frantically wave his Mickey Mouse book at me and I'd read to him and Doreen when Georgie and I were through. The book was in Italian, and every day I made up a different story to go with the pictures, but the kids didn't seem to mind, or notice.

"Here's Mickey Mouse, so happy in his new job," I'd say as they'd point to the picture of Mickey Mouse. "And here's Minnie Mouse," I'd ad-lib as they pointed. "Minnie Mouse is reading books to children who won't even talk to her. She's thinking, *For this I went to graduate school?*" Brian would nod solemnly as Doreen turned the pages. "Look! It's Donald Duck and he's driving over Mickey and Minnie's front lawn. Don't they have driveways where Donald Duck is from?

"And here's the three little ducks, Huey, Dewey, and Louie! Quack,

quack, quack." Brian continued to stare silently. Doreen cracked a tiny smile. "Quack, quack, quack," I'd repeat until Doreen giggled.

"Quack, quack, quack, all the silly little duckies have big important jobs to do. Quack, quack, quack," I'd say until Doreen quacked back. "Why can't Minnie Mouse have something important to do, too?" Then I'd get out some paper and crayons and we'd color. Brian in stony silence; Doreen and me quacking.

John loved his work. He and Adam would be implementing a microlending program much like the highly successful Grameen Bank project in Bangladesh and India. Farmers and small business owners without any collateral could guarantee one another's loans by forming borrower groups. Only one member at a time could get a loan and had to pay it back before someone else could apply. Community support helped the borrowers' businesses thrive and peer pressure kept them repaying their loans.

But before they could give out any loans, they had to help establish a bank. The last (and only) bank in Arua had collapsed after Idi Amin helped himself to all the money in it. John and Adam had developed a partnership with a bank that served southern Uganda and recruited some of their staff to come up to Arua. They had recently opened the bank in a temporary building while overseeing the construction of a permanent one. Now John and Adam were going out to villages explaining the project and encouraging people to use the bank. This would be no small feat in a region where people generally stashed their money under the mattress.

I'd amble over to the bank during the day, mostly just to enjoy the bank's cleanliness and all-day electricity. John would be laughing with Adam or strategizing with the bank's outreach workers. I tagged along when he went out to the villages. I watched as he patiently explained the principles of savings and credit to people who had never been to school, much less to a bank. He couldn't be more different from them, and yet he connected with them as if he'd lived among them all his life.

Who knew, for instance, that John was fluent in "Special English"? He happily dispensed with bothersome verb tenses, articles, and other unimportant words, speaking oh-so-slowly and clearly in his kindergarten English so that everyone could understand him. Well, everyone except, perhaps, those of us who were schooled in English!

Following after John and occasionally going to workshops still left me with plenty of free time. So what is an educated woman to do with herself in the bush? Well, there's always tennis. And golf. Quite surprisingly, Arua had tennis courts and a golf course. Neither was anything to write home about, which, of course, didn't stop me from writing home about them. The nine-hole golf course was maintained by a guy who hacked his way through it with a machete once a week, and the two dirt tennis courts usually had goats tied to the fences. But expats in remote outposts of war-torn countries can't be choosy.

Coby and I began to meet at the tennis courts nearly every afternoon. Two *mzungus* playing tennis in the African bush couldn't help but attract all the neighborhood kids. Which was fine by us. We paid them to chase errant balls and pick up the goat turds.

"Oh, good one, Eve," Coby congratulated me as I finally managed to serve one inside the lines on her side of the court. I was not the best tennis player.

"It only took, what? Six tries?" I said, counting the half-dozen children who were scouring the tall grass for my overzealous balls.

"Well, you're getting better. This is good!" She pronounced it like the Dutch *goed,* so it sounded really emphatic, heavy on the "o" and "d."

"Sorry I'm not much of an athlete." I envied Coby's lean, athletic body and had begun to think of her natural athleticism as another Dutch trait. Right up there with cheery competence and a fondness for cheese.

"You're very good," she assured me. "Anyway, it is just fun to be playing."

"And out of the house," I added, thinking of *eau de Rose.*

"And away from Simon," she said, using, of course, the correct Dutch pronunciation of her son's name so I had to squelch a giggle.

"Simon . . . er, Semen," I said, forcing myself to say it her way, "doesn't mind when you leave him?" I asked.

"Ah, he loves Florence and the girls. He's getting to be very spoiled with all of them around all the time." Coby seemed to have the proverbial African village over at her compound. As far as I could tell, she only employed Florence, the house girl, and Valeri, the cook. But Florence usually brought along her daughters and Valeri occasionally brought his wife, and everyone doted on the towheaded two-year-old. "Now Simon expects Bernard and me to carry him all the time, too!"

"Enough tennis for today?" I asked, looking at my watch.

Coby looked up at the sun. "Yah, it look like it's time for tea. You come for tea? I made cheese!"

"Oh, *kaas!*" I said, showing off one of the Dutch words that I was learning along with Simon.

"*Goed!*" said Coby.

"And *boom*," I said, pointing to a tree. "*Wolken,*" I said pointing up at the wispy clouds floating on the deep blue sky.

"*Zeer goed!*" Coby pronounced. "So come for tea and more Dutch lessons."

"I'm free as a bird until it's badminton and cocktails time. I was just going to go over to John's bank."

"Are you going to open an account?" she asked.

"No. I just wanted to look in the mirror!" The inside of the bank was decorated in a modern, Italian style, right down to the mirrors on the walls. We put our tennis rackets in their cases and were quickly surrounded by a scruffy assortment of small boys and girls, waving our errant tennis balls at us. I collected the balls and handed each child twenty-five shillings.

"Tomorrow?" one of the boys chirped. "You play again tomorrow?" he asked.

"Yes," I said as we left the tennis court. "We will probably play again tomorrow."

"Okay!" he shouted. "Bye-bye," he said, and the rest of the kids echoed him from the tennis court.

"It's a good life, yah?" Coby asked as we walked through the field toward the road.

"Yah," I had to agree. "It is. I guess. Weird, though."

"Not working, you mean? I know." Coby had worked when she and Bernard were in Nicaragua. But in Arua she was the "tagalong spouse," like me. "I haven't given up looking for work yet. I still go over to Kuluva Hospital every week. But I am not so hopeful about it anymore," she said, shrugging.

"And this," I said, turning around and waving at the phalanx of kids following a few feet behind us. "All these people wanting to do stuff for us. All these people wanting something from us. It's just weird."

"Yah, you'll get used to it. I think I got used to it from being in Nicaragua. Now Arua doesn't seem quite so strange." We came to the edge of the field and stepped onto the dirt road. The children behind us scattered as we headed toward Coby's compound on the other side of the road. "You know what helped me?" Coby asked. "Having Simon. I know it sounds silly, because he hardly needs me. He has so many people to look after him. But becoming a mother made me feel, somehow, less useless."

"Yeah, I've thought about it. John and I always planned on having kids. But back home I was too busy with school and my career. Well, I seem to have solved my busyness problem!" I said as we reached Coby's gate and a barechested *askari* jumped up to open it for us.

Rose had taken over the bulk of my domestic duties at home. And frankly, when she was in the house, I really had to get out. She was a fine worker and a decent cook. But the body odor, which at first seemed like a mildly unpleasant scent, had now aged to a full-blown stench. Put plainly, Rose reeked.

"Bathing is a luxury that not all Ugandans enjoy, Eve," John said when I complained about it. *Ah, there was Saint John being culturally sensitive again, while I was smelling it and telling it like it was.*

"Well, Rose can enjoy it all she wants," I moaned. "I told her to use our shower. I took her to the dead *mzungu* market and bought her new dresses. Well, new used dresses." A huge portion of Arua's economy depended on the brisk business of selling clothing donated by the Salvation Army and Goodwills of the world. The locals called them "dead *mzungu*" clothing, because they couldn't conceive of any other reason to give away clothing. But new dresses or not, Rose continued to stink, and I took to finding reasons to get out of the house each day. But one could only spend so much time quacking and coloring with the neighbors' kids.

I hadn't quite given up all hope of finding work, but I had decided to stop running around the country like a jobless hussy. So far, it had only left me frustrated and still unemployed. And besides, I figured, I hadn't followed John halfway across the world just to spend the bulk of my time halfway across the country. So I tried to find ways to keep myself occupied in Arua.

"I would like to volunteer to do AIDS education in Arua's schools," I told Arua's district health educator when I went to meet him in his office. "I used to set up AIDS education programs in schools in America."

"Yes, that would be good," he said as his secretary handed me a plastic mug full of dark, sweet tea. "If only we had the resources."

"Well, it really wouldn't take much. I mean, I would volunteer my time and I'm sure I could get any materials we needed donated from my friends back home." He offered me a plate of groundnuts. I took a handful then remembered that one of the Italians recently told me that the red papery coating causes cancer.

"Yes, but we'd need a vehicle to get around," the district health educator said, popping a handful of the red nuts into his mouth and chewing. "Perhaps CARE could give us a vehicle."

"Well, I doubt that," I told him, trying to unobtrusively scrape the papery coating off the nuts, one at a time, before I ate them.

"But you work for CARE. They have many vehicles. I see them around town all the time."

"I don't work for CARE," I reiterated, although I had made that clear when I introduced myself. "But many of the schools are right here in town. We wouldn't even need a vehicle to get to them. We could walk."

"Oh, imagine that!" he said, laughing so hard I thought ground-nuts might start shooting out of his nose. "The district health educator walking to school! Yes, very funny," he said, sipping his tea. "And don't forget my per diem."

"Per diem?" I asked. "Doesn't the district pay your salary?"

"Of course they pay my salary," he said, helping himself to more groundnuts. "But if you want to go out in the field, then as the district health educator I must accompany you. And for that, I have to get a per diem." Ah, yes, Elizabeth Marum had warned me about this. Bureaucrats who do next to nothing and who ensure that no one else does anything, either, since that might cause them to look bad and lose their jobs.

"Oh," I said, giving up and popping the whole damn handful of groundnuts in my mouth. *If they really were carcinogenic, maybe I could eat enough to kill myself.*

In the end, the district health educator did invite me to make a presentation at Arua's HIV educators meeting the following week and I gladly accepted his invitation.

At the meeting I handed out index cards to the thirty community educators who had gathered in the bare cement-walled hut on the out-skirts of town. The cards were all blank except for three that each had a small X on the back. I instructed everyone to go around the room, shake hands and get the signatures of three different people. This was an instant hit, as Ugandans are very fond of meeting and greeting. I was immediately inundated with people wanting to shake my hand—although I wasn't playing the game.

"Okay, turn your cards over," I instructed when everyone was finally back in their seats. "Stand up if your card has an X on it." Three people stood.

"They are in trouble!" a young man shouted from the back of the room.

"Well, not trouble," I said. "But for the purposes of this game, the X on their card represents being HIV-positive." Great peals of laughter erupted from everyone—including the three who were standing.

"Unlucky!" someone else yelled.

"Now, remember, this is only an illustration. I am not saying that these three people actually are infected." My days of doing this in New York had taught me to be very careful about insinuating that someone was HIV-positive, even if it was just pretend.

"Yes, yes, we understand," the district health educator interrupted my disclaimer. "No need to be worried." Apparently Ugandans were not nearly as touchy about this as Americans.

"Now, would the three people who are standing please read the names of the people you shook hands with. And would those people please stand." With each name that was read, the group erupted in laughter and applause. "Each of you have now been infected, too," I said to more howls of laughter.

"Now," I said to the newly standing. "Would each one of you—"

"Yes! We know what to do," shouted someone who was standing as he began reading the names on his card. And without further instruction from me, the reading and standing continued until nearly everyone in the room was "infected."

"Oh, very good. Very good," said the district health educator, standing up beside me. "This is a fine illustration of how HIV can spread throughout a community."

"And good fun!" someone called from the back of the room.

The day ended, of course, with a closing ceremony. I was seated up front, as the "Guest of Honor," as was John, who had only come to take me home.

"Would you be so kind as to say a few words?" the district health educator asked John when he arrived.

John looked over at me and mouthed, *What are we doing here?* But he smoothly turned to the group. "Thank you for all the work you are doing to help your communities," he said. "And thank you for letting my wife join you today. She really knows a lot about AIDS, and I think she can help the wonderful people of the Arua district." The group applauded as John sat down beside me.

"Oh, yes, she has helped us already," the district health educator said. "In fact, the group is so grateful for her help today that they have prepared a special presentation for her."

A group of women stood in a semicircle in the front of the room. "Please come join us," one of the women said, pulling me up by the arm and holding on to my hand. "You have taught us something which we will use to the benefit of our communities. We thank you for that," she said, bowing slightly at me. "And now we have a something for you."

A job, perhaps?

The women broke into a raucous song whose words—being in Lugbara but not a shopping list—I couldn't quite make out. But the stomping, hand clapping, and trilling told me it was a happy song. I smiled and swayed and saw John stomping his feet.

When the song finished, the woman holding my hand said, "Today, Eve, you are one of us. Living together with us and helping the people of Arua. Because of this, we give you a new name. A Lugbara name. We call you 'Ayikoru.' "

"Ayikoru," I repeated. "It's beautiful." I looked at John, who was beaming back at me.

"It is from the word *ayiko*. It means 'joyful.' "

"Joyful . . . I like that. *Awadifo saaru*," I thanked them.

Dear Susan,

Well, it's 9:30 p.m. and the lights keep going off. No problem for us, though, since my handy-dandy husband installed two solar panels on our roof and a couple of solar lights in the house. (He also fell through the kitchen ceiling while installing the lights, thus also creating a sunroof in the kitchen.) He says we can get a battery that stores solar power, too, and maybe even be able to run the TV and VCR when we have no electricity. We will be living the high life then! Things are great with John. Even when everything else stinks, I'm glad we are together. Sometimes it's like a honeymoon. When the lights go out, we have dinner by candlelight and plenty of romantic evenings. The nights are long and full of stars and not a lot of other entertainment options. Hey, maybe that explains why developing countries have such high fertility rates!

Speaking of which (hold on to your cervical cap), we have decided to try to get pregnant! I know, you think it's a horrible place to be pregnant. But I know a bunch of expat women who've had babies here and they all say it's fine. And three of them are married to doctors! So after trying for a month, my period came early. Of course, I'm disappointed already. Have you ever known me to be patient?

I'll keep you posted,
Eve

Chapter Nineteen

A Little Bit Pregnant in Uganda

The last thing my mother yelled before we got on the plane to Uganda was something along the lines of, "YOU'D BETTER NOT GET PREGNANT OVER THERE!" This was not so much out of concern for my health or even the baby's, but rather out of fear that she would miss all the fun of watching my belly grow and of buying me maternity clothes. But I knew she couldn't wait to be a grandmother. She's a Jewish mother after all; it comes with the territory.

But getting pregnant—or not—wasn't even on my radar screen at the time. It wasn't that I was determined *not* to get pregnant in Uganda. But at that point in my life my focus was on my career. I had assumed—erroneously, in retrospect—that I'd be too busy fighting AIDS in Uganda for the next two years to even think about having a baby. But three months of fruitless job searches, combined with all the healthy expat mothers and babies around me, convinced me—and John—that now might be the perfect time to have a baby.

"Don't forget, Evie, it's not always so easy to get pregnant. My gynecologist said it might take a whole year at your age." I was all of thirty-one. But this was my mother's response when I wrote to tell her of our plans. I actually thought it rather uncouth to tell people we were trying to get pregnant. It was like announcing: HEY, WE'RE HAVING LOTS OF UNPROTECTED SEX OVER HERE! But hell, everyone was having lots of unprotected sex over here. And besides, being uncouth had never stopped me before.

It was just after Thanksgiving, a regular day in Uganda, although all the Americans in town did get together for a turkey supper after work. I didn't really think that I was pregnant after just two months of lots of unprotected sex—er, I mean trying—even though my period was a few days late. When my breasts started aching and I had steady cramping, I was sure these were signs that my period was on its way. But when the cramping didn't subside and my period didn't start, I began to wonder if I might be pregnant.

"Hey, didn't you swipe a bunch of pregnancy tests from the hospital before you left?" John asked, remembering a box we had brought with us and stashed away in a closet.

"I didn't swipe them," I said defensively. "They were given to me." Susan had swiped them for me from a supply cabinet of the hospital where we both had worked.

"Don't even think about getting pregnant while you're over there," Susan had warned at the time. "An ectopic pregnancy in the middle of nowhere can kill you. But take these just in case," she said, handing me a box full of pregnancy tests. "There ought to be enough here to do one a month—just for fun. At least then you'll know if you should worry."

"Why don't we just do one of them and find out?" John suggested.

So first thing the next morning I did one of the tests. Pee on a stick; now what could be simpler? Not much, except that our tests, pilfered from a case that was never intended for individual sale, did not come with instructions. I figured out the peeing-on-the-stick part, no problem. But I had no idea when—or how—to read the results.

"I don't know what this means," I said to John, waving the stick that now had a line that had gone from pink to blue. This was before the days when they figured out how to make these things simple enough so that even an illiterate—and hormonally imbalanced—woman could tell whether or not she was pregnant. "But I guess we'll figure it out eventually. Why worry about it now?"

There really was no reason to worry about it—until the continuous cramping became sharp enough to wake me in the middle of the night. So I went to see David Morton, the American missionary doctor at Kuluva, the mission hospital just outside of town.

"Sharp pains in your abdomen and a missed period?" he said. "We need to rule out an ectopic pregnancy. That's where the developing embryo attaches to one of the fallopian tubes."

"Yeah, I know what that is. But first we need to rule in a pregnancy, David. Can't you do a pregnancy test?"

"We don't have those here. Honestly, by the time a woman comes to us, it's pretty obvious that she's pregnant."

"Well, I brought one of the tests that I have from the hospital where I used to work," I said, producing a pee stick from my bag. "Maybe you'll know how to read it."

"Eve, I've been practicing medicine in the bush here for eight years now. I don't know how to read those things. But let's do a physical and we'll see what we can find out. Just slip off your underwear, hike up your skirt, and try to get comfortable on this examining table."

"Here?" I asked, looking around the bare cement room. Just outside the wide-open window on one side of the room I watched people shuffling in the dust on their way up the road to the leprosy clinic and down the road to the church. Through the other window I saw a long line of haggard-looking people waiting to collect medicines from the pharmacy. I've never been a whiz at physics, but if I could see them clear as day, couldn't they see me?

"Oh . . . um, just a second. Let's see if we can rig up something here." David scrounged around and found a folding screen to provide me with some privacy. The lengths that he had to go to in order to provide me with this told me that this was an unusual request.

"Well, your uterus does seem slightly enlarged. But without further tests I really can't be sure," he said after poking around gently on my insides. "If you are pregnant, you'll be fine. We can do your basic prenatal care right here." He turned his back while I pulled myself together. "And since it's your first pregnancy, I'd strongly recommend that you go back to the States, or at least to Kampala, to give birth."

Like I was going to give birth in a place that couldn't even tell me if I was pregnant! "But I am concerned about the sharp pains in your abdomen. So let's get you to Kampala as soon as possible and have them rule out an ectopic pregnancy."

"John and I are going to Kampala tomorrow," I told him.

"Good. Radio down today and have someone get you an appointment right away at the Surgery."

"Surgery?" I croaked.

"They're British doctors." David patted my arm. "Their office is called the Surgery. Try not to worry."

"We're planning on driving down. Do you think that's safe?" I asked.

"I haven't heard of any hijackings in Murchison Falls in the last few months. I think it's safe."

"No, I mean, if I am pregnant. The awful tarmac. All that bouncing. Is that safe? For the baby, I mean. If there is one."

"Eve, if you are pregnant, that baby is in the safest place there is. Trust me. If bouncing over these roads could induce a miscarriage, well, no one here would stay pregnant for very long. But you could probably get a seat on MAF if that's more comfortable."

"We were hoping to do some shopping," I said. "Need anything?"

"No. I think we're good. But thanks," David answered. What was it about the missionaries and their damned simple lifestyles? Didn't they hanker for a nice Italian salami now and then? Didn't they need Tupperware like the rest of us?

I drove to the CARE office and sent a radio message to Kampala asking the CARE secretary to schedule an appointment for me at the Surgery.

Driving to Kampala would be much less pleasant, not to mention seven hours longer, than going by plane. But flying meant we could only carry back what we could fit on our laps. Whereas driving to Kampala meant stuffing the Pajero full of things we could only get in Kampala. So the awful drive down would be worth it for the goodies we could bring back home. Smoked meats, cheeses, and breads from

Kampala's new Italian deli; gin, tonic, and Baileys Irish Cream from the duty-free shops; modern-day wonders like tin foil and canned cat food from the more cosmopolitan stores; and magazines, videos, and books passed around by Kampala's sizeable and generous expat population.

"There is a boy at the gate who would like a ride to Kampala," James told us as we loaded up the Pajero early the next morning.

"Who is this boy?" John asked.

"I myself do not know him. But his name is Robert. He is thirteen and he lives up on the hill by the Catholic diocese and he is going to Kampala to stay with his uncle."

"Well, how does he even know we are going to Kampala today?" I asked.

James shrugged. "You are *mzungus*," he said. As if that explained precisely how everyone in town knew our business.

"Well, we have room. Of course we'll give him a ride." It would be no trouble. Or so we thought, until midway through the trip when we stopped for lunch and Robert had no lunch. But it was no trouble to share our lunch with him and no trouble to buy him a warm soda at a roadside shop, because he had no money of his own. And then we got back on the road and Robert vomited up his entire lunch onto the back of my car seat.

"I did not wish to trouble you to stop," he said.

Oh, no trouble. We mopped him up and said good-bye to Robert when we reached Kampala, hoping he'd be no trouble to his uncle either.

"You are unequivocally pregnant," Dr. Stockley said when we went to see him at the Surgery the next morning. He was looking through the small microscope at the slide that contained a drop of my pee along with some chemical that he had mixed with it. "Or maybe not," he added. "Have a look for yourself." He slid the microscope across the table to where John and I were sitting. Dr. Stockley's many years of living in Uganda gave him a distinctly African outlook on life. He had a you-could-die . . . but-then-again-you-might-not kind of air that I wasn't finding especially reassuring at the moment. But if anyone suddenly needed a tracheotomy while out in the bush, I suspect Dr. Stockley could do it with a ballpoint pen and a rusty pocketknife.

"What exactly am I supposed to be looking for?" I asked, peering down the barrel of the microscope. Seeing nothing that I could decipher, I passed it along to John.

"Well, you see, when we mix the urine with this chemical, it will clot at precisely three minutes if there is enough hCG hormone in it, indicating that you are pregnant. It seems your urine here made a half-hearted attempt at clotting, but not until four minutes. And now it seems to be trying to unclot."

"Hah!" I let out a tortured laugh. "My mother always used to tell me that there's no such thing as being just a little bit pregnant. But my mother has never been to Uganda!"

"Let's get you up on the table and do an exam," Dr. Stockley said.

"Ah . . . yes . . . this ovary feels a bit boggy," he said with his hand still inside me. "Now the normal size of a uterus is that of a chicken's egg. Your uterus feels to be more like a duck's egg."

"Well, what does that mean?" I asked. What the hell did I know about the size of a duck's egg relative to that of a chicken's? Or what the word "boggy" meant, for that matter.

"Well, it might mean that you are pregnant," he said, removing his hand and signaling me to get up from the examining table. "But then again, it might mean nothing at all. I have an idea," he said as if something novel had just occurred to him. "Let's take your blood pressure." My blood pressure, never low on the best of days, was off the chart.

"Hmmm . . . I say, this doesn't look too good. If you are pregnant, you'll never get by with this kind of blood pressure. Here's what I think we ought to do." He looked from me to John. "I think the two of you ought to go out this evening and have a nice cold Nile." He was referring to Uganda's national beer, which came only in 20-ounce bottles. "And try to relax. Then come back here tomorrow and we'll see what kind of lab tests we can do on you."

I found this to be an unorthodox prescription—especially for a potentially pregnant woman. But Dr. Stockley seemed to be an unorthodox physician. I liked his recommendation about the beer and I was beginning to like him.

"So what does this mean?" I asked in frustration the next morning as we watched my urine once again coagulate and then uncoagulate under the microscope.

"Well, it could mean any one of a number of things," Dr. Stockley said. "It could mean that you are not pregnant. It could mean that you are pregnant but that the level of hCG is very low. And that could mean that you are about to miscarry. But I could be wrong."

John and I both stared, dumbfounded, at the doctor.

"But here's what I think we should do. I think we should get you two to the pantomime show tonight over at the International School. It should be hilarious. I'm in it. Want a couple of tickets?" He rummaged through his desk.

"No thanks. We've got dinner plans with the Marums," John offered as if we needed an excuse. "Do you know them? Elizabeth runs the AIDS programs for USAID."

"Oh, nice family. One of the twins impaled herself on their fence a while back. Missed all of her major organs. Lucky. Nice family," he repeated. "And Larry's a pediatrician! Works at your embassy, I believe. Great! He'll know what to do in case you do start bleeding. Feel free to call me, though, if you need me."

I was beginning *not* to like this guy.

Dinner at the Marums' was at least as good a diversion as seeing Dr. Stockley again, even if he was doing his comedy act onstage for a change.

"Welcome, welcome. So nice that we could finally do this," Elizabeth said as we stood on the front porch of her huge house tucked behind a high metal fence. "Larry and the kids are up in the treehouse," she said, pointing up into a misshapen flame tree in the front yard. A good twenty feet off the ground was a Swiss Family Robinson chateau, complete with a thatched roof and something that looked like a dumbwaiter.

"Larry! Paul! Sonja! Look who's here," Elizabeth called up.

A tall, bearded man stepped out onto the porch of the treehouse. "Hey, come on up and see the view."

A blond-haired boy poked his head out of a window. "Yeah, you can come up. There's plenty of room."

"Hey, Mom," a girl called out from the same window. "Can you put one of the cats in the basket and send her up?"

"Later, Sonja," Elizabeth called up.

"Great house!" John said.

"Larry and the kids built it," Elizabeth said.

"Wow! A doctor and a carpenter," John enthused. "I gotta see this." John headed for the rope ladder.

"I'm not exactly feeling up to the climb," I said. I followed Elizabeth inside the house.

"Malaria?" Elizabeth asked. She led me into her spacious living room.

"No. I might be pregnant," I blurted.

"Oh, that's wonderful!" she gushed enthusiastically. "Have a seat." She pointed me toward a stylishly upholstered couch.

"Only, I might not be," I added, sinking into the couch beside her.

"Well, have you been to see Dr. Stockley?" she asked.

"Only every day this week." I hadn't intended to burden our burgeoning friendship by pouring out the whole sorry tale of my impending pregnancy-cum-miscarriage. But there it was dribbling out as I sat next to Elizabeth on her soft couch, admiring the vase of flowers on the piano.

"You want to hear a pregnancy horror story?" Elizabeth asked when I'd finally brought her up to date on my tale of woe. "No, on second thought, you really don't need to hear a pregnancy horror story right now. Let's go see what we can find to settle your stomach." She led me through the dining room. From the furniture to the place settings on the table to the bric-a-brac on the sideboard, it looked like I had stepped into America.

"I'm USAID," Elizabeth said, as if she were answering my unasked question. "They ship stuff over from the States."

We walked through the dining room and into a small hallway.

"There's a powder room if you need it," Elizabeth said, pointing out a small bathroom. "There's the kitchen," she said, waving toward a large, very modern-looking kitchen that at first seemed like a mirage to me. I took a peek and saw a two-door refrigerator and a standing freezer along one wall and a big, square island in the middle of the room that held a blender, a food processor, and a toaster oven. The sudden appearance of this all-American kitchen seemed downright miraculous to me.

"Wow, something sure smells good," I said, inhaling.

"It's chicken Marbella," Elizabeth said. "One of our favorite recipes. I hope that's okay with you. I forgot to ask what you guys eat."

"Oh, we have learned to eat pretty much anything," I said.

"Well, let's see what we can find to help settle your stomach."

Elizabeth led me into an attached garage with a metal shelving unit that was stocked with cases of macaroni and cheese, peanut butter, jellies, breakfast cereals, granola bars, juices, chips, toilet paper, soap, pet food, and, there it was . . . soup. I stood there for a moment, reminded of the time I had fallen apart in the supermarket. Ah, what I wouldn't give now to be overwhelmed by so many choices.

"Where did all this come from?" I asked.

"Well, when you work for the U.S. government, you can get a consumables shipment."

"Wow," I whispered. It was the first time I had ever coveted another woman's canned goods.

"It's nice. Especially for the kids. When Larry and I decided to come here, the twins were eight and we knew we were disrupting their lives. So the food and the stuff from home, well, it helps them have a bit more of a normal American childhood." She perused the stock. "Oh, crackers. How about some saltines?" she asked.

As I nibbled on saltines, Sonja and Paul bounded in from outside, looking every bit the average American kids. They were both blond and lanky, with long arms and legs poking out of their shorts and T-shirts. "I heard about the fence," I said as Sonja poured me a drink.

"Yeah, I won't try to climb over that again," she said, pointing to the spearlike fence posts. I drained the glass in one grateful swig. "Wow, you were thirsty!" Sonja said.

"Oh, my God! That was the best drink I have ever tasted!"

"Umm, it's just apple juice," Sonja said and held up a plastic bottle of Juicy Juice.

"Don't you have apple juice in Arua?" Paul asked. His hair was gelled to stick up in the front, just like I remembered boys in the States doing.

"No," I said with a laugh. "We don't have much in Arua."

I felt considerably better about everything by the time we'd finished our delicious dinner. By the end of the evening, the entire Marum family knew all the details of the possible pregnancy saga. Elizabeth sent me off with a box of saltines and an invitation to stay with them the next time we came to Kampala. Sonja handed me a bottle of apple juice of my very own.

"Now, you be sure to keep us posted," Elizabeth said as we were pulling down the driveway.

"And you know, if you do have a baby, I can be your pediatrician!" Larry yelled after us.

The next morning's urine test was as inconclusive as the previous ones. But Dr. Stockley had another idea.

"I say, let's jab you and get some blood and do a serum hCG test," he said. "Yes, that's a fine idea." I thought so too. And knowing that blood tests can detect pregnancies earlier than urine tests, I wondered why he hadn't thought of this days ago.

"I'll have someone rush it over to the lab now," he said as he finished siphoning off a tube of my blood. "Come round at five this evening and we should have some reliable results." I was starting to like him again.

At 4:30 p.m. John was in a meeting at the CARE office and I was outside stamping my feet. I poked my head into the meeting, caught John's eye, and pointed to my watch.

"If you'll all excuse me," John said as he stood.

"It seems that John Waite has something more important to attend to now," Stan said to the group. But he smiled at John and said, "Some things are more important than work." I was relieved and then appalled as I realized that the country director and probably the entire CARE staff knew of our dilemma. But what did I expect? The expat world was pretty close and we all knew each other's business. And it was the CARE secretary who'd made our doctor's appointments.

We stepped out of the office into the bright, late-afternoon sunshine and found that our vehicle was missing. The yard around the office was a small parking lot of CARE-emblazoned jeeps and Land Rovers. It was gated and guarded, so when a vehicle went missing, it usually meant that someone had borrowed it for an errand because their vehicle had been blocked in or broken down.

"Ah, Mr. John Waite, madam," the guard replied when we went to inquire about our vehicle. "Your Pajero was quite dirty from the road. The color of Arua was all over it!" The dirt in Arua was a burned red and after a long drive, we—as well as our vehicle—were always covered in it. "It is now being washed out back." He took one look at my face and added, "It will be finished in ten minutes."

I looked at my watch. It was already nearly five o'clock. I didn't trust my shaky sanity to survive if we got to the Surgery and found that Dr. Stockley had left for a night of pantomiming and I still didn't know if I was pregnant or not.

"Can you give me the keys to another vehicle? Any vehicle," John asked in quiet desperation. "Give me the keys to Terry Cross's Land

Rover. If he comes looking, just give him the keys to my Pajero. Tell him I said we can trade tomorrow."

We hopped into the Land Rover and crept along as fast as we could, over the potholed roads that were clogged with bicycles, pedestrians, and dangerously overloaded commuter vans called *matatus.*

"It's not five o'clock" was the first thing Dr. Stockley said upon our breathless arrival in his office at 5:15 p.m. "And it seems that I jabbed you for nothing" was the second thing he said. "Our lab can't do a serum hCG test. You'd have to go to Nairobi for that."

"What??? Well, what do we do now?" It was John being indignant and frustrated for both of us. I was just speechless.

"Well, I have one more idea," he said, sitting behind his desk and scribbling on a piece of paper. "First thing tomorrow morning—"

"Pee in a cup!" I said, finishing the sentence that I thought surely would come.

"No, we've had enough of your pee. No. Go over to see this radiologist," he said, and handed me a piece of paper with an address on it. "He's a Ugandan fellow. I've heard quite good things about him. He'll do a sonogram. That ought to tell you what you need to know. He ought to be able to tell you if you are pregnant and if it is ectopic or not."

"Oh, a sonogram in Uganda?" I bit my tongue to keep from saying, *Why hadn't someone thought of that earlier?*

"And let's take your blood pressure again," the doctor said, motioning for me to hop up on the examining table. "Just for fun."

"Your pressure is sky-high, again," he said, letting the air out of the pressure cuff. "This uncertainty is really bothering you, isn't it?" he asked. "Well, you know, I can recommend one more thing."

John and I waited to hear what diversion the good doctor would recommend next—opium, perhaps?

"If all else fails, find yourself a traditional African doctor. Some of these guys are so good that just by looking at you they can tell if you are pregnant, when the baby will be born, whether it will be a boy or a girl, and maybe even what it will be when it grows up!" He said it with a straight face, and I didn't have the faintest idea if he was being facetious or not.

The next morning we reported to the address that Dr. Stockley had given us. I was pleasantly surprised to find a nice, well-appointed radiologist's office. A nurse kindly took our information and then handed me a large glass of water.

"You must drink until you cannot hold any more," she instructed. I sat down in the waiting room and drank. When I'd finished my glass of water, the nurse came over with another. And then another.

"Can you hold any more?" she asked pleasantly while waving a fourth glass of water at me.

"No, I really don't think I can. In fact, I need to pee!"

"Good!" She laughed. "Then you are ready." She led us down the hall to a modern sonogram room. "Here," she said, handing me a dressing gown—the first I had ever been offered in Uganda. I nearly cried with relief. "You can take off your clothing and put this on. Doctor will be right with you."

I was certainly impressed. All I had seen of this office so far gave me confidence that I would soon have a reliable answer.

"Hello, Mr. and Mrs. Waite. I am Dr. Nnangwe Joseph," he said, offering his sturdy hand to both John and me. "I understand that you are anxious to be pregnant," he said, looking at me.

"I am anxious to *know* if I am pregnant," I said.

"Well, get up on the table and we will see what we can do about that."

He ran the greased-up wand over my flat belly—which made me have to pee even more—and punched in buttons on what looked like a big computer console.

"Here are the fallopian tubes." He pressed the wand down first into one side of my abdomen and then into the other. He pointed to some hazy squiggle on the screen. "They look clear. No pregnancy there."

He swished the wand around some more on my belly. He punched some more buttons and stared at the screen, before making his final pronouncement.

"You are definitely not pregnant, Mrs. Waite," he said rather sadly.

"Well, then why is my period so late? It's now ten days overdue. And what about the cramping and the sharp pains? What are they?" I asked.

"I can see by this sonogram that your period will be coming. See, right here, there is a thickening," he said as he pointed to an indecipherable blob on the screen. "This means that your period is surely coming. I can confidently say that you will get your period in . . ." He paused and looked as if he was making a methodical calculation. "In two days."

He must have taken the look of amazement on my face for disappointment.

"How long have you been married?" he asked.

"Um . . . just over two years," I answered, wondering what that had to do with my diagnosis.

"Well, I can see why you are so anxious to be pregnant, then." He turned his attention to John. "Two years married and no babies! What a shame," he said while sucking his teeth. "Has your mother picked out a second wife for you yet?"

John and I left the radiologist's office in a kind of quiet shock. Until I had been told that I was definitely not pregnant, I hadn't even been sure that I really wanted to be pregnant.

"How are you feeling?" John asked, putting his arm around my shoulders.

"Disappointed and numb. And worried. 'Cause if I'm not pregnant, then what's wrong with me? My period is ten days late and my boobs are killing me! And I didn't want to say anything before, but I'm beginning to feel nauseous and exhausted all the time." I began to cry. "And if I am pregnant . . . well, what the hell were we doing thinking we could even have a baby here?"

"Don't worry. It will all work out." John said this a lot, and though he was usually right, it didn't make me feel any better just then. Then he kissed me on the top of my head, which did make me feel better. "Dr. Stockley said to come see him after the radiologist. Let's go see him one more time. At least we can be sure that it's not an ectopic pregnancy—and that was the real worry. Tomorrow we'll just go home."

I wasn't usually in much of a rush to give up the relative luxuries of Kampala for Arua. But after all the running around and confusion, I couldn't wait to get back to our quiet life.

"Hmm . . ." Dr. Stockley read the brief report that we had been given on the way out of the radiologist's office. "Says here you are unequivocally not pregnant. But if I had to wager a bet, I'd say you are pregnant."

"Wait a minute!" Now I was thoroughly exasperated. "What about the inconclusive tests? The clotting and unclotting? The 'I'm going to miscarry' theory and the really good radiologist you sent us to? You told me you thought I was pregnant, then you thought I wasn't pregnant. Now this guy tells me that I am definitely not pregnant and now you think I am! What am I supposed to think?"

"I don't know about how it's done in America, but medicine here is definitely not an exact science. There could be any number of explanations for all your inconclusive tests. But the main thing is that we can reasonably rule out an ectopic pregnancy. So you can go back to Arua and relax a bit. If you feel pregnant, then you may well be pregnant. Nothing more we can do but just wait and see."

"Well, what about the sonogram? Could he have been wrong?"

"Sure. Don't radiologists ever make mistakes in America?"

"So what if he was wrong about my not having an ectopic pregnancy?"

"Try not to worry too much about that. My guess is that if it is an ectopic pregnancy, you'll have so much pain and bleeding before your fallopian tube bursts, there'll be time to get to Kuluva Hospital and David Morton will have a good chance at saving you, if not your reproductive organs."

Oh, yeah. I was feeling better already!

Dear Jean,

I'm writing from Kampala, where I'm miserable and nauseous and no one can figure out if I'm pregnant or not. Or if I am pregnant, if I'm miscarrying. Oh, God! What were we thinking trying to get pregnant over here? What have we done? I suppose there is nothing we can do at this point but wait and see. John says it'll all be just fine. But he always says that!

To help take my mind off of my misery, we rescued a desperate-looking rat of a puppy that we found hiding in the CARE compound and we're taking him up to Arua with us tomorrow. We caught him, fed him, flea-dipped him twice, and bathed him in puppy shampoo. He's all clean and shiny now and has warmed up to us. Me especially, which is too bad because his puppy smell is really making me want to puke and then die.

Oh, yeah, we took the puppy to the vet because he looked so mangy and malnourished. This guy was truly amazing—barely lifted the dog two inches out of his box for all of two seconds and began prescribing medicines. No need for a pesky examination or anything. Hmmm . . . maybe I should go to see this guy about my situation!

Well, if I am pregnant I'll be nearly seven months by the time I come home for your wedding. With you all tall and skinny and me short and round, we ought to look like a bat and a ball coming down the aisle!

I'll keep you posted,
Eve

Chapter Twenty

No Good Deed Goes Unpunished

We were certainly hoping for an uneventful trip back to Arua. Well, as uneventful as can be when you're driving five hundred kilometers on dirt roads. With an unexpected cargo of four children. And a puppy. Only the puppy belonged to us.

As we were preparing for our return trip, John's secretary, Nasra, radioed down from Arua and asked us to give a ride to her four young nieces and nephews. "They will be no trouble," Nasra assured us. The memories and the smell of vomit still lingered from our ride down with Robert. As it turned out, he never did find his uncle and so came to the CARE office every day we were in Kampala, asking for food, money, and a ride back to Arua.

One of the *askaris* shook his head as I gave Robert money for a bus ticket to Arua. "*Your* boy will never leave you alone now," he said.

"He is *not* my boy," I answered. "I'm just helping him out."

"Well, he is your boy, now," the *askari* said, as if he were imparting to me a basic lesson on Ugandan culture. "Madam, in Uganda if you pull a drowning man out of the Nile, you had better be prepared to buy him some dry clothes." *And feed him supper and maybe even give him a place to stay.*

But we just couldn't say no to Nasra. And so we were headed to Arua with four children and a dog and things were going surprisingly well. The children had been very well behaved, sharing a package of cookies that their mother had packed for them. Our puppy, Armstrong, however, had climbed out of his box and thrown up all over the back of the Pajero (what was it with that vehicle and vomit?). But the kids were happy to keep him company in the backseat.

Suddenly, like a mirage out of the flat distance, a group of people came running toward us. As we got closer we saw that they were actually running toward a Land Rover that had flipped onto its side and was teetering precariously on the edge of the road just up ahead of us. We carefully maneuvered our way through the crowd and toward the vehicle. Two wheels were up in the air and its roof, now lying sideways, was scraped as if it had been dragged along the ground. Someone waved us over and asked if we could help transport the wounded.

"John?" I put my hand on his arm as he pulled the vehicle over to the side of the road. "What about what the embassy told us?" We had been told of stories of *mzungus* who had pulled over to help and were then accused of causing the accident in an attempt by the victims to extort money. *And then, of course, there's the whole drowning man thing.*

"We have to help, Eve. Don't worry. It will be fine." Saint John actually believed that if you pulled a drowning man out of the Nile River you ought to at least teach him to swim.

We were directed by several bystanders to a round, genial-looking white man, the only *mzungu* in the crowd. Despite the wadded handkerchief he held to his bald head, blood was trickling onto his face, settling into the creases around his eyes.

"This Italian father is a good man," we were told by a young Ugandan as he walked the bleeding priest toward our vehicle. "Could you take him to the police post up the road?"

"Certainly," John said. "But wouldn't he rather us take him to the clinic for treatment?"

"No, no," protested the injured priest. "This is just a superficial head wound. I'd rather go directly to the police and report the accident." We had also been warned by the embassy about the severe punishments for being involved in an accident and not reporting it to authorities.

"Are there any others who need help?" I scanned the group.

"No," one of the bystanders assured me. "It is only the father who is seriously injured."

"Shouldn't he be taken too?" I pointed to a man sitting in an obvious haze on the side of the road. Blood was oozing from the top of his head.

"Oh no, he is Ugandan," someone piped up. "He will be okay."

I walked over and saw that his head and arm were both bleeding heavily. "Do you need help?" I asked. He said nothing and stared off into the distance. We decided to take him with us.

We squeezed the children and Armstrong into the back with the luggage and all the goodies from my shopping binge, and guided the two injured men onto the backseat.

"The police post is just ten kilometers up the road," we were told by someone in the crowd. "You cannot miss it."

We drove for fifteen kilometers not seeing anything that resembled a town or a police post, until we were stopped by a huge, spiked metal slab lying in the middle of the road. Three soldiers were reclining on the side of the road, against the trunk of an ancient baobab tree. Seeing the CARE logo on the side of the vehicle and a *mzungu* at the wheel, the soldiers waved us on from the shade of the tree's gnarled branches.

"Officers," John pulled over and called out to the still-reclining soldiers. "We need some help."

"Was there a shooting?" one of the soldiers asked with a look that can only be described as glee.

"No. No shooting," I answered. "But a car accident. We need to get to a police post." One of the soldiers got up, slung his AK-47 over his shoulder, walked to our vehicle, and stared into the backseat.

"We need a police post," I repeated. The two other soldiers also stood and began peering into the window.

"Was there a shooting?" one of them asked again.

"No," I answered again. "But there was a car accident. A vehicle accident," I corrected myself, remembering that in Uganda we traveled in vehicles, not cars. "And we need to get help."

"Was there a robbery?" the other one asked, clutching his rifle excitedly.

"No, a vehicle accident!" I repeated as the soldiers continued flinging questions at us.

"What happened?" asked one.

"Was another vehicle involved?" chimed another.

"Is the vehicle still there on the road?" asked the third.

"Where is it?" pinged number one.

"Should we go?" ponged number two.

"Can you take us there?" Shoot and score from number three. I had been wondering just how long it would be before the soldiers asked us for a ride.

"The vehicle these men were driving swerved off the road and turned over," John said. "It happened about fifteen kilometers back." The soldiers listened, nodded earnestly, and began questioning us again.

"Five kilometers back?" one asked.

"Can you take us there?" asked another.

"Was there a shooting?" asked the third.

"We need a police post," John said.

"Oh, yes," one of the soldiers said. "You need a police post."

"Well, where would we find a police post?" John wasn't even trying to mask his frustration.

"Continue on this road," one of the soldiers offered. "You will get to Myenga. There is a police post there. There is a sign on the road so you cannot miss it."

John shifted into gear and began to pull to the left of the roadblock when one of the soldiers put his face into my window.

"By the way, do you have any cigarettes?" he asked.

"No," I said.

"Then how about a newspaper?"

We left him in a cloud of red dust and found the Myenga police post, which amounted to three tin roundhouses scattered in a dirt clearing. Three half-naked children, a woman with a baby on her exposed breast, and a monkey were sitting in the tiny sliver of shade made by the slight overhang of one of the tin roofs. A man dressed in dark pants and a blindingly bright orange shirt came out of one of the huts to greet us.

"Yes, *mzee*," he said, addressing John, who, while not an old man, often got the respectful Swahili title of *"mzee"* simply because he had a beard. I asked around a lot, but no one could tell me the equivalent for respectfully addressing an older woman. "How can I help you?"

"There's been an accident on the road a few kilometers back," John explained. "The people involved would like to make a police report."

"Ah . . . then you have come to the right place. I am the chief of police."

"We've got two people with head injuries," I said, getting out of the car. "And we need to get them some medical attention."

"Why yes, madam," the police chief said, gingerly taking my arm. "You can come right inside here and we will take care of you." He began to lead me into one of the huts.

"Not me. I'm fine," I said, yanking my hand free. *Well, I might be pregnant . . . might not be . . . but I doubt you can help me with that.*

"These men need help," I said, pointing to the bleeding and dazed passengers in the backseat of our car.

"I will direct you to the clinic and take their report there." He jumped into the backseat, shoving aside the injured men, and directed us to a small cement building that was just across the road.

People seemed to appear out of nowhere as we helped the two men out of the car. A man in a dirty lab coat came out of the clinic building. "Welcome to Myenga Clinic," he said. "You will receive good medical care here." Whatever slight confidence this might have instilled faded immediately as he left the bleeding and shocked Ugandan on the front step and rushed the Italian inside. It was fifteen minutes more before someone came out to attend to the ashen and shaking Ugandan.

Something else to tell my friend who was convinced that black people couldn't be racist, I thought. If not racism, what was it that caused white people to be singled out for special attention, while black people were ignored. It's just Ugandan hospitality, I'd sometimes tell myself, because let's be honest, I enjoyed the special treatment. (Who wouldn't?) Being white branded me as a foreigner and Ugandans are unfailingly kind to guests. Maybe being bumped to the front of the line or given a seat in the shade is not the same as letting a black man bleed while a less injured white man is attended to. But maybe they are simply two not-so-distant points on the same discrimination spectrum.

I tried not to think too much about this dilemma—for it was constant—as John and I cleaned the blood off of the backseat. I'd worked around people with AIDS long enough to not be particularly frightened of simply wiping up the nearly dried blood; we had no open sores that it would get into. But the man in the dirty white lab coat ran out and handed us gloves. "You must be careful of HIV slash AIDS," he warned.

As we cleaned up and reorganized the children and the dog and got ready to go, the chief of police tried to get us to drive him back to the scene of the accident. We were saved only by the intervention of the bandaged-up priest who insisted that we'd already been helpful enough. By the time we finally got back on the road to Arua, the entire population of Myenga had gathered to watch us. Everyone was abuzz about the accident—or perhaps the shooting—that had happened and the three *mzungus*—one with a bleeding head—who'd come to the clinic.

The rest of the trip on that long, red road was uneventful. Well, as uneventful as anything ever was in Uganda.

Dear Mom,

Well, John has really taken to our new dog, Armstrong, which is a good thing. Even though I was the one who insisted we rescue him from the streets of Kampala, as soon as we got home, I discovered that I

can't stand the smell of him. (The dog, not John!) You
should see John out there with him—he's building a
doghouse. It's hysterical. John mentioned to one of the
guards that he wanted to put a thatched roof on it. So
at eight o'clock this morning the guard showed up at
our house with two old women carrying huge loads of
dried grass on their heads. Well, there was no way in
hell that we were going to tell these women that they
had just walked God knows how far with grass on
their heads so that we could use it to build a doghouse.
So John told everyone that he's building a house out
back for his (very short) mother-in-law! And they just
think he is the sweetest guy in the world.

　　It stopped raining weeks ago. And now everyone
stinks more than usual. I smell my own armpits. Still
think my life is adventurous?

I'll keep you posted,
Eve

Chapter Twenty-One

The Smell of Sweat and Old Sex

Let's face it: It was hard being in Uganda. Well, maybe not so hard for the Ugandans. In fact, I was always surprised at how happy everyone around me seemed to be. As long as it didn't kill them, they took their bouts of malaria in stride. They stepped their bare feet over the snakes, giant black ants, and palm-sized spiders that kept me from ever walking barefoot. No postage stamps this week? They did without mail. No meat in the market? They made stews out of the stinky dried fish that I felt guilty even feeding to my cats. No water? They cheerily dispensed with bathing.

So let me rephrase my earlier statement: It was hard being *me* in Uganda. And it didn't seem like it was about to get easier. I still didn't have a definitive pregnancy diagnosis. The two days to my period predicted by the radiologist had come and gone with no period.

I went back to see David Morton. "Let me try something a very wise professor taught me in medical school," he said when I'd concluded our tale of medical misadventures in Kampala. "He taught us to ask our patients what they think is going on in their bodies. So what do you think, Eve? Do you think you're pregnant?" he asked.

"Oh, yeah," I said, thinking of the nausea that had recently become my constant companion. "Yeah, I think I am pregnant."

"Well, then I'd say you're pregnant."

Here's the thing about being pregnant in Uganda. Just about everyone is pregnant in Uganda. Well, all the women of child-bearing years, that is. They were pregnant and walking for miles with huge loads of wood balanced on their heads. They were pregnant and nursing toddlers. They were pregnant and hoeing the fields. They were pregnant and nursing toddlers and hoeing the fields with huge loads of wood on their heads all at the same time. And smiling. Did I mention smiling? But me? I was pregnant and sick. Not much else. Forget tennis and badminton. Retching and whining soon became my only pastimes.

We planned to celebrate our first Christmas in Uganda at a luxury resort in Entebbe. We'd spend the day lounging by the pool and then call our families to break the good news that night. Everyone at CARE had the week between Christmas and New Year's off and we were planning on joining a few friends on a real (not a bank) safari through a few of Uganda's national parks.

On Christmas Day we did enjoy the pool and the phone calls. And after that we enjoyed nothing. The next day as we drove to Kampala, I was wrenched by intestinal cramps. We arrived at our friends' house, where I went immediately to the bathroom, explosively emptied my intestines, and proceeded to pass out on the floor. Since this scene repeated itself several more times over the next few hours, our friends went on safari without us. I couldn't possibly get back in a vehicle, so we stayed in their house and I spent the next two days running between the bed and the toilet. On the third day, John mopped me up and carried me to dear old Dr. Stockley.

"Enjoying this pregnancy, I see?" chuckled the good doctor/humorist.

"No, I am not enjoying it. But this shitting my brains out is a whole new dimension."

"Do you think you can produce a sample for me?" He handed me a plastic cup.

"Let's see, it's been twenty minutes since my last bout of explosive diarrhea. Without a doubt." I took the cup and went into the bathroom while John and the doctor chatted in his office.

"Oh, you've got a good case of bacterial dysentery," the doctor pronounced while peering through a microscope. "A bloody good case. Excuse the pun. You'll need a strong dose of antibiotics." He handed me a vial of pills. "And even these may not get at it. Come round in a few days if it's still hanging on."

"Is it safe to take these during pregnancy?" I whimpered. The baby wasn't even born yet and I was already worried about it.

"Looking at you, I don't think it'd be safe for you not to take it."

Antibiotics or not, the dysentery hung on through another three days and another round of antibiotics. I celebrated New Year's Eve by limping out of bed at midnight long enough to stand on the balcony to watch as gunfire rained down on Kampala.

"What are they shooting at?" I asked John, glad that we were staying far from the center of the city.

"I think they all just shoot up into the air. For some reason, shooting up into the air is celebratory in some countries," he explained.

"Not so celebratory when the bullets come back down, I bet." I hobbled back to bed.

When the dysentery finally subsided, it was replaced by increasing nausea.

"It's morning sickness. It'll pass," Dr. Stockley said when I called to tell him I was now wracked by nausea and hadn't eaten much of anything since Christmas.

"Morning sickness? Hah! That's a misnomer! More like twenty-four-hour-a-day sickness. Isn't there something I can take for this?"

"You can't take anything. You're pregnant. Well, except of course for those antibiotics—but let's try to avoid that again. And then, of course, your daily dose of Paludrine—do take those. And don't forget the prenatal vitamins I gave you. And the folic acid. But aside from that you shouldn't be taking drugs," he said.

"I don't know how I am going to get through this," I wailed as I hung up the phone.

"Why don't we call Larry Marum?" John suggested. "Maybe he can give you some advice."

"The first time we socialized with them, I told them my whole sob story. Now I'm gonna call them again and whine about how nauseous I am?" But I called him. That's how desperate I was.

"Dr. Stockley says it's just morning sickness. But this just can't be normal. If every pregnant woman felt this bad, the human race would end. I'm afraid I'm starving the baby," I sobbed. "I'm sorry, I'm crying. I feel like an idiot. I just feel so sick."

"It sounds like it. Want me to come over and take a look at you?" he asked.

"No. I've seen Dr. Stockley. He says I'm fine. I just wondered if you had any advice?" I sniffed. "I'm sorry I'm being such a baby."

"Oh, Eve, you feel awful. It's hard. You don't have to be sorry. You know, there is an antihistamine that's okay to take in pregnancy," he offered.

"Yeah, but I don't have allergies." Although my nose had been continuously stuffed up since I got pregnant. But breathing was the least of my worries.

"Yeah, but the antihistamine might take the edge off your nausea. But it might also make you drowsy."

"Well, if I'm sleeping, then I won't care that I'm so nauseous."

"Elizabeth says come by for more saltines—and anything else you'd like—before you head back to Arua."

By the second week of January, we were back in Arua. I wasn't quite through my first trimester and had already lost eight pounds, which wasn't surprising considering my diet consisted mainly of drugs. But now I was so dopey from the antihistamines that I didn't care.

And I was glad to be home. I didn't do much besides lie around and moan. But I preferred lying around my own house where at least I had Beijing and Berlin to keep me company. Since they didn't smell, they were allowed inside the house. Armstrong and his pukey puppy smell were banished to the outside, where he'd bark at the goats that always seemed to be hanging around just outside my gate. With the near-constant nagging noise they made, on some days I'd wish he'd catch one.

"Yoo-hoo. I brought you some bread," Pauline called in through the screen door. "Just out of the oven."

"Haven't you heard? I'm off all food," I told her.

"Well, I'll leave it in the kitchen for John. And whenever you're feeling up to eating, come on by and I'll feed you." I couldn't imagine ever feeling up to eating again.

A few days later, I woke up in the morning feeling like my head was full of cotton. Then the wrist I broke when I was twelve started to ache. Then my hips hurt whenever I lay down, but I got dizzy whenever I stood up. Then my ears started buzzing and I ran a slight fever. John took me over to see David Morton at Kuluva Hospital.

"Hmmm . . . it's hard to see. There's not a lot of parasites in your blood," David said, looking through a microscope at a slide smeared with my blood. "But there it is. You definitely have malaria."

"I can't have malaria. I take those damn awful Paludrine pills every night."

"Yeah, I know you do. We all do. But they don't come with a guarantee. You can still get malaria even if you take all the precautions. It's just endemic here. And pregnant women are more susceptible to malaria. It doesn't seem to be a terrible case. But you'll have to take the chloroquine anyway."

"Is it safe to take chloroquine while I'm pregnant?"

"All the pregnant women here take it. And you really have no choice. Malaria doesn't clear up by itself. It tends to get worse. And we can't have you walking around with malaria for another six or seven months. That definitely would not be good for you or the baby."

So I added chloroquine to my daily diet of drugs.

"Well, halloo there, Eve. I heard you were feeling under what? I heard you were feeling under the weather." Adam's wife and children had finally joined him in Arua and the whole family had moved to a house about half a mile from ours. We didn't see him as often outside of work. "I've come to check up on you."

"Hi, Adam," I said. I was embarrassed at how sick I was.

"Not feeling so what? Not feeling so good, I hear."

"Oh, just a little bit pregnant. And a bit of dysentery. And a touch of malaria. I have no idea how I'm going to do this," I moaned.

"Oh, Eve." Adam was smiling as usual. "You will just have to get on with it! And when you are feeling better, Sarah says to invite you over for supper. She says you have fed me enough, now it is her turn to feed you. We will have *matoke*. Yum!"

"Yay!" I tried to sound excited. But it was hard to imagine ever being excited about eating *matoke*—or anything—again.

No, I was definitely not a pretty little pregnant gal. And it wasn't only my body that seemed to be conspiring to make me as miserable as humanly possible. Even the damn weather had turned on me. I assumed that because Uganda was subtropical and on the equator, the weather would always be the same: beautiful. So wasn't I surprised to learn that Uganda actually has four seasons: wet, wetter, dry, and drought.

We had arrived in August, during the wet season. The "short rains," as they were called, came every day, arriving usually late at night or early in the morning and lasting just a few hours each time. Then came the wetter season of the "long rains." What had previously politely confined itself to late at night now poured down in sheets all day, every day. This was quite handy, a national bonanza of sorts, providing a perfectly acceptable excuse for everything that was late, canceled, or went wrong during the long rainy season. And in Uganda, an excuse was as good as actually doing whatever it was you were supposed to do in the first place.

On the first morning of the long rains, I was confused when Rose, due at 8:30 a.m., didn't show up until 10:00 a.m. "The rain delayed me," she said, shrugging her shoulders and shaking fat drops of water off of her umbrella.

Maybe the rain bathed you, too, I thought. But no such luck.

But by December the rain had stopped completely and everything changed. At first I enjoyed the continuously sunny days that soaked up the mud we had been living in for months. But that was before I learned that the absence of the rain can be just as fierce as the rain itself.

In a few hot weeks, the lush tropical landscape turned hard and brown. Grass burned. Flowers blew away in the hot winds. Rich jacaranda and flamboyant trees that had been covered with purple and pink flowers now stood stark naked. Thirsty elephants left the game parks and wandered onto the roads with the baboons and monkeys in search of water. The roads that had been rutted and muddy turned to beach sand.

But it wasn't only the land and animals that suffered. The drought was an equal opportunity dilemma. We privileged *mzungu* in our fancy cement houses suffered along with our Ugandan neighbors in their mud and thatch huts. We all watched as the last precious drops of water disappeared from our tanks.

Most people in Arua collected rainwater in big barrels or tanks. In addition, fancier houses, like ours, were hooked up to the town's water supply. The town sent water to us, via a rudimentary system of water mains, which we could collect and store in our water tank. But the town's source of water was the same as ours: the rain. This meant that they sent us water during the rainy season, when we needed it least, but not in the dry season when we needed it most. When we finally ran out of water, I was forced, like everyone else, to pump water from the nearest borehole—now that I learned what a borehole actually was—and carry it home in a brigade of bright yellow jerry cans. Okay, *I* didn't have to pump the water and carry it home. Rose and our *askaris* did. But still, those were tough times.

In the dry season, we used our water sparingly, aware that our tanks would not be replenished until the next time it rained. Well, we were *supposed* to use it sparingly, because we were *supposed* to be aware that it wouldn't be replenished. But I swear, I missed that page in the handbook. So it took me a while—and a few admonitions from Pauline—before I caught on to the whole plan. That, and it was hot and dusty. I mean, those winds blowing down from the Sahara really make a mess. I'll admit it: During that first dry season I took more than my fair share of showers.

But bathing was one of the few things I had left to enjoy at that point. And of all the hardships I had to endure, the hardest by far was . . . How to put this delicately? People stunk. It wasn't only Rose. Some days it seemed to me that the whole damn country was funky. I know I should be politically correct here and say that there was a world of disparity between what was comfortable for my American nose and what was normal for Ugandans. I could explain that the lack of water and indoor plumbing, combined with the effort it took just to stay alive, understandably pushed bathing way down onto the bottom of people's priority list. And I could tell you what I was told again and again—that Ugandans have very active sex lives (three times a night was a very common boast). But to put it plainly, I was surrounded by people who smelled like sweat and old sex.

How unfortunate for me, then, that I am possessed of an exceptionally sensitive sense of smell. Even with a cold, I can smell someone in need of a bath at ten paces. And practically everyone in Uganda was in need of a bath! Pregnancy only enhanced my strong sense of smell, and now, as far as I was concerned, everyone needed to bathe, wash their clothes, and put on a little deodorant. I guess it was my own illogical attempt to ward off the body odor of others that caused me to bathe as often as I could.

But even I had to relent on my personal hygiene campaign when the dry season got even drier. John and I stopped showering altogether and started taking "bird baths," using just four cups of water each. It became nearly impossible for me to wash my body and my thick, curly hair with that amount of water. John had studied up before we left Brooklyn and had been trimming his own hair since we'd arrived. Thus far I had declined his haircutting offers and I now had a mop of heavy curls.

"It's a hundred degrees in my head," I said one day when the heat, the drought, and another case of malaria had all converged on me. "I am begging you to cut my hair."

"Oh, I knew you'd come around," John said and ran to get the scissors.

He seemed quite pleased with his handiwork when it was all over. I felt better and thought it looked surprisingly good from what I could see in the back of a spoon, since we had no mirror in the house and I wasn't quite up to going to the bank to look in theirs. But on a trip to Kampala a few weeks later, Stan's wife took one look at me and said, "Let's get you to someone who can fix that!" Which effectively ended John's tenure as my hairstylist.

Meanwhile, the drought went on. We saved the dirty rinse water from mopping, laundry, and dishes and used it to flush the toilet once a day. Rose reluctantly cut back on her daily floor-mopping but not before she abdicated all responsibility for what might move in. We washed our clothes less and less often and found ourselves smelling more and more . . . well, African.

Speaking of that African smell, I found it harder to be around Rose at all. I also found it harder to stay out of the house since I needed to be horizontal most of the time. I wondered if body odor constituted legitimate grounds for firing someone. But Rose herself provided me with the solution to this problem.

"Madam Eve," she said one day. "I have always wanted to finish my schooling. I am still not too old to go back." She was standing clear across the dining room and I could still smell her.

"No, you are not too old at all," I said, backing up till I was leaning against the opposite wall. "I think it would be a great idea to finish your schooling. What would it take to get you back into school?" I walked into the kitchen as if maybe I could find what she needed there. Way over on the far side of the kitchen.

"I would need two thousand shillings for my school fees. And a bit more for my uniform and building fees," she said, following me into the kitchen. "That is why I left school and started working in the first place. My parents could no longer afford to pay my school fees."

"Well, Rose, a dream deferred is a dream denied," I said. "Wait here a minute." I held my breath and walked past her toward the back of the house. I got five thousand shillings from John's dresser drawer.

"Here you go, Rose. Go back to school with our best wishes," I said, handing her the money.

"Shall I still come and work for you on the weekends?" she asked.

"Oh, no. You concentrate on your studies. Don't worry about us. We'll find someone else. You just concentrate on your schooling."

"Oh, thank you, Madam Eve. Thank you." She came in close to shake my hand.

"Oh, my pleasure," I said, not inhaling until she left for good.

I was relieved to be rid of Rose but knew I'd need to hire someone soon. I was far too food averse to set foot in the market or near the stove. John had been doing the shopping and cooking since I got pregnant. But I knew we'd need someone to sweep and dust, even if we had called a moratorium on mopping. Six months in Uganda seemed to have cured my earlier reluctance to hire a (or even say) house girl. Now I couldn't imagine how I'd ever survive without one. And as Pauline had said, women were lining up for what was a good job.

"Hello, Madam Eve," Regina said when she showed up at my door two days later. "I am Embati Regina. My husband's sister knows Mr. Waite John of CARE. I understand you need a house girl."

The first thing I noticed about Regina was that she didn't smell. And trust me, I did the whiff test. Another thing I noticed about Regina was that her breasts were enormously lopsided.

"Can I ask you a question?" I said after I'd interviewed her once, had John meet her, and had her come back again to make sure she still didn't smell. "Why are your breasts so uneven?" It was an unusual question, but not particularly awkward in Uganda. Legs were supposed to be covered, but breasts, which were on display everywhere, were not considered particularly private. At four months pregnant, I had no belly to speak of but several of my Ugandan women friends would pat my enlarged boobs and say, "Oh, you are beginning to look pregnant!" Regina looked down at her uneven cleavage and shrugged. "I do not know, madam. But they become this way whenever I have a baby. My youngest is now three months."

I had come to accept the fact that maybe I was not going to play a part in reducing the scourge of AIDS in Uganda. But here, at last, was a health mystery I just might be able to solve. I hired Regina, vowing to get to the bottom of her mysterious breast imbalance. I had a cause. And the house immediately began to smell better.

Now one very real risk of living in the developing world is that your feces may become a major preoccupation, as well as a perfectly acceptable topic of dinner conversation. In fact, back in Peace Corps training, a nurse gave us an entire lecture about shit. She warned us about all the creatures that could take up residence in our intestines. There were amoebas, parasites, bacteria, dysentery, cholera—an entire itsybitsy parallel universe waiting to get into our guts. She warned us to pay attention to our poops, to check them regularly for blood, worms, strange colors, or extra pungency. And this was a warning I took to heart.

One morning—late in the dry season and early in my pregnancy—I went to the bathroom and, as I was wont to do, looked down to check it out. I thought it was damn funny at first when I imagined I saw a creature with a tiny black nose staring up at me. On closer inspection, I noticed little whiskers beneath the tiny nose and the whole thing seemed to be trying to claw its way out of the toilet bowl.

"Oh my God!" I screamed to John. This was definitely not something the Peace Corps nurse had warned us about. "John! Get in here! Now!"

John came racing into the bathroom.

"Look! In the toilet. Oh my God. Look!" I screamed. "Is it the baby? Did I shit the baby?" Okay, I knew under normal circumstances it would be impossible to pass a baby out of my anus, and besides, if I did, it probably wouldn't have whiskers. But these were not normal circumstances. John, good man that he is, peered into the toilet.

"No. I think it's a rat."

"Oh my God! I shit a rat!" I screamed and ran back to bed.

John came in a few minutes later. He sat beside me on the bed and stroked my back.

"Is it gone? The rat? Is it gone?" I whimpered.

"Yes, honey. It's gone. And you didn't shit it. It didn't come out of you. It was probably already in the toilet when you sat down. I asked James and Nasser. They say the rats climb up into the drainpipes when it gets very dry. They are looking for water too."

"You mean the rat was in the toilet the whole time?"

"Yeah, it was already there."

"Oh my God, I shit on a rat! A rat was in the toilet when I sat down. Oh my God!" I didn't know which was worse, but I knew I would never enjoy a leisurely sit on the toilet again. "Can I go home?" I wailed.

John rubbed my back some more. "Eve, this is home. For now, anyway."

I sat up and reached for a tissue. "I could go to my mother's. She has air-conditioning. And television. And water!" *And no rats in the toilet.*

"Eve, I know you're miserable right now." John put his arms around me. "But it's gonna get better. I promise. And I don't want you to leave. I want you here with me."

I blew my nose. "But how can you want me? I'm useless. I lay around all day feeling miserable and whining. I don't *do* anything!"

"Eve, you are making our baby. You are doing the hardest work anyone can do. I know that. Stay here with me. I'll take care of you while you take care of the baby. It's all right if you're a little whiny and miserable." *A little?* "Just stay here. I don't want you to go anywhere."

I wouldn't have left him even if I could, which I couldn't, because, let's face it, I could barely get out of bed. So I continued my regimen of lying around and doing nothing. Luckily, we now had Regina, so at least the house got clean and John and the cats got fed. I quietly moaned on the couch as Regina cheerily went about running the household, trying to make it seem as if I was in charge.

"Eve," she said. Regina was one of the few Ugandans who did not call me "madam," and I loved her for that. "If it is okay with you, I will wait to make the cats' food until you go out." This was Regina's polite way of telling me that (a) we were out of the dried fish porridge that we fed to the cats, (b) she had taken care of it, (c) she knew the smell of it cooking would make me wretch, and (d) I really ought to get off the couch at least for a little while.

"Hoi," Coby greeted me when I dragged myself down the road to her house. "Have some tea?"

"I'll try some. Thanks."

"Feeling any better yet?" she asked, pouring tea out of a thermos that always seemed to be at the ready on her kitchen counter.

"Well, the dysentery and malaria are gone. So that's an improvement. But I wonder if I will ever feel like eating again. And this can't be good for the baby."

"It will get better. I promise. At least I hope so. I'm not feeling so good myself lately."

"Coby?"

"Bernard didn't want me to say anything until I was through the first trimester, but I'm pregnant too!" *I told you there wasn't much to do around here at night.*

"Coby! We'll be pregnant together!" That was the best news I'd heard in weeks.

"Yah. We can go through this together. Why not?" She smiled. And I smiled.

I continued to feel miserable. Coby, tough Dutch cookie that she was, fared somewhat better. But because I now had Coby to commiserate with, things were a little bit easier on John.

The dry season wore on and everyone beseeched the heavens for rain. Of course, we each did it in our own ways. So while our neighbors banged on their drums nearly every night, we expats kept threatening to wash our cars. But absolutely everyone watched the skies.

"Ah, see those clouds? See how they are curling up?" Nasser pointed to the wispy white clouds in the watercolor blue sky. "That means the rains are on their way."

"When?" I asked, looking up into the damn postcard-perfect sky. Nasser shrugged. "When it rains."

Finally, in March, after four scorched months, I woke to a gentle tapping on our tin roof.

"John." I nudged him awake. The glowing blue face of the battery-operated clock on the dresser read 3:10 a.m. "John, what's that noise?"

"I don't hear anything, honey. Go back to sleep."

I rolled over but the tapping continued, growing heavier and louder until it was beating down with the certainty of drums.

"John! Wake up. It's raining!"

"Oh, it's raining. That's good. We need rain," he mumbled and rolled over.

I lay there listening to the glorious symphony of water pounding the ground and pounding my roof. I imagined it beginning to fill my parched water tanks. The smell of must, like old smoke, escaped from the scorched earth like a sigh. The air suddenly felt lighter. "Thank you," I whispered to no one.

"Did you say something?" John yelled over the steady pounding that had fully woken him—and probably everyone—by now.

"You know how I'm always wishing for things from home? Television and telephones and decaf cappuccinos?" I asked.

"Snapple iced tea, bagels and lox, the Sunday *New York Times*, and—"

"Yeah, yeah, all that. Well, right now, I don't want any of that. All I have wanted for days is this rain. This rain is better than all of that. Put together."

"I'm glad," John said. He wrapped himself around me.

"Hey, I'm a little hungry," I said.

"All right." He leapt out of bed. "What can I get you?"

"Well, you know what I'd really love. I'd love some cottage cheese."

"Yeah, well, that would be a tall order. Let me go see what I can find." He padded off to the kitchen with a flashlight and returned a few minutes later. I could make out a bowl in his hand.

"Pineapple?" he asked. I popped a piece in my mouth. It was sweet and juicy and perfect.

"That's good," I said and ate the entire bowl.

We went back to bed and for the first time in months, I didn't want to be anywhere else.

Dear Susan,

Hi. I'm writing to you from the reception area of the district administrator's office, waiting for John to come out of a meeting with the men who run the Women in Development office. (Did I hear you say, "Duh"?) Three people are looking over my shoulder this very second because anything a mzungu writes must be interesting.

So far pregnancy seems to be a lot like old age. Lots of weird aches, lots o' gas, backaches, gotta pee all the time, constipation and/or diarrhea. And don't even get me started on the nausea! I guess it's a bit like old age. And I don't just mean the symptoms. I mean, you feel so lousy that maybe death starts to look not all that bad. And with pregnancy, you feel so lousy that giving birth starts to look not all that bad.

Did I tell you that last time we were in Kampala, we had dinner with a whole bunch of other CARE expats and that some of these folks have been with CARE for nearly twenty years and have been everywhere? Compared to these guys, John and I have never left the farm! But I don't think I'll still be doing this twenty years from now. Deep down inside, I think your brave friend Eve is really a scaredy cat. Sometimes I think what I want is to be able to say "I lived in (fill in the exotic location here) and did (fill in the bold adventure here)." But I'm not sure I'm really prepared for actually having to deal with the hardships of living in the exotic location or the discomfort of dealing with the bold adventure.

Thank God, it started raining a couple of nights ago. But then all these termites came out of their giant termite mounds and it was like night of the living dead. Well, not dead, just flying white ants. And they got in everything, and they are really gross, and even more gross is that people here eat them! And two nights ago we had a bat flying around inside the house. I don't know who was more scared, me or it. But we were both running for cover. It eventually parked itself (wounded) in our bathroom sink (but we didn't know that). This, after John says to me, "It's out of the house, dear. Now go brush your teeth!"

I'll keep you posted,
Eve

Chapter Twenty-Two

Law and Order in the Wild West (Nile)

"I want my tea now, madam!" the policeman on my front porch bellowed. It was both what he said and the way he said it that told me something was wrong. I put a thermos of tea out on the verandah every night for the guards. But no guard had ever asked for tea that early in the evening or in such a demanding tone. In fact, no guard had ever asked for tea. Few Ugandans I knew, and certainly none who worked for *mzungus,* would have thought it polite to ask so directly for anything.

We had just cleaned up from dinner when the policeman made this unusual request. My friend Jane, who had so tidily packed up my undies when I left Ecuador, was visiting us. Just finishing up her final year of medical school, she was on her way to Kenya to do an internship. Stefano, one of the Italian doctors who lived on our road, had also joined us for dinner.

"Congratulations, Eve," Stefano said when he arrived, holding out a bottle of Italian red wine in his hand. "I hear you will soon be increasing the *mzungu* population of Arua by one!"

"Stefano!" I said, feigning shock. "I can't drink this! I'm pregnant." In fact, I had only recently begun to eat or drink *anything* again.

"*Beh,*" he said in an expression that was the Italian equivalent of "pshaw!" "You Americans are too nervous! It's fine to drink a little bit of wine when you are pregnant. Italian women do it all the time! Just don't drink the whole bottle at once!" I immediately swore to return in my next life as an Italian woman!

Since the bombing at the White Rhino Hotel back in October, we'd had armed police guards in our compounds at night and I never felt comfortable with them. Our own *askaris* I trusted completely. James and Nasser looked after us—and Armstrong—as if we were part of their families. When I went to Pauline and Terry's house now, it was usually their *askari*, John, who Pauline respectfully called "our *mzee*," who greeted me. *Mzee* John shyly admitted to being a distant cousin of Idi Amin's, and, like Adam, he was a fascinating storehouse of knowledge about Ugandan politics and history.

"You know after World War Two, the United Nations tried to give Uganda to the Jewish people to make a homeland," *Mzee* John told me during one of our conversations. "I am sorry they did not accept it," he went on. "Those Jewish people are clever and they would have done good things for Uganda."

Damn, I thought, practically drooling. *If the Jews had accepted, maybe I'd be able to get some bagels and lox around here.*

Whenever we visited the Hatchards' house, it was usually Busiya, with his spear at his side and a cigarette hanging out of his mouth, who opened the gate to greet us. I had given him carrot sticks and lectures about smoking whenever he was in our compound. I never knew what he actually understood until one night he showed up to substitute in my compound with a carrot hanging out of his mouth.

"I have a dream," he told me. "My girl tell me to leave cigarettes. So I leave them."

But the police guards rotated constantly, so we never got to know them like we did our *askaris*. And we didn't know what to make of that night's guard. We were settled in the living room after dinner, taking advantage of the night's electricity to watch a video, when the policeman made his second unusual announcement of the evening.

"The compound is secured for the night," he yelled in through the screen door. "No one is to enter or exit!"

"Well, we have a guest here who will need to leave," John stepped out onto the verandah to speak with the policeman.

"NO! I am on duty. The compound is secure. No one can enter or exit after twenty-one hundred hours!"

John shot a questioning glance over to Nasser, our regular night-time *askari*. Nasser shrugged at John, then gently tapped the policeman's shoulder.

"You may be on duty, *mzee*," Nasser said in a deferential tone, "but this is Mr. John Waite's home. His guest should be allowed to leave at any moment."

The policeman spun around and pointed his AK-47 at Nasser. "I am in charge here. I say who can come and who can go. And I say no one can leave this compound. This compound is secure."

Armstrong began yapping. It was Nasser who had bathed him and fattened him up after we'd first brought the mangy puppy home. It was obvious that the two of them felt protective of one another.

"I will shoot this dog!" the policeman announced as he turned his gun from Nasser to Armstrong.

"No, *mzee*," said Nasser in a soothing tone. "This is a silly little dog. I will take him away from you." Nasser grabbed Armstrong's collar and, walking backward and keeping his eyes lowered the whole time, disappeared around the back of our house.

"I want my tea now, madam!" the policeman yelled again, this time putting his face right to the screen door that separated the living room from the verandah.

"Come help me make tea," I said, grabbing Jane by the arm and pulling her into the kitchen. "What kind of drugs do you have in your medical kit?" I asked. "Do you have something that we could spike his tea with and knock him out?"

"Well, I've got some sedatives. We can grind them up and dissolve them in his tea." Jane ran to the guest bedroom and came back with a bottle of little white pills. We smashed one up and put it in the thermos.

"I think we'll need more than that," I said.

"How many do you think we need?" Jane asked.

"Well," I said, thinking this whole scene was eerily like the movie we had been watching, in which a woman ineptly tries to kill her philandering husband by lacing his spaghetti sauce with vast quantities of sleeping pills. "We want to be sure to put enough in to really knock him out, but not so many that we kill him.

"Yeah, we want to knock him out but not kill him," I said. In my mind I repeated that sentence over and over. Because if you think of yourself as a good girl from a bizarre but nice Jewish family who's followed her husband here to help people, you never really imagine yourself saying the words "Yeah, we want to knock him out but not kill him."

"I'll go peek at him and see if I can figure out how much he weighs," Jane said nonchalantly.

"*Mzee*," Jane inquired sweetly. "*Mzee*, do you take sugar in your tea?"

"Of course!" he huffed. "Lots of sugar."

Jane came back. "I don't know, I guess he weighs about a hundred and sixty pounds or so." She thought for a moment. "Let's put in two more."

"What if he doesn't drink all of it, though?"

"Okay, let's put in four just in case," Jane said, grinding up another tablet. "That way one cup ought to knock him out. But it shouldn't kill him even if he drinks the whole thermos."

"Yeah, Jane, let's not kill him. That would probably ruin both of our careers."

We crushed up the tablets and dissolved them into the hot tea. "And more sugar, lots of sugar so he won't taste it."

"Our police guard seems a bit on edge this evening," John said as he walked into the kitchen. I told him about the tranquilizing tea that Jane and I were brewing.

"Okay, but you don't take it out to him. I'll give it to him." John walked through the kitchen to the back door that looked out onto a small garden and James's house. Nasser was out there with James, who must have heard the racket and Armstrong's barking.

"Nasser, come in here and look after my family," John called softly out the door. "I'm going to take the policeman his tea." A surge of warmth ran through me. For two and a half years I had been John's wife. But now that I was pregnant, I was his family.

"No, *mzee*," Nasser said taking the thermos from John's hand. "You stay inside the house with your family. I will bring the tea. I was an army man. I know how to deal with this crazy policeman. I can disarm him if I can get behind him."

"Well, don't do anything dangerous, Nasser," I said. "We put some tablets in the tea, lots of them. We think that if he drinks the tea, he will fall asleep and then you can take his gun."

Nasser smiled. "Madam is a very clever woman!" He took the tea and walked around to the front of the house.

"Yes, *mzee,* I will tell them," we heard Nasser say a moment later as he headed toward the back of the house.

"Mr. John Waite and family," Nasser announced loudly. "The policeman has secured this compound and requests that you lock up for the night."

John complied by closing and locking the French doors, which was all there was between our living room and the front porch. The thin glass doors would offer little protection, however, against a madman with an AK-47. With nothing else to do, the four of us huddled together in the living room. Feigning normalcy, we returned to the movie about the woman trying to kill her husband with sleeping pills hidden in the spaghetti sauce, because now we were all dying to know how that worked out for her. But each of us sat with one eye on the television and the other one on the door. We turned the sound up just enough to cover our hushed whispers.

"Okay, what do we do now?" I was completely panicked. "We can't get out. We can't call for help." The radio was in the Pajero, which was parked in the driveway, right next to where the policeman had stationed himself. "This lunatic could kill us and no one would even know that we need help." I felt more vulnerable than I had ever felt since coming to Uganda. I took some comfort in the fact that a palm reader in Ecuador once told me I would die young, but not before giving birth to a daughter.

"There's not much we can do but wait it out. Let's try not to worry too much." John had his arm around my shoulder, but I was keenly aware of how isolated we were.

"*Beh,* he's just a little psychotic," Stefano said with a shrug. "Nothing to worry about. He'll calm down soon."

"He'll probably pass out soon," Jane added. "I think we put enough sedatives in his tea to put an elephant to sleep."

"But not kill him," I added quickly.

We stopped talking and strained to hear any movement from the front porch. All we heard were the usual night sounds: a symphony of crickets carried on a gentle wind and a slow, steady beat of drums from somewhere off in the distance. John walked quietly to the back door.

"Nasser," he hissed. "What's going on out there? Are you all right?"

"It is me, James, sir. Nasser has left the compound." James spoke barely above a whisper. "He has climbed over the fence here," he said, pointing to the seven-foot-high, razor-wire-topped fence. "He has gone to Mr. Terry Cross's house to get help. He has told me to watch over your family."

"No, James, you go inside and watch over your family. We are fine."

"I am sure Nasser will return soon with help," James said.

Ten minutes later, we saw lights coming toward our house and heard the bouncing of a jeep over the deeply rutted dirt road. Terry's vehicle stopped in front of our gate.

A broad man in a uniform stepped out of the passenger's side. "Officer," he barked. "You are relieved of this post. Come with me now."

"But, sir, I have not yet finished my job here," the policeman said as he got up from his seat on our front porch and walked quickly to the front gate.

"Officer, you are relieved of this post. Come now or I will have you removed."

"Yes, sir." The policeman walked quietly out of the compound and got into the back of the Land Rover.

"Sorry for the problem, Mr. Waite," the police chief said to John. "This man is usually a fine officer. One of our best. But he is drunk. I will return him to the barracks and he will sleep it off."

Jane and I looked at each other. *He'll sleep it off, all right,* I thought. *He's got enough sleeping pills in him to sleep for a very long time. But not enough to kill him!*

"He will not bother you any further." The police chief got back into Terry's vehicle.

"A bit of excitement in there tonight?" Terry asked, popping his head out of the driver's window.

"Yeah, a bit of an unusual night, you might say," John answered.

"Ah, another great tale to tell the folks back home. You gotta love this expat life!" Terry smiled as he drove off.

Giddy with relief, we poured a fresh round of beers and even a glass of Stefano's wine for me and decided to watch the end of the movie.

About a half an hour later we heard hollering and banging on the gate. "Let me back in! I have come to finish my job!"

"Shit! He's back," said John and Stefano in tandem, staring out the front door.

"Let me in! Let me in! I have returned to assume my post," yelled the policeman.

"*Mzee.*" It was James, speaking slowly through the gate. "I think you have completed your job well. This compound is secure. You should return to your barracks now." I was struck by how incredibly brave this slight young man was. There was nothing between him and that guy but a chain-link fence.

James came around to the kitchen door after talking to the policeman at the fence for a few minutes. "He wants to be let in."

"I thought the chief hauled him back to the barracks. I thought they would keep him there for the night!" I felt suddenly dizzy as if

I had been plunged into an absurd episode of *The Twilight Zone*. "Shouldn't he be passed out by now?" I asked Jane.

"Gee," she said. "Maybe we shouldn't have worried so much about killing him."

"He has no shoes," James said, explaining the security measure that was supposed to have kept him from returning.

"Did they take away his gun, at least?" John asked.

"No, sir. He still has his gun."

"Well, don't go out there again, James. Stay out back. At least he's outside the fence this time. We'll be okay in here." John didn't sound terribly reassuring.

"Nasser has gone over the fence again," James said. "He will go get help."

The policeman was still banging on the gate and howling to be let in when the Land Rover's lights shone down the road for the second time that night. But this time, the policeman fled into the woods when he saw the vehicle. The police chief and another officer jumped out of the jeep and ran after him. Terry kept his headlights shining into the woods.

"Hmmm . . . I guess it's not so funny now, is it?" Terry asked when we all joined him by his vehicle.

"Why the hell did they take away his shoes but not his gun?" John asked in amazement.

"The police chief thought he was drunk," Terry shrugged. "Unfortunately that happens quite often. They usually just sleep it off."

"Oh, that's just great! I feel better than ever about having an armed guard every night." Terry was well aware of my concern about having a gun in my yard. "These guys are psychotic to boot!"

After a few minutes, the police chief came back and asked us for a torch. Flashlight in hand, he headed back into the woods.

"We have lost him," the police chief announced when he returned ten minutes later.

"So what do we do now?" John asked.

"We will go back to the station. He will no doubt return tomorrow.

We will discipline him then," the chief said. "You and your family can go to bed. I am sure this man will not bother you again tonight."

"Go to bed?" I asked. "How can we just go to bed? The man is obviously psychotic, and now he's in trouble and we're the ones who got him in trouble. And in case you forgot, he still has his gun!"

"This officer will stay here tonight," the chief said, pointing to the officer who had come with him from the station. "He has a gun, too. You will be fine."

"Oh, goodie," I said. "Now we can look forward to a gun battle in our yard later tonight!"

"Maybe you should all spend the night at our house," Terry offered. He didn't have to offer twice. Stefano went home and John, Jane, and I went to Terry and Pauline's house. I was half expecting to hear gunshots coming from my house all night. But the rest of the night was quiet, except for the annoying drone of mosquitoes, and our muttered curses as we slapped at them. In our haste to get out of our house, we'd forgotten to take our mosquito nets with us. We decided to risk getting malaria rather than go back to the house and chance a third run-in with the crazed police guard.

We went to the police station the next morning. The runaway officer, apparently refreshed after a night in the bush, reported to work as if nothing unusual had happened. Fearful of losing the lucrative business of providing private protection to the half-dozen international aid organizations in Arua, the police chief asked to be allowed to handle the matter internally. He assured us that the man in question would be immediately transferred to another district and we could forget all about this unfortunate incident.

Beh, I thought. *I never forget anything!*

Dear Susan,

It was delightful to get your package of goodies yesterday. Thank you. Thank you. Yes, the huge stack of videos is towering in our living room. But, nay, it is not left dusty and nigh onto toppling over in the corner! No! We have built a shrine around it in the center of the room next to the TV and the VCR. And it is here that we make a nightly pilgrimage, light candles, and pray to the great gods of industry that someday soon we, too, may put on our bouncy Air Jordans (bought for twice the per capita income of most Ugandans) and live within commuting distance (in our sporty new Mustang) of a McDonald's! Hell, it's not the sitcoms that we watch over and over. No, we fast-forward to the commercials: That's what reminds us of the world we left behind!

I'm finally beginning to feel a bit better. I've rediscovered my appetite. Unfortunately, there's nothing here I want to eat. I swear some nights I could kill for ice cream. Last night I woke John up at three in the morning whining about that episode of M*A*S*H where they got the ribs sent all the way from Chicago. "If they could get ribs in Korea during a war in the 1950s," I said, "can't you find a way to get bagels and lox here in Uganda?"

We started thinking of baby names. But John says I am not supposed to tell you what they are. For now though, s/he is referred to as "Mowgli Hyphen" as suggested by John's brothers. "Mowgli" after the kid in The Jungle Book and "Hyphen" because John's family keeps wondering if the kid is going to be a Waite, a Brown, or a hyphen!

I'm also not supposed to tell you how we were recently held hostage in our own home. But I promise it'll make a great story someday!

I'll keep you posted,
Eve

Chapter Twenty-Three

My African Pregnancy

"Skim milk!" I yelled, thrusting the book at John. My girlfriend Patti, who'd recently given birth, had sent me a copy of *What to Expect When You're Expecting*. "I'm supposed to be drinking skim milk. Where the hell am I supposed to get skim milk around here?"

"Well, the cows around here are pretty skinny," John said. I glared at him. "I think they just don't want you to gain too much weight. I don't think you need to worry about that, Eve."

I had finally started to feel better in my fifth month. My appetite had improved. But except for what we could haul back from Kampala, it was difficult to find anything that I really wanted to eat. Whenever I craved anything other than the bananas or pineapples that I usually had on hand, I'd wander over to Pauline's house. She practically always had some wonderful leftovers, or a cake or bread that she'd just pulled out of the oven. But even with Pauline's treats, I was plagued by the fear that I was not eating enough and therefore damaging my unborn child. The book was only adding to my guilt.

"Oh my God. Look at this. It says here our child is going to be brain-damaged if I don't eat folic-acid-fortified bread. Where the hell am I supposed to get that?"

"Um, Eve," John said, gently taking the book from my hands. "I don't think you should read this book anymore."

"But every pregnant woman is supposed to read this book," I said. "It's supposed to be very helpful."

John took the book and slammed a mosquito against the wall with it. "Yup. It is a very helpful book."

Regardless of what it said in the book, it did seem like my pregnancy was progressing just fine. David Morton had heard the baby's heartbeat with his stethoscope and I could now regularly feel the baby kicking. After a rocky start, my pregnancy, like my life in Uganda, was beginning to feel better. And like the weather around me, my work life had gone from desperate drought to near downpour.

"How would you like to be our computer teacher at the bank?" John had asked recently.

"Because I'm such a computer whiz myself?" I asked. It was early 1994, and while computers had made their way into most offices and plenty of homes in America, they were still a fairly new technology in Africa, and almost unheard of in Arua.

"You know how to cut and paste and save. So you're light-years ahead of pretty much everyone else. The three new computers we got are just sitting there. Everyone is afraid to touch them."

"So what would I teach them?"

"Well, you could come and give them some lessons in the basics. Just get them started."

"Well, I do know WordPerfect!" This is the program I had been using to write my short stories and letters home.

"And you could teach them Lotus 1-2-3."

"I'd have to teach that to myself first."

"Yeah, but you could. These guys are still afraid the computer will blow up if they touch the wrong button. Most of them are still petrified to turn the damn things on."

So three afternoons a week, I'd go with John to the bank and teach basic computer skills to the assistant branch manager and some of the outreach workers and clerks. In addition to having never seen a computer, most of them had never even typed on a keyboard. So I made up little typing exercises; the kinds I remembered from junior high school. I was the Mavis Beacon of the jungle! It was hardly what I'd hoped to be doing, but it was something. And I was happy with my little job, for the most part. It was pleasant enough, except late in the week, when a particular bank staffer was especially rank. He was a very nice guy and always wore a neat suit (the same neat suit), but we strongly suspected he only bathed on weekends—and never washed that suit.

"Take the afternoon off," John would occasionally warn me when he came home for lunch. "Even I could smell him today." Which, coming from John, must have meant he was unbearable.

In addition to my little gig at the bank, CARE had hired me to teach basic health classes for the *askaris* and drivers and their families. I was thrilled and created participatory lesson plans about basic first aid and preventing the spread of communicable diseases, including, of course, HIV and other sexually transmitted diseases. But the classes posed some interesting dilemmas.

"Madam," one of the *askaris* said as he pulled me aside after I'd told the class to bring their wives to the next week's class on HIV and sexually transmitted diseases. "I have two wives. Which should I bring?"

Hmmm . . . that was not something I'd had to deal with back in New York.

"You can bring as many wives as you'd like, I guess." *When in Rome—or Africa—as they say . . .*

"But, madam, I cannot bring them both at the same time."

Silly me! "Um, don't they know about each other?"

"Yes! Of course they do. But if they are both here with me, who will be at home watching the children and preparing the *matoke?*"

Duh! So I started offering each class several times so that various wives could have a chance to come.

I was also hired to conduct a training class for the Rakai AIDS Information Network. And, thus, I finally got my chance to work in the epicenter of Uganda's AIDS epidemic. This group restored my faith in the outlook for HIV prevention in Uganda. But the highlight of the week was the eggs Benedict my hosts served me for brunch. *Hey, I was six months pregnant and ravenous.* So now that I was finally feeling better, it was May and nearly time for me to fly back to the States for

Jean's wedding. But John and I had one more safari planned before I went home to give birth.

Jane went to Kenya shortly after our hostage crisis, but we met up with her and her fiancé, Matt, a few weeks later for a safari through the southern part of Uganda. So that's how I found myself six months pregnant and trekking through the Virunga Mountains in search of the elusive mountain gorillas. I couldn't help but wonder what *What to Expect When You're Expecting* would have to say about that. But all we used that book for these days was swatting mosquitoes. We'd leave their little dead bodies plastered to the walls, like teeny tiny hunting trophies or warnings to other mosquitoes.

So there we were, after hours of following our guides as they slashed a path through the thick undergrowth, in literally a no-man's-land somewhere between Uganda, Zaire, and Rwanda. There was absolutely no way to tell which country we were in because it was jungle as far as the eye could see—which wasn't very far since it was really thick jungle. At one point I was quite convinced that we were no longer walking on the ground but were actually clawing our way forward on the thick ropy vines in the canopy of growth above it all. Our guides certainly seemed to know their way around the jungle—I only hoped they knew their way out as well.

After five hours of hellacious climbing, we reached the spot where the guides had last seen the gorillas. As soon as we got there, rain began pouring down in sheets. The gorillas knew enough to get out of the rain; they were nowhere to be seen. We humans stood there with no protection from the cold downpour.

"I can't take another step. I can't lift my legs. I have arthritis in my hips," I whined.

"You don't have arthritis," John said.

"I think I developed a spontaneous case of it about two hours ago. Can't we just go down?"

"We are not going back down until we see the gorillas!" Jane yelled. She was standing right next to me but had to yell in order to be heard over the waterfall of rain. "I've climbed for the last five hours and I am not leaving until I see them!"

"But they aren't coming out. I'm drenched. I'm exhausted. My hips don't work anymore." I was being a big baby and I knew it. But this had been the most physically punishing thing I had ever done. I had been in excruciating pain as we'd climbed straight uphill for the last two hours.

"You guys live in Africa," Jane insisted. "You might get another chance. But this is my one shot. And I am not leaving until I see the gorillas!" I realized that this was my one shot, too, as I was not going to sign up for this torture again. So I whimpered quietly and huddled in the rain.

In case I haven't said it yet, Uganda is an incredibly beautiful country. Sure, I had whined, moaned, and been frightened an awful lot during the past ten months here. But I had also been awestruck by sights so picture-book perfect that it was hard to believe they were real: the pack of elephants that had nearly charged us when Matt had gotten too close; the school of baby giraffes that had loped along beside our Pajero; the hippos and crocodiles that sloshed in every available body of water; the rainbows of tiny, twittering birds that decorated nearly every tree and hillside. Whenever I witnessed such a scene, I felt incredibly lucky to be in Africa. Yes, it was hard at times. But perhaps this was the price we paid for the chance to witness such beauty.

As the rain slowed to a drizzle, a gorilla strutted out into the clearing not more than two or three yards away from us. We humans got very still, as if we were petrified; and truly we were as this silverback stood up to his full six feet and blew up his chest like a baritone about to perform for us. He stripped a handful of wet leaves off some nearby branches with his black, leathery—yet very familiar-looking—hands and stuffed them into his mouth. He stared straight at us, but we averted our eyes as our guides had taught us, so we wouldn't be perceived as a threat to this alpha male. My stomach growled and I remembered anxiously that I didn't have so much as a groundnut to tide me over, because the guides had made us leave our food back on the trail so that the gorillas wouldn't smell it. After a few minutes of staring, he walked off into the woods and soon an adult female with a baby clinging to her belly came into the clearing. They completely ignored us as they yanked leaves from the trees, stuffed them in their mouths, and groomed each other's fur. We sat silently for an hour, absolutely transfixed, and I knew that this was one of those amazing experiences that was worth every moment of discomfort I'd had to endure to get there.

Jane and Matt went back to the States a few days later. And soon it was time for me to head back to the States as well.

> Dear Patti,
>
> I can't thank you enough for sending me my very own copy of What to Expect While You're Expecting. It's come in very handy (although I won't tell you for what). I am thinking of writing my own book someday: Things You'd Never Expect When You're Expecting in Africa.
>
> Well, according to the book, I should be nesting. But so far it's John that's doing the nesting. He's decided to build a crib for the baby—completely by hand, out of local mahogany. This ought to keep him busy for the rest of my pregnancy—at least!
>
> So how's motherhood going? And when I get home can I borrow some of your maternity clothes? So far my entire wardrobe consists of drawstring pants and dresses with no waistlines that I picked up at the dead mzungu clothing market. I'm not showing, but it makes me feel better to wear something loose. Of course, I recently caught myself going to the market in hot-pink pants. But I guess one of the nice things about

this place is that no one even noticed. Certainly not the ten-year-old boy wearing the bright yellow sweatshirt that said "Sexy Grandma!"

I'll keep you posted,
Eve

Chapter Twenty-Four

🍃

Return to the Land of Plenty

"But I don't want to go home," I whined from the floor of Entebbe Airport, where I was lying in the fetal position in an effort to stave off a fainting spell. "I want to stay here with you." I was now nearly seven months pregnant and the fainting had recently started.

"You have to go, Eve. My parents will be waiting for you at the airport." John knelt beside me and spoke soothingly. "And Jean is counting on you. Besides, you'll have to leave soon anyway. They won't let you fly in another few weeks. So go and have a good time."

"But I'll miss you!" I wailed. The crying jags had come along with the fainting.

"I'll miss you and Mowgli Hyphen, too. But I'll be there before you know it."

"But it will be awful without you!" I sobbed.

"You'll finally get to eat anything you want." John dangled this statement like a sugar-coated carrot.

"Well, I am hungry," I sniffed as John lifted me off the floor and gently guided me to the departure gate. So with tears in my eyes and visions of dairy products dancing in my head, I got on the plane.

The trip to America required a short flight to Nairobi followed by an eight-hour flight to London followed by a seven-hour flight to Boston.

"Are you Eve Brown?" a surprised-looking flight attendant asked me as I prepared to disembark in London.

"Yes, I'm Eve Brown. Is something wrong?"

"Oh, no, it's just that I had a note here that says you are a pregnant woman traveling alone, so we wanted to assist you. I kept looking for a pregnant woman. But you're not pregnant," she said, eyeing my nondescript midsection.

"Yeah, I am pregnant," I said. I rubbed the little bulge that only I could detect. "Almost seven months."

"Wow! Sorry I didn't find you sooner. Is there anything I can help you with now?"

"You wouldn't happen to have any cottage cheese, would you?"

"No, I'm afraid I don't. But I can request an extra meal for you during the flight to Boston, if you'd like. And I'll get you through customs and maybe you can find some cottage cheese around Heathrow. You have a long layover."

"Well, there you go," the flight attendant said after she expertly swept me through customs and into the waiting area of the airport. "I'm sure you'll find whatever you're looking for here." She pointed in the direction of a dizzying array of shops and kiosks.

I was overwhelmed. After ten months of living in a place where there was never that much going on, it was like the unfortunate supermarket incident all over again. Only Heathrow Airport, with its cacophony of sights, sounds, and unbelievable amount of stuff, was worse than the soup aisle any day. It was ironic that for the past ten months I had dreamed of just these types of bright, shiny things. And now, with the bright, shiny things all around me, I found myself unable to move. It was, as my mother would have said, as if I had been afflicted by the worst case of "mall glaze" ever.

I fought the urge to grab the flight attendant's hand and follow her back onto the plane. Instead, I shuffled over to a row of chairs, sat down, and gaped. It wasn't just the stuff. I had never seen so many white people. As I stared openmouthed, I kept expecting to see someone I recognized. After all, I knew just about every *mzungu* in Uganda. It seemed inconceivable that I could be surrounded by thousands of them now and not know a single one. But absolutely no one looked familiar.

I sat, stuck to the black vinyl chair, feeling alone and small. Then I looked across to the row of stores with stuff in them; stores where you could touch things; stores that might actually have something I wanted to buy. And then it hit me: Reverse culture shock or not, I had an opportunity to shop and time was a-wasting! I took a deep breath and steeled myself by focusing on a single task. I would search for the one thing I had craved more than anything else for the past few months.

"Do you have cottage cheese?" I asked in the first store I entered.

"Cottage cheese?" The salesclerk looked amazed. "This is a Body Shop."

"Oh, yeah." I was not in Uganda anymore. I had to remind myself that in the rest of the world, stores that had tires in the window probably sold tires.

"Then ChapStick," I said, running my tongue over my cracked lips. "You must have ChapStick!"

"We have lip gloss. All sorts of flavors." She pointed me toward the display of small containers of lip products.

I bought six containers of lip gloss. Pleased that I had done so well on my first purchase in the new world, I powered on in search of what I really wanted.

I soon discovered that while Heathrow Airport sold Belgian chocolate, Irish butter, Italian wines, and French cheeses of every kind, they did not sell cottage cheese. I remembered from our flight to Uganda that we had laid over in a hotel that was attached to the airport. I also remembered this hotel had a restaurant. Feeling slightly cocky with my fancy new British lip gloss, and with plenty of time to kill, I headed to that hotel. After all, I told myself, I had survived a hostage situation and tracked gorillas through the Impenetrable Forest. Surely I could make my way around a British airport.

"Do you have cottage cheese?" I asked when the waitress sat me down and handed me a menu.

"Cottage cheese? I don't know. Is it on the menu?" The waitress and I perused the menu together. "Nah, I don't see it here," she said.

"Listen, I've got to have some cottage cheese. Please."

"Is this some sort of weird American diet?"

"No, I'm pregnant," I said, doing my best to stick out my tiny belly. "And I've been in Uganda for the past ten months. And I'm craving cottage cheese like mad. Please, can you help me?"

The waitress looked at me. "You're pregnant? And living in Uganda? Ah, poor dear. Just wait right here." She disappeared into the kitchen.

"Here you are, dear." She placed a bowl of cottage cheese topped with a cherry in front of me. "Is that enough for you? I can bring you more if you'd like."

"Oh, this is beautiful. Thank you."

"Is there anything else you want?"

"No. This is all I need. Thank you. Thank you." I dug my spoon into the bowl while tears of joy ran down my face.

When I arrived in Boston the next day, my in-laws were waiting. They ushered me into their car and, bless their souls, took me immediately to a medium-sized convenience store.

"John called after your plane took off," my mother-in-law said. "He said you'd be hungry, and that you'd want to pick out your own food. But he warned us not to take you to a big supermarket."

"Oh, isn't he sweet? He doesn't want you to have to pick me up from the floor of the soup aisle."

"Uh-huh," my mother-in-law murmured.

"Oh, this is wonderful. Just wonderful," I sang as I picked up two large containers of cottage cheese and six bottles of Snapple iced tea. "America really is a great and glorious country," I gushed.

"That's what you want to eat?" She looked at me. "No wonder you haven't gained any weight."

I went to Jean's house a few days later, cottage cheese in hand, to assume my responsibilities as her maid of honor.

"You're the pregnant bridesmaid?" the seamstress looked at me in disbelief as she draped me in raw silk the color of emeralds. I was so grateful that Jean and her sisters had good taste and that I was not going to look like a bowling ball covered in pastel frills. "Honey, looks like we're going to have to take this skirt in, not let it out!"

"Well, leave a little extra room," Jean said. "This little pregnant lady has been eating up a storm since she arrived. And we've still got five days until the wedding!"

"Yeah, can we go to Friendly's right after this fitting?" I begged. "Last night I dreamt of chicken fingers in sweet-and-sour dipping sauce."

"So! Where's your belly?" I was getting a little tired of that question. But I wasn't too worried, since David Morton had heard the baby's heartbeat and had assured me that all was going well. "Where's my grandchild?" my mother said when she saw me for the first time at Jean's rehearsal dinner. She looked disappointedly at my little tummy.

"Just watch her eat," Jean said to my mother. "She seems to be making up for lost time." Jean had invited my mother to the wedding and all the prewedding festivities, which was a good thing. I had flown into Massachusetts—where my in-laws lived and the wedding was taking place—and wouldn't get down to New York—where my mother was—until after the wedding. If Jean hadn't invited my mother, she probably would have crashed.

"That's my daughter. The preggo from Africa!" My mother announced this to everyone, as if I, not the bride, were the star of the show. After the wedding, I went to New York with my mother and had my first real prenatal doctor's visit.

"So," said my obstetrician as she read my chart. "You had malaria and dysentery in your first trimester. And you've had antibiotics, antihistamines, and antimalarials." She stared at my flat belly. "You're sure you're still pregnant?"

"Oh, yeah!" my mother declared. "She's pregnant all right. I felt the baby kicking."

I put my hand on my active little belly. "Yeah, Mowgli here is kicking up a storm."

"Well, climb up on the examining table," the obstetrician said, looking at me with some disbelief, "and let's have a look."

"Well, you and the baby do seem to be doing fine," she declared after a thorough examination. "You need to put on some weight, though. Eat! Have ice cream and whole milk and whatever you're craving. You really have got to gain some weight. But other than that, you're doing fine. And I want you to start taking a childbirth preparation class. They teach them here at the hospital."

"But John won't be back for another month. Don't you need to have someone with you for that?"

"You won't have time if you wait for John. Why don't you start by bringing your mother or a friend with you? And John can join you when he gets here."

"Ooh, can I come? Evie, I'll come with you." My mother was practically jumping up and down.

I stared at her.

"Oh, I'll be good. I'll sit quietly in the corner. Just like I'm gonna do when you give birth. You won't even know I'm in the room."

It was impossible not to know when my mother was in the room.

"Let's tell everyone we're a couple," Susan said when I took her with me to my first childbirth class.

"Yeah, but what will we do when John shows up in a few weeks?" I asked.

"We'll tell them he's our sperm donor!" But as it turned out, the truth of our situation was far more interesting. There were two other lesbian couples in the class, but I was the only mother-to-be living in the African bush.

Before I left Uganda, John reminded me of what he had advised me when I first came home from the Peace Corps. "Everyone will ask about it," he warned. "But most people really only want to hear about the weather and what you ate. More than that and their eyes will start to glaze over."

So I did as John advised and I tried not to bore people too much with all the details of my life for the past ten months. I sublet an apartment near our old neighborhood in Brooklyn and marveled at how easy life seemed with round-the-clock electricity and all the water and television I could want. Even though New York City was hot and steamy, no one seemed to smell. I made a daily pilgrimage to the corner supermarket, the Italian deli, and the ice-cream shop, and did as the doctor ordered.

"You can lay off the Ben and Jerry's now" is what I believe she said when I waddled in for my second prenatal visit.

When John arrived at the beginning of my ninth month, life was perfect. Well, until that incredibly painful day in August when I had to pass an eight-pound human being through my vagina.

But that's another story.

Part

Three

🌿

Chapter Twenty-Five

It Takes a Village

Sierra Rose Waite, who had once been an indecipherable blob on a sonogram, was born perfect and healthy, on August 12, 1994. Three days later, she took her first road trip from Brooklyn to Cape Cod, where John's parents had rented us a house on the beach for a month of R & R and visits from family and friends.

"I think I'll go take a look at the ocean," my father-in-law said a few days later, as I plopped down on a bench in the middle of Hyannisport and gingerly put a fussy Sierra on my exposed breast. There was never any question of whether or not I would breastfeed. The only question was whether I would nurse discreetly, like an American, or boobies flashing in the wind, like a Ugandan.

With everyone around—and my boobs flashing in the wind—it really did feel a bit like the proverbial African village. There was always a grandparent, godparent, aunt, or uncle around with a willing hand to hold the baby. But unlike our African village, this one had electricity and television twenty-four hours a day, a beach, supermarkets, pizza parlors, ice-cream shops, and restaurants. It was heaven. And it was also the countdown to our returning to Uganda. I had mixed feelings about going back. Having quickly gotten over my mall glaze, I was now thoroughly enjoying life in the "Land of Plenty." But Arua was home and I was anxious to get back to our life there.

"What did you decide to do about diapers? Cloth or disposable?"

Susan asked as we scoured department stores and supermarkets trying to load up on stuff to take back.

"That whole debate is a nonstarter for me. There are no Pampers in Uganda. And if there were, I'd have to bury them in my backyard!" I imagined the neighborhood kids rummaging through piles of dirty diapers.

"Ma!" I yelled as I watched my mother put a case of Desitin in my shopping cart. "How much diaper rash do you think this kid is gonna have?"

"I don't know. But better to be safe than sorry. And here," she said, putting a case of Anbesol into the cart. "She's bound to start teething eventually."

"And take a snot sucker," my friend Patti said, handing me one of those bulb-shaped suction things. "Every new mother needs a snot sucker. You probably won't be able to get one there."

"Y'know, Evie, maybe you shouldn't go back there." My mom and I were ogling Sierra's passport. Her eyes weren't even open in the photo. "You guys have to think of Sierra now."

"Mom, Arua is the perfect place for Sierra. Fresh air, sunshine, a big house, loads of help, lots of kids. Don't worry. She'll be fine."

"Well, maybe you should just stay home. I'm sure John could get a job here."

"Ma. Arua is home now. And if we stayed here, I'd have to get a job, too."

Despite my mother's threats to lie down on the runway in front of our plane, we went back to Uganda when Sierra was five weeks old. I did feel bad about taking Sierra away from her grandparents, and I also wondered if we were doing the right thing by bringing her up in the Ugandan bush. Would she be forever scarred by missing out on the Mommy & Me and Gymboree classes that Patti had talked about? But I also watched as she and others juggled motherhood and work because almost no one could afford to live on one salary. I figured having a mommy who wasn't stressed out by the demands of life in America would more than make up for Sierra's lack of extracurricular activities. Of course, I had completely forgotten about how stressful it can be when hand grenades are blowing up while you're eating supper or when you're being held hostage in your own home. But those things were ancient history in Arua. Or so I thought.

"Ah, thank you for coming back," the customs official said to John and me as he stamped the new visas in our passports next to the old ones.

"Thank you for coming back," Alex said when we saw him at the airport. He immediately took Sierra from my arms; with eighteen kids of his own now, I trusted that he knew how to hold a baby.

Everyone at CARE headquarters thanked us for coming back and immediately began passing Sierra around. We spent that first night at Stan's house, Sierra sleeping in a suitcase, since they didn't have a crib. It seemed to suit her just fine.

"And don't forget, you've got the big house now," Stan reminded us before we got on the road the next day. Somewhere between giving birth and nonstop breastfeeding I had forgotten that Terry and Pauline had been transferred down to Kampala and we had been given their old house.

"No! I don't think I can survive in Arua without Pauline. Give them their house back and tell them to stay." I wasn't really worried about surviving in Arua now. Besides, I had Regina to help me. But we had grown quite attached to Pauline and Terry. I had kind of envisioned them as surrogate grandparents for Sierra. But people were always coming and going in the development world.

Somehow, Sierra slept through the long, bumpy ride to Arua. I wondered if it felt familiar to her from all the times she'd made the drive in utero. And just like I did when we'd made that first trip a little more than a year before, I stared out the window and waved at the children, although this time I knew better than to look for a restroom.

"Here, watch me do it one more time." Regina bent over, held Sierra against her back with one hand and then whipped the *kitenge* over both of them with the other. Then Regina cinched, pulled, and tied the cloth tight over her breasts and stood up straight with both hands free and a smiling Sierra snuggled securely against her back. "It is simple," she pronounced of the clever papooselike contraption that let women go about their business, hands free to hoe the fields or shuck *matoke*. It was never simple for me, but I didn't have to hoe fields or shuck *matoke*.

Which was a very lucky thing indeed. Because for our first few months back in Arua, it seemed like all I did was nurse Sierra. I began to wonder if, in the long history of motherhood, anyone had ever been nursed to death? When I wasn't nursing—or pumping milk so that John could feed Sierra a bottle laced with her malaria prophylaxis—I was changing diapers.

As soon as we got to Arua, we made the switch to cloth diapers, which meant that Sierra—and everything she came in contact with—was nearly always sopping wet. Except, of course, when she—and everything she came in contact with—was covered in the mustardy yellow poops that squished down her legs and up her back. John and I felt like total idiots. Two master's degrees between us, and the cloth diaper technology was totally beyond us.

Luckily, I didn't have to do much of anything beside lactate and change diapers. I could hardly imagine how my friends back home did even this without all the help I now had. Along with the bigger house, we had also accrued a bigger cast of characters around the house. While we got unpacked and settled, we temporarily hired a second house girl to help Regina. Cissie came recommended by another of the Italian families in the neighborhood. She was quiet as a mouse, but such a good worker that we kept her on permanently.

Besides nursing, I spent most of my time dealing with the nearly unending parade of daily visitors, many of them part of what I called the "Home Shopping Network."

"Look, madam, I made this just for you," said a young man outside my gate who waved a woven tray at me. It was made of bright strips of red, green, and yellow straw—like the two or three dozen other woven trays, baskets, and coasters we already had. Woven into this one, however, were the words "I love you." What could I do but buy it? And the hat he'd made especially for Sierra; the one that said "Arua Boy" on it. We also bought goatskin drums and carved wooden masks. And the ebony nativity scene with the giant baby Jesus and the three wise men who carried spears.

"Oh, madam-o," said Erneste, limping to my gate pushing his bicycle, just as he did two or three times a week. I don't know why he called me "madam-o." Maybe he learned English from an Italian. "Today I have spinach!" He knew I was a sucker for spinach. And broccoli, lettuce, or carrots—basically any vegetable besides the ubiquitous okra and *matoke*.

"Erneste, I brought seeds back from America." I showed him the seed packets I'd stashed in my luggage. "I thought I'd try to plant my own *mzungu* vegetables."

"Ah, a *mzungu* growing vegetables!" Erneste laughed. "*Mzungu* don't know how to farm. But I will come and help you, madam-o."

I might have argued that point with him, except for the fact that this *mzungu* didn't have the faintest idea how to farm. After helping me plant my little garden, Erneste used all my extra seeds to plant his own, bigger garden right next to mine—from which he would later sell me the harvest.

Regina's husband, Steven, also made the rounds of the Home Shopping Network, selling me enough *adungus,* a traditional stringed instrument, to start a *mzungu adungu* band. When our living room was full of *adungus,* Steven came just to visit and to tell me his problems. Regina cringed when she saw Steven at the gate, but I found his tales of woe oddly compelling and entertaining.

And then there was Richard, who I found waiting on my verandah not long after we'd moved in. I knew him as "Terry and Pauline's Boy Richard" because that is what all the Ugandans called him. That is, until they all started calling him "*Your* Boy, Richard."

"What is this, Richard?" I asked that first morning when the tall fifteen-year-old handed me a list: *aspirin—20 tablets; white shirts with collars—2; black pens—5; blue pens—5.* The paper itself was worn but the writing was painstakingly neat.

"It is the things I need for school, madam," Richard answered, looking slightly embarrassed. Elementary and secondary schools were not free in Uganda, and the fees were high enough to keep lots of kids out of school. It was common for foreigners, as well as better-off Ugandans, to pay the school fees of neighborhood kids or relatives. I was still paying the school fees for Jane, one of Erneste's daughters, and a couple of other neighborhood girls.

"Two jars of skin lotion? One comb? These are not exactly what I consider school supplies."

"Well, I will use these things in school, madam. And Madam Pauline always bought them for me."

"Chloroquine?!" I asked.

"No doubt, I will get malaria this year, madam."

"Let me get this straight. If you get malaria, I have to pay for your medicine?"

"Well, only if I get malaria while in school, madam. Then it is a school fee. If I get malaria while on holiday, then I will have to find the money elsewhere.

"I will do what I did for Madam Pauline," Richard continued softly. "In exchange for your assistance, I will work at your compound on weekends and holidays. I used to help Madam Pauline with the garden. See," he said, pointing to a small stand of young banana trees in the far corner of the yard. "Madam and I planted those banana trees."

"Well, John was talking about putting up a *paillote* right next to the banana plantation. I guess you're hired."

So our house was getting fuller by the day. Regina had started to bring her one-year-old son, Billy, and Billy's babysitter, or *aya*. We turned the back room, where Solomon used to live, into a nursery of sorts, with mats on the floor, a bed, and lots of toys. Sometimes Coby and her new son, Job, would come by, as did an American woman and a British missionary woman and their new babies. Soon, we had our own Mommy & Me group—expat style, which meant after we nursed the babies, our *ayas* took them so we could play tennis.

Alison, a young, single Brit who'd recently come to town, didn't join our mommy group, but she did join us on the tennis courts. Alison was a volunteer with VSO, which is the European equivalent of Peace Corps. She reminded me of myself when I was in the Peace Corps. Or rather, of how I would have liked to be.

"Fuck's sake," Alison yelled. "It really throws off my serve when the goats wander onto the court."

"Ah, quit yer bellyaching!" I yelled back. "Just serve." Alison gracefully set up a picture-perfect serve to my side, and I, of course, missed it. "Wow, I guess I was too busy admiring that to hit it. Where'd you learn how to serve like that?"

"Miss Haversham's Finishing School for Girls," she snorted. "Hey, Coby, take over for me. I need a ciggie." She walked over to where she'd parked her motorcycle, pulled a packet of rolling papers and a tin of tobacco out of her saddlebag, squatted in the dirt, and expertly rolled herself a cigarette.

"Hey, I found lemongrass growing in my yard. I'm going to make lemongrass fettuccine this afternoon. Why don't you guys come over for supper?" I asked.

"Oh, I was wondering who had the pasta machine," Coby said.

"I got it when Daniella was through with it. And I'm supposed to pass it to Anna Hatchard next." The hand-cranked pasta maker belonged to one of the Italian families, but it—like someone's ice-cream maker—got passed around so much, it was practically community property. "And, Alison, I have some yogurt for you."

"Thanks. It never comes out right when I make it."

"Well, first you have to pasteurize the milk. Then let it cool down to body temperature. Just stick your finger in it—it shouldn't feel too hot or too cold. Then mix in a spoon full of yogurt that you already have. Wrap the pan in a towel, then put it in your sleeping bag and leave the whole thing overnight. It's simple, really. Anyway, come over later and I'll give you some. And stop by the CARE office on your way home and tell John we're having a party at his house tonight. And invite Mark, too."

So this is what my life had come to: philanthropy, gardening, cooking, and tennis. I felt like I was thoroughly enjoying my retirement; having skipped the whole bothersome thirty-odd years of working first. But John was working hard enough for the two of us. His project was progressing so well that CARE was talking about extending our two-year contract for a third year. Which was a good thing, because with the help of my very own African village, I was starting to get the hang of life in Arua.

Dear Mom,

Well, Sierra is finally sleeping through the night and in her own room, too. Although John absolutely refuses to let her cry herself to sleep, so it's hard to get her into bed at night. John finally finished making the crib he's been working on for . . . well, longer than it took me to make Sierra! It's really beautiful, with tiny carved elephants on it and a side that's hinged so mommy can reach in. It is incredibly special. Do you think Sierra will somehow be shaped by her unusual beginnings? Will she even have memories of this place? Will she know she spent the first months of her life in a crib that her daddy made for her, totally by hand?

John brought me a small desk and chair from the CARE office and we made me a little writing space in Sierra's bedroom. It feels nice to sit here and type away quietly while she sleeps. I'm starting to write some short stories. I have a fantasy of writing the next Out of Africa. Okay, it's just a fantasy, but it gives me something to do—besides nurse—and gives me hope that maybe someday I can combine motherhood with something else.

There's a swarm of nasty African bees that live in a hive that's right outside of Sierra's window. If one of them gets in here, I swear, I will kill it with my bare hands. There's a beekeeper at CARE who has promised to come and take this hive away for over a month now. If a bee stings Sierra, I swear, I'll kill this beekeeper with my bare hands! Is this what you meant by maternal instinct?

I'll keep you posted,
Eve

Chapter Twenty-Six

Package Hell

Sierra was healthy and happy as long as she was attached to my boob or being held. Now that I was no longer actively looking for work, it came looking for me. The Peace Corps occasionally hired me to conduct in-service health trainings and to facilitate COS conferences for departing volunteers. I'd also gotten several requests from USAID and various other agencies to work with them on trainings, conferences, and evaluations. Of course, this usually meant traveling down to Entebbe or Kampala—which could be somewhat problematic with a baby attached to my boob.

Luckily, most women in Uganda seemed to have an infant attached to some part of their body at all times, and when I wore Sierra on my back to a job interview, everyone cooed at her and I got offered the job. Luckily, I didn't have to wear Sierra while I was working; Cissie, who unlike Regina had no family of her own to look after, usually came with us on out-of-town jobs.

When Sierra turned six months old right before Christmas, I began to try to interest her in something other than breast milk. I borrowed a food mill from one of the Italians (what would we have done without the Italians and their well-stocked kitchens?) and began mashing bananas, grueling rice, and pureeing peas. I became so fond of pureed peas that I started serving them to John. But Sierra smeared the baby food on her face and showed no interest in giving up nursing anytime before kindergarten.

John's work was going well, but as a few of his counterparts at the bank became more and more possessive and demanding of CARE's resources, he began to figure out that not everyone was involved in the project for altruistic reasons. But missing computers and AWOL vehicles aside, things were progressing more or less as hoped. The opening of the brand-new bank building in January was marked, of course, by great fanfare. The ensuing ceremony was complete with visiting dignitaries and long, wordy speeches. John was pleased as he sat through the ceremony up on the dais. And I was proud of him as I watched with Sierra from my seat of honor. By February, the new bank was bustling and entrepreneurs were starting to make use of the credit and loan program.

As Sierra spent more time with Regina, Billy, and Cissie, I spent more time writing: my usual long, newsy letters home as well as short stories about life in Arua. Most nights I'd charge up my laptop computer when the power came on, and most days there'd be something to write about. In Arua, you never knew when something ordinary, like a trip to the post office, would end up being anything but ordinary.

"Sierra," I sung over my shoulder one day as we walked home from the post office. "Who do you think sent us a package?" The post office service counter was already closed when we found the three little notices in our mailbox. That meant we'd have to wait until the next day to collect our packages.

"Bahbahbahbah," Sierra drooled down my back.

"Maybe your Christmas and Hanukkah presents arrived. It is February." It could take a few days or months for a package to arrive from the States. There seemed to be no reliable pattern.

"Gahgahgah," Sierra said.

"It could be just another box of ant and roach traps."

"Gaaa!" she screeched. We'd been receiving packages of ant and roach traps ever since I'd sent home a videotape of the thumb-sized humming ants that surrounded our house one day.

It was after four o'clock the next day when I left Sierra with Cissie and Regina and set off down the road to get my packages. I should have wrapped a *kitenge* over my shorts to make it look like I was wearing a skirt like most Ugandan women do. But even in a *kitenge* I attracted attention. It was hot and the post office was just at the end of the road; I'd decided to throw modesty to the sub-Saharan wind.

"*Ife mani sende! Ife mani sende!*" a flock of neighborhood children greeted me just outside my gate with their familiar chant.

"*Ife* mani *sende!*" I yelled back at them. I put the emphasis on *me,* which sent the children laughing and scattering in all directions.

Arua's new post office was cool and airy, and had a long wooden counter with six half-moon windows cut into the glass partition above it. Each window had a wooden sign that listed the services available there. I thought most of it was just wishful thinking or flat-out lies. Imagine purchasing a money order or making an international telephone call in Arua!

There was only one clerk behind the counter. He was seated behind the window labeled "Stamps/Post Office Boxes/Registered Mail." I jaunted up to his window, greeted him, and presented my slips like winning lottery tickets.

"You have to go over to that window," he said, pointing to the window below the sign that read "Small Packets/Packages."

"But no one is over there," I said. He leaned out of his window and pointed to the wooden sign above his head that read "Stamps/Post Office Boxes/Registered Mail."

"This window is for stamps, post office boxes, and registered mail," he said. Then he pointed to the window next to his underneath the sign that read "Money Orders/Telex/International Telephone." "That window is for money orders, telex, and international phone calls." Then he pointed once again to the window at the far end of the counter beneath the sign that said "Small Packets/Packages." "And that window is for small packets and packages." I didn't dare to ask what was available at the three windows beneath the signs that were still blank. I just headed to the other end of the counter.

"Bloody hell." I looked over my shoulder and saw John Hatchard standing by his post office box, reading a letter.

"Problem, Hatch?" I detoured over to him.

"I keep telling these idiots we need an underground water storage tank."

"USAID turned down your request to fund a swimming pool again, eh?" I asked.

"Well, if ya tell 'em it's a swimming pool, of course they're gonna turn ya down. But I keep telling 'em that Arua needs an underground water storage tank. We need an underground water storage tank. Wouldn't you agree?"

"Yeah, definitely. And have them put it in my backyard while you're at it."

"Yeah, I might just do that. You've got the big compound. Would go nice there."

I walked over to the Small Packets/Packages window and, wouldn't you know, the same clerk from the Stamps/Post Office Boxes/Registered Mail window came over and took my three package slips, went into a back room, and came back a few minutes later with one small box. "Fifty shillings for this one, but you will have to go see the customs officer about these." He handed me back two of the package slips. "He is at the Customs House, over on Transport Road."

"Where?" I asked.

"To get to Transport Road you go out of the post office and—"

"No. I know where Transport Road is," I said. "I just don't know where on Transport Road the Customs House is."

"Oh, it is right at the end of the road. Where the Uganda Revenue Authority is." I thought I knew where that was, having seen a sign once.

It was now 4:30 and I was desperate to get my packages before the post office closed at 5:00. I nearly ran the two blocks to Transport Road and I was now painfully aware that I was wearing shorts. I found the corner where I remembered seeing the Uganda Revenue Authority sign. But all the signs had been removed since a 2,000 *Ush* tax had been imposed on signs. Even the Uganda Revenue Authority—the Ugandan tax collectors—took down its sign rather than pay the tax.

It took a few minutes, but I finally found the customs officer. "Good afternoon. How are you?" I offered my hand and the usual Ugandan greeting that I still found annoying as hell. In New York City I had perfected the art of not even making eye contact with people. Now I was expected to shake hands with and inquire about the health of every stranger I met.

I was expecting "I am fine. How are you?," which was so automatic people often answered before they were even asked. But he just grunted at me and continued drinking his tea.

"Oh, these packages are not here," he said when I presented him my slips. "You have to go to the post office to get these."

"But I was just at the post office," I reported. "And they sent me to you to get my packages."

"No, no. The packages are in the post office."

"Then why did the post office send me here?" I asked.

"Because I am the customs officer." He popped a handful of groundnuts into his mouth.

"How do I get my packages?" I pleaded.

"Oh, you want your packages! Well, then I have to go with you to the post office to look at your packages, assess the customs tax, collect it, and affix my stamp on your receipt. Then you can have your packages."

"Okay, then," I said, enthusiastically enough, I hoped, for both of us. "Let's go to the post office."

"Oh, no," he said, pointing to his watch. "We cannot go now. The post office is closed."

"The post office is open," I said. "I just came from there."

"Yes . . . umm . . . but by the time we get there it will be closed," he said. I looked at my watch. It was 4:42.

"Look," I said, "we have eighteen minutes before the post office closes. We can make it."

"Okay." He stood up grudgingly. "Where is your vehicle?"

"I don't have a vehicle. We'll have to walk."

"Oh, no vehicle." He sat back down. "We will never get there in time."

"We can easily make it, it's just around the corner and down the street." And then I remembered all the time I had spent drinking tea and eating groundnuts with the district health educator in his office, never going to schools because he wouldn't walk. Farmers, merchants, and laborers regularly walked for miles and never complained. But once people got into a position of power in Uganda, they refused to walk. So how did things get done with so few vehicles and so many people averse to walking? Well, many times, they didn't. And so I was sure I would never get my packages and began to imagine my once-glorious packages decaying in some forgotten corner of the post office, the cardboard dust blending in with the red dirt of Uganda.

The customs officer drained his teacup. "Well, let us go then." He stood. As we turned onto the main road, I flagged down a passing CARE vehicle with Adam at the wheel.

"Hello there, Eve. How are you? And where is my little friend Ascienju?"

"Adam! I am fine. The baby is at home. I am just trying to get my packages from the post office. This is the customs officer."

"Yes, I know this fellow. We went to school together. How are you? How is the family?"

"Oh, Adam. Good to see you. We are all fine. Fine." We got into Adam's vehicle.

"So I see you have met what?" Adam asked the officer. "You have met my good friend Eve. Adam and Eve! Don't you just love that? I work with Eve's husband, John. A good, good man."

Adam dropped us at the post office, hurrying home to catch BBC's daily wrap-up of the OJ Simpson trial, Adam's latest American fascination. I presented my slips, fees, and the customs officer to the clerk. He went off to the back room and returned with two huge boxes.

"I'll bet those are my daughter's Christmas presents," I said, knowing he'd have no idea what Hanukkah was.

The customs officer looked severely at the boxes.

"My husband works with your friend Adam at CARE. Do you know about CARE? They're doing so much to help the people of Uganda. We love Uganda. We've lived here for a year and a half now. Beautiful country. Did you know that CARE is tax-exempt?" I hadn't come all this way to go home empty-handed.

The customs officer read the customs slip pasted onto the outside of each box. *Ten pieces of baby clothes* it said on one; *twelve stuffed animals* it said on the other. Holiday presents from my father.

"It's for my daughter. Ascienju," I stammered.

"Your daughter is a *mzungu*?" he asked.

Who else but a mzungu *baby would get ten pieces of clothing and twelve stuffed animals for Christmas or Hanukkah?* "Yes," I said.

"Where did she get such a beautiful African name?" he asked.

"Oh, my husband—and Adam—did some work in the village of Cilio, and the people there made her a traditional naming ceremony."

"Ascienju," he said slowly. "It means peaceful heart."

"Pissy-full heart" was how the children of Cilio had pronounced it. But who was I to argue?

"I love babies," the customs officer said. He stamped the slips and handed them back to me.

"So, what do I have to pay?" I asked nervously.

"Nothing," he said. "Tell Ascienju 'Happy Christmas' from me."

I couldn't help but wonder if he had noticed that it was February.

Dear Dad,

Sierra says thank you for all the goodies you sent her, which just recently arrived. (Of course, it sounds like "baaaa!!!!" when Sierra says it.) I can't believe I never filled you in on your granddaughter's first big holiday adventure in Kenya and Tanzania. It was a great vacation, but traveling with a six-month-old through East Africa is not the carefree getaway you might imagine. But, of course, you haven't really experienced the joy of parenthood until you've schlepped a poopy baby, a car seat, and a porta-crib through the steamy streets of Dar Es Salaam. After the longest day in history—which included three flights, one rental car, and a ferry ride—we arrived in Mombasa, where we relaxed and enjoyed Christmas in a lovely cottage on a beautiful beach. The beach was unspoiled and fairly empty (perhaps the three plane rides, rental car, and ferry ride are keeping tourists away), yet just a twenty-minute drive from a town that had everything.

After Mombasa, we headed to Zanzibar, which really has its own distinct flavor (lobster, shrimp, and coconut), language (Swahili), and customs (literally—as in having to have your passport stamped when you arrive on the island from the mainland). We thought, like the rest of the world, that Zanzibar is part of Tanzania and so didn't get our passports stamped when we got to the island and were actually there illegally for two days! We rang in the New Year by staying with the Marums in a luxurious U.S. Embassy house (complete with AC, private beach, and marvelous cook).

So of course it was a bit of a letdown to come home to landlocked, lobsterless Arua. But what we lack in sea life, we more than make up for in insect life. I came home to find that my kitchen has been overrun by more species of ants than I ever knew existed and just one species of roach—HUGE.

I'm glad you're enjoying Sierra's latest video. "Sierra on the Road" is actually her second feature film. Unfortunately, her first—"A Very Clean Girl," noted for its many bath scenes—seems to have gotten lost in the intercontinental mail. We are now working on Sierra's third film, "Screeching and Babbling with Baby," which is due out next month.

I'll keep you posted,
Eve

Chapter Twenty-Seven

Can You Hear Me Now?

To the uninitiated, it could look like Arua was stuck in the world of yesterday. Sure, most of our neighbors cooked over open fires and, clearly, no one had ever heard of the recent prohibition against wearing plaids with stripes. But if you looked closely you could see signs of the modern era encroaching. For the past few months we'd been getting an extra hour of electricity every night, with the town generator working from 7:00 p.m. until 11:00 p.m. A brand-new bank had been built for John's project. A building, I might add, that had not only all-day electricity (thanks to its own generator) but also a flush toilet. Progress was not as obvious with the Anti-AIDS Club that I had started at the local secondary school. After training every Friday afternoon for nearly a year, the students had gone out to share their newly acquired knowledge about AIDS.

"So how did it go?" I asked when the trainees convened the next week.

"Oh, madam," said one of the students, raising his hand. "I was talking with a neighbor and I could not answer this person's question."

"Well, what was the question?" I asked.

"Well, this person asked me if HIV could be transmitted through an infected tomato. And I did not know the answer to that."

"You didn't know if HIV could be transmitted by a tomato?"

"Well, it's true, madam," another student piped up. "You never told us the answer to that one!"

"Okay." I took a deep breath. "Let's review again. Someone tell me the three ways that HIV can be transmitted."

"By sex," one girl said.

"By sharing needles or blood," another said.

"And from mother to baby," a boy said.

"And those are the only three ways, right?" I asked. I should have known better.

"Yes," said the most promising student in the class. "Except, of course, for voodoo hex." So progress was not exactly being made in leaps and bounds on the educational front. But modernity was coming to Arua in the form of the telephone. Until now there had only been one telephone in the whole town. It was housed at the post office and if you wanted to make a phone call, you'd have to go down there, fill out a form, and then wait outside on a bench in the hot sun while the operator attempted to connect your call.

If your call did connect, you got to go into the small, airless room where the telephone was housed. But you usually didn't go alone. Everyone else on the bench—whether you knew them or not—would come with you. After all, yours might be the only successful call of the day and everyone wanted to get in on it. The operator listened in on his own extension, having little else to do once the only line in town was engaged.

"Are you finished yet?" he'd ask every few minutes. He'd disconnect you whenever he felt you were done.

So we were among the first to apply when the Uganda Post and Telephone (UPT) announced that we could get home telephones. The three-page application required two passport-sized photos, the signature and stamp of our local government representative, and a personal reference from a present UPT customer, which was a slight problem since no one in town had a phone yet. But we got Mark to vouch for our good character, the fact that we knew how to use a telephone, and that—so far as he knew—we had never intentionally damaged one.

He added the official CARE stamp and his signature with a flourish, for good measure.

"A technician will come out to your place soon to see if it is an appropriate site for a telephone," said the man who took my application. I felt more anxious than I'd expected. *Was my home, indeed, appropriate for the care and feeding of a telephone?*

And then, of course, nothing happened for weeks, and I had almost forgotten about the whole thing when three technicians showed up in our compound to inspect the place as promised. This inspection consisted of a tall, fat man looking from my house to the road and grunting. To strengthen our case, however, I showed him the ancient black telephone that I had found in a closet. I had no idea how or why it had gotten into our house. But discovering it had given me hope that a highly advanced civilization had once lived in Arua and might come again.

"Ah, yes. There was talk of telephone in Arua during Idi Amin's time," the big man said when I showed him our rodent-nibbled relict.

Two other men jumped out of the UPT truck and joined the big man in my house. A man in a garage mechanic's jumpsuit rummaged around in his toolbox and then asked me for a tape measure so that they could figure out how much wire they'd need when they actually did get around to installing the phone. The third member of their team smiled and sat down on my couch. I wondered if I was supposed to offer him tea.

A week later the three of them showed up again, this time with a new telephone. The fat man gave the instructions, the man in the jumpsuit installed the phone, and the third guy sat on my couch and smiled. Within a half hour, an impressively modern-looking phone was hung on our dining room wall.

The guy in the orange jumpsuit picked up the receiver and pressed "0." "Your telephone is working, madam." He handed me the phone.

"This is Arua," I could hear the operator say. "Hello?"

I suppressed the urge to ask if he had Prince Albert in a can. Instead, I giggled and hung up the phone. *Who knows, maybe soon they'll invent talking pictures.* "So now," I asked, "can I call America from my house?"

"No," the technician chuckled. "But you can call the operator at the post office and he can call America for you."

"But I can call Kampala from my house, right?" I asked.

"Uh, no," said the technician. "But you can call the operator from your house and he can call Kampala for you."

"Okay, but I can call Coby from my house. Right?"

"Well, no. But you can call the operator and he will call her for you." *Okay, it was a whole new world, but it came complete with the same old glitches.*

We wrote home and told everyone. "It's like a game of telephone," we told them. "You call the international operator and ask him to connect you to the Kampala operator, who can connect you to the Arua operator, and then ask for Arua 71." And in a few weeks, we got our first phone call. Unfortunately, it was my mom calling to tell me that my grandfather had died.

Regina's husband, Steven, was waiting on my verandah the next morning. "I have come to express my condolences." He took my hand in his. "May our Lord Jesus Christ welcome your grandfather into the kingdom of heaven." I thought it best not to tell Steven that my grandfather, an observant Jew, had probably been hoping for a seat on the Jesus-free side of heaven.

"May our Lord Jesus Christ ease your pain." Steven crossed himself. Then he crossed me. Then he crossed the entire house. I think he was trying to show off what he was learning in his Christian correspondence course, since John and I were subsidizing much of it.

"You cannot know how sorry I am that now you will be leaving," he said. He had tears in his eyes. "And who is to know if you will ever return."

"We're not leaving," I told him. Steven, who was never at a loss for words, was actually silent. "The United States is too far and costs too much money just to go back for a short visit," I explained.

"But won't you go home for any of the funerals?" The Lugbara traditionally had a series of funerals when someone died. It began with the first one in which the deceased was actually buried—usually right in the family compound—and culminated a year later with the raucous, booze-soaked last funeral rites.

"I've already missed the funeral," I told him.

"How could you miss the funeral?" he asked. "Didn't they wait for you?"

"In my culture funerals are over very quickly. In my religion, we have to bury the dead within twenty-four hours. We can't always wait until all the relatives arrive."

"You mean there is such a rush over there that the dead can't wait for the living? Here, even our dead are not in a hurry!"

After the phone call from my mother, the phone went dead. A few weeks later, I walked down to the post office to report the problem. The operator dialed up my number, got a ring, and declared that my phone was indeed working.

"Then how come you don't answer when I dial '0' so I can make a call?" I asked.

"Your phone works fine, madam," he said. "It's just that there is no electricity to light up the switchboard to inform me that you are trying to reach me." *A small problem.* "Why don't you just send your *askari* down to the post office when you want to make a phone call and I will ring you?"

Before we leapt into the modern age, Coby and I sent messages back and forth several times a day with our *askaris*. Now, apparently, we were supposed to send our *askaris* to the post office, which meant that Coby's *askari* had to pass my house on his way to the post office. Pretty soon we were bypassing the post office and sending messages the old-fashioned way.

While jogging up Arua Hill one day, the guard in charge of the telephone transmitter showed John around. "This," the guard said, pointing to a big lever, "turns the whole phone system on and off. I must shut it down when rain is coming. You see now it is on and these little lights mean that someone is talking." Then, pulling the lever down, he proudly announced, "Now it's off!"

The whole phone system seemed pretty useless, but we were assured that everything would change once Arua got its own exchange.

"The exchange," the folks at UPT said, looking kind of glassy-eyed, "will connect our system to all the other telephone systems." The exchange was going to grant us all real telephone numbers, too, so that we would no longer be merely "Arua 71." No. When the exchange came, we would be "200-71."

"The exchange," the operator sighed, "will allow us to phone direct, from our own telephones, to anywhere else in the world. Even Kampala!"

"Well, when is this exchange gonna get here?" I asked.

"We were actually due to get it last month," the operator said. "But someone took it to Fort Portal instead."

Other than the first three digits of a telephone number, I had no idea what an exchange actually consisted of. But I had visions of a huge switchboard, complete with an operator, loaded onto a flatbed and hijacked to Fort Portal, a town northwest of Kampala that had electricity, water, and even a pizzeria. *How unfair! Certainly we in Arua—with barely any electricity or water and only fantasies of pizza— are far more deserving.*

"But don't worry," he said. "The next one is ours."

The telephone that had once been such a promising sign of development quickly became a wall decoration. Sure, it gave my heart a little flutter just to look at it, but it was no more useful than the Zairian masks that were hung on the walls. (Somehow word got out after we bought the first one and now masks were showing up regularly on the Home Shopping Network.) I gave up all hope that my fancy new telephone would ever be more than a conversation piece.

Dear Jean,

Wow, what a thrill to get your phone call last week, even if we did get cut off after a minute. Oh, well, thanks for trying. My mom also got through a few weeks ago. Long enough to tell me my grandfather had died, and then we were cut off. No luck getting through to her since. But maybe when the long-awaited exchange gets to Arua, we'll actually be able to talk. But don't hold your breath!

Well, last night took the cake . . . and then threw it up. This had to be the most disgusting night in a life full of disgusting events (lancing your butt blisters no longer even makes the top ten). I get home from tennis to Sierra splashing in a puddle on the floor (she had spilled water) and John nauseous and headachy and straw from a broom strewn all over the place. (John was trying to sweep up the water. I told you he wasn't feeling well.) John proceeds to get sick all over the bathroom, Sierra gets cranky, and then it's the invasion of the white ants.

White ants are actually huge winged termites that live in these humongous anthills all over the place. They are considered a delicacy around here (not by me). They come out one night a year, after the first big rain of the rainy season. And they come out by the zillions and the whole place is alive with them, like a bizarre but miniature Alfred Hitchcock movie. They were an inch thick on the doors and windows because they are attracted to the lights from the inside of the house. The noise was tremendous as they beat their zillion pairs of wings against the screens. And they managed to get in no matter what I did. And then the house started filling up with them. They swooped around our heads. We tried to avoid them by walking in between them. Then there was no in between them. They dropped into our dinner. They squished under our feet. They were absolutely everywhere. I put Sierra in her crib under her mosquito net, where she starts to scream and flail and get herself completely tangled up in the net. Meanwhile, John was vomiting violently in the toilet. After I got John to bed and Sierra finally passed out, I swept up a ton of termites and flushed them down the toilet. When Regina came this morning, she thought I was crazy. If I'm lucky enough to get all those white ants in my house, she asked, why don't I just eat them?

Oh, gross . . . I just found a squished giant ant stuck to the bottom of my foot—and no, I am not wearing shoes! Do I love this place or what?

I'll keep you posted,
Eve

Chapter Twenty-Eight

❦

To Market to Market (to Buy a Fresh Fish)

John's contract was due to finish in August of 1995. But in April of that year, CARE asked us to extend our contract. I laughed at that idea at first, recalling how desperate I'd been during our first few months here. Back then I couldn't fathom how I'd survive for two years. Now they were asking us to stay for a third year, and the funny thing was, I was seriously considering it.

Sierra's first eight months had been healthy and happy. And though everyone in the States assumed that raising a baby in Arua was some kind of hardship, I probably had it easier than a lot of my friends back home. I had all the help in the world—especially since Cissie had moved into the refurnished "nursery" after a particularly ugly fight with her brother and her father. I had a husband who loved his job and came home for lunch most days and was home in time for sunset gin-tonics most evenings. Our weekends were free for socializing with a fascinating circle of expat and local friends. We never had to worry about cleaning our house, fixing our car, or even mowing our lawn! Like the Ugandans around us, we had pretty much learned to ignore the rumors about an impending war with Sudan and/or a rebel invasion of the West Nile. Life in Arua, for the most part, was calm and peaceful and we assumed it would stay that way.

There were frustrations, of course. I had once heard Uganda referred to as "the Land of Waiting." Ugandans were always waiting: for transport, for petrol, for money, for the plane to bring the mail, for the man with the key to return. I had been known to call it "the Land Where an Excuse Is as Good as a Deed." To put it bluntly, not a whole lot got done. And we high-strung, fast-paced, New York types could easily go bald pulling our hair out as things moved along—or didn't—at glacial speed. But John and I had slowed down enough to see and appreciate the almost imperceptible signs of progress that had been made, and much of it was due to John's project.

There were more women who were making a living by brewing beer or selling handicrafts. There were more farmers who'd been able to open stalls in the market. There was the potter who now owned his own wheel and the banana farmer who'd built a solar dehydrator for drying bananas into banana chips, which, because they could be easily transported, could be sold to a wider market. For these people and for others, there was now the chance to live above a bare subsistence level, the hope of sending a child to school or of being able to build a house out of bricks rather than mud. They were tiny baby steps toward development, indeed, but they were there. John was proud of his role in this. And I was proud of him. All in all, the good outweighed the bad. And we happily agreed to stay on for a third year.

Since we wouldn't be going home for another year and a half, John's parents came to visit us. I was tremendously excited—visitors from home were a rare thing and a cause for celebration. But I was also more than a little nervous. Arua was home to us now, and we were used to it. But would it seem like some backwoods outpost to Grammie and Papa? Would they find it uncomfortable? Would they get sick? We eased them in slowly when they arrived that May, letting them adjust to Kampala before we shocked them with Arua. But I think their first shock came when we took Sierra for her checkup while we were in Kampala and Larry Marum weighed her by suspending her from something that looked an awful lot like a meat hook attached to a grocery scale.

"Why don't you leave Sierra here with us in the hotel?" Grammie asked the next day as I was about to go on a marathon shopping trip in Kampala.

"Do you think she'll be okay with you?" At lunch the previous day, Sierra had screamed when Papa tried to hold her. It was even more heartbreaking when she squirmed out of her grandfather's arms and went happily into the waiter's.

"I know we're not black," Grammie said, "but she seems to be getting used to us."

We flew home the next day on one of the bigger airlines that had recently started flying to Arua. John thought his parents would be more comfortable on a twenty-passenger plane than MAF's tiny puddle jumper. But good Catholics that they are, I thought they would have appreciated MAF's preflight prayers.

"Now, don't go to too much trouble for dinner tonight," Grammie said a few days later as they were about to go off to a village meeting with John. "Just something simple is fine for us." She didn't get that nothing was simple in Arua. But I was determined to do my best imitation of Pauline while they were here. We'd already eaten the chicken that a neighbor had given as a gift to my in-laws. And we'd butchered and grilled a goat for the party we'd hosted the night before so that our friends and colleagues could meet them.

I know, I thought, *I'll get some fresh fish.* Luckily it was Friday, one of the two days that you could get fresh fish in Arua. Besides, you get extra points for serving fish to Catholics on Fridays, don't you? Normally I avoided the madness of the market on fish days by sending Regina or Cissie. But Regina was cleaning up from last night's party and Cissie, with Sierra on her back, was washing the nappies. So I set off on my bicycle, aiming to get to the market when the fishermen did, sometime around 3:30 p.m., and before they were completely sold out, as they always were, by 5:00 p.m.

"Hey, you *mzungu*! *Ife mani sende!*" I looked over my shoulder at two young boys at the side of the road, selling chewing gum and cigarettes. *What? Did they really think that one day I would finally break down and start flinging shillings around just to shut them up?*

Behind the boys' rickety table was an old tree with a cross scraped roughly into its huge trunk. The tree had been there forever, but the cross had only recently appeared. Some people thought it was a sign from God. But most said it was the Seventh-day Adventists who'd recently arrived in Arua. One of them had come to my gate to bring me the "good news."

"I've heard the news, madam," *Mzee* John warned me. "And it is not good!"

I locked my bicycle up in front of a shop where I knew the shopkeeper would keep an eye on it for me. Then I walked past the beggars and lepers, emptying my pockets of my five- and ten-shilling notes as I went.

"Hello, madam," shouted one of the ladies who sold sugar, salt, tea, and coffee in half-kilo bags and in pencil-thin tubes.

"How is your husband?" someone else yelled. I recognized her as one of the women who had recently taken a business class at the bank.

"Where is the baby?" someone else called. "Is she walking yet?"

"Oh, we are all fine, thank you," I answered the whole group. Aside from the woman I recognized from the bank, I knew nothing about these women who I'd greeted several times a week for the past year and a half. Yet they knew so much about my life.

I walked quickly past the rows of stalls, waving and shaking my head as everyone tried to get me to come over to buy their wares. "Just fish today," I called to them. "I'll be back tomorrow," I said. *With my mother-in-law.* And I thought back to my first trip to the market. Wasn't I freaked out by the begging lepers; overwhelmed by the noise and everyone vying for my attention; grossed out by the fried termites? Now it was hard to remember what it was like not to shop like this. Yet I couldn't help but wonder: What would my mother-in-law think of the cow carcasses?

"How is my husband, Solomon?" a woman selling potatoes asked. Constance had been living with Solomon, when he was Terry and Pauline's *askari.* "Will you take me and the baby with you to Kampala the next time you go?" Constance had recently given birth to the tiny baby girl who was now tied to her back.

"I thought Solomon told you to stay in Arua." I knew he had another wife and several children down there. I wondered if he told her *never* to come to Kampala and that's why she named her new daughter Never.

"Well, then, can I marry your husband?" she asked. I didn't know if she was joking or not. Polygamy was perfectly acceptable to many people in Arua. And there was no shortage of women who wanted to marry John. He was, after all, an excellent husband.

"No," I answered. Joking or not, I wanted it understood that I did not wish to share John.

"Hello, Eve," shouted the young ladies who sold cooking oil.

"Hello, ladies," I shouted back although I didn't know their names. I wondered how they had learned mine.

I hopped over the trench of dirty water and walked over to where the Banana Ladies sat on plastic sheets covered with bunches of bananas. Our little banana plantation hadn't matured yet and I still bought bananas from Zila. All the Banana Ladies cheerily told me who was overcharging me for a papaya or which pineapple would be ready today, which one was good for tomorrow. They all let me stow my shopping bags with them when they got too heavy to lug around and I still had more shopping to do. But none of them except Zila had ever tried to sell me bananas.

"You are *my* customer," Zila explained when I'd asked her why none of the other ladies ever competed for my business. Then she looked down at the obnoxious pink pants I had been wearing that day, part of my dead *mzungu* maternity wardrobe. "Will you give me your pants?"

"Well, I'm using them right now," I had told her. "But I'll give them to you when I'm done."

"*Karibu,*" Zila said today as she clapped me on the shoulder. "Where is Ascienju?"

"I'll bring her when I come to do my regular shopping tomorrow. But today I just came to get fish."

"There is no fish yet," she told me. But I knew this from the relative calm of the market. "The rain has delayed them," Zila offered. It had indeed rained that morning. "They will come soon. Sit down and wait." She scooted over and offered me half of the empty crate she was sitting on. I knew that "soon" had an extremely broad definition in Uganda that bore no resemblance whatsoever to the Western definition. But if I was determined to make fish for dinner, I had no choice but to wait.

The Banana Ladies all whooped and clapped as I sat down next to Zila, and pretty soon word spread that a *mzungu* was selling bananas and a crowd gathered in front of us.

"*Karibu* (you are welcome)," I said. "*Abuaaaa* (bananas)," I yelled. "*Turu alu* (one hundred)," I said, pointing to the smallest bunches. "*Turu iri* (two hundred)," I said, pointing to the medium-sized bunches. "*Turu iri kalitowi* (two hundred and fifty)." I pointed to the biggest bunches. A woman with a camera pushed her way through the crowd and snapped a photo of Zila and me selling bananas. I wondered what kind of commotion I would cause if I rented my own stall and started selling the *mzungu* vegetables from the garden that Erneste helped me plant.

"The fish has arrived," Zila announced as a line of raggedly dressed men appeared and spread huge plastic sheets between the rows of vegetable stalls. "Go," she said and pushed me to where the fishmongers were now pouring out buckets of wet fish onto the plastic sheets. Suddenly, I was surrounded by a mob of people and was pushed, pulled, and jostled toward the general direction of the fish. I seemed to be carried along by this wave of people, although I wasn't actually walking.

For the first time in Uganda, I was just one of the crowd, and I wasn't sure if I liked it or not. But I resigned myself to the Ugandan way of waiting, and eventually, as if by peristalsis, I was spit out in front of one of the fishmongers where whole tilapia were strung together like odd necklaces and hunks of Nile perch were piled up on his wet sheet.

I bent down to inspect the fish and the salesman ruffled a finger against the gills so that I could see the deep red color. "Fresh, fresh," he said.

"I'll take a kilo of the tilapia." I held a plastic bag out toward him. He cut two big fish loose from the twine that bound them together and gingerly dropped them into my bag. I handed him 1,500 shillings, about a dollar fifty. I turned around and was immediately absorbed back into the stream of people. I moved my feet in the direction of the edge of the crowd, although I was not making any discernible progress. I kept my bag and my head up and reminded myself to breathe. I kept making persistent rhythmic motions, like swimming, until eventually I could make my way out of the mob.

I congratulated myself for how far I'd come since that first trip to the market with Pauline nearly two years ago. Now I could buy the buggy meat at the butcher shop. Now I knew how to bargain down the already ridiculously low price of tomatoes. (All right, I was still overpaying, but it was my way of sharing my "wealth.") And as of today, I could buy my own fish. Today, I told myself, I am a Ugandan! *Well, sort of.*

I looked over and saw Zila sitting calmly behind her bananas. I thought about the pants that I had never given her and about the many bananas that she had given me, always as a gift for Sierra. I turned around and dove back into the mob and slowly, persistently made my way back to the fish. I asked the man what he could give me for 500 shillings. He pointed to a moist white hunk of Nile perch, still attached on one side to its shiny black skin. I nodded and handed over the 500 shillings. He dropped the fish into a second plastic bag, and, once again, I dove back into the maelstrom of shoppers.

"A gift for you," I said when I'd made my way back to Zila.

"Thank you," she whispered. She took the bag and put it beside her crate.

"It's a fish," I said.

"Yes, I know," she answered. "I will cook it for supper."

I turned to leave. "And maybe next time," she called after me, "you will give me your pants!"

"I hope you didn't go through too much trouble," Grammie said that night after we'd all devoured our supper of poached tilapia with pasta on a bed of sautéed spinach.

Oh, no trouble at all!

Dear Grammie and Papa,

We were glad and relieved to hear that you made it home safe and healthy after our wonderful safari together in Kenya. We, on the other hand, all got sick within a week of returning to Uganda. On the Sunday of our return, Sierra awoke with a temperature of 103. She had never had a fever before and I would have been much more nervous had we not been staying at the Marums' house. But Larry quickly diagnosed an ear infection and gave her antibiotics and she recovered so quickly we were able to fly to Arua on Monday morning. I, on the other hand, came down with malaria shortly after getting home, and then John and I both caught a particularly nasty stomach bug. Thankfully that only lasted twenty-four hours and we are all now healthy once again.

Sierra is doing wonderfully. She's recently reached three benchmark achievements: She stood by herself, her first tooth began to make an appearance, and Regina saw her take her first steps! I told her that in my family the person who sees a baby's first steps has to buy their first pair of shoes. But she's off the hook since my mom has already sent enough shoes to last a lifetime! (Don't tell my mom, but I gave half of them to Regina's kids.)

We really enjoyed having you visit and you were great sports about all the usual African discomforts. Sorry about the overnight train. They assured me that a second-class compartment would fit five comfortably.

But perhaps they meant five Pygmies! And who knew it could get so cold between Mombasa and Nairobi? But I agree with Papa: Where else can you see elephants while a waiter is pouring hot coffee onto your lap?

Now we're getting ready for a visit from Susan and Brad. They've probably already got their nonrefundable tickets. Should I tell them about the cholera epidemic?

When we were in Kampala, we watched on CNN about the bombing in Oklahoma City. Then we missed our flight back to Arua, and John was fuming and huffing around the airport because the airline changed their schedule without bothering to tell us. "This is terrible," he said. "No, it's not terrible!" I told him. "Our daughter wasn't blown up in a day care center in Oklahoma City! That was terrible. This is merely an inconvenience."

I'll keep you posted,
Eve

Chapter Twenty-Nine

*

Go White Team!

In Arua, I was always being asked for something. Would you be so kind as to offer your generous assistance with my school fees? Can you buy me a bus ticket to Kampala? Can you inject my dog with this medicine? Will you give me your bra? Can you fly the plane? Okay, it was actually John who was asked to fly the plane so that the pilot could eat his lunch. Being about the same weight as the pilot, he was already sitting in the copilot's seat. And out of the five passengers, we all agreed that John was the most qualified since his brother is a pilot.

It was like the Ugandan version of trick or treat. People just came up to us and asked for what they wanted. Only this particular holiday wasn't limited to one day a year. Here, every day was Halloween—or Christmas, as the case may be. And I was Santa Claus.

It's not just that I was perceived as wealthy. In Uganda, for the first time in my life, I actually *was* wealthy. I was wealthy because even the few possessions that I had brought with me to Arua were more than most of my neighbors would ever have in their lives. I was wealthy because I didn't have to live solely by what I could grow or catch; because I was educated and because I was American. I was wealthy because, in the end, I could go home.

And so I was usually happy to help; that's what we were here to do, weren't we? But by the beginning of our third year there, fixing people's problems felt like my full-time occupation. Maybe I ought to hang out a shingle, I thought. One that said, "The Social/Miracle Worker/Philanthropist Is IN." And preferably it would have a flip-over sign that read "OUT" so that at least I could control my own hours.

By then I was paying Richard's school fees and buying his school supplies, malaria pills, and toiletries. I had also paid for his sister's malaria treatment and bought the coffin for his father's funeral. I was also paying the school fees for one of Erneste's daughters and two other girls I hardly even knew, although twice a year they each came by to show me their grades. I had paid the hospital fees for another of Erneste's daughters when she gave birth. I gave Regina and Cissie anything they needed—which most often was new shoes, and for this we carried cardboard tracings of the feet of all of their family members whenever we traveled. John lent money to several of the *askaris* for various family emergencies and business enterprises. Sometimes it felt like we gave and gave and gave. But the asking never ended.

But it's not like Ugandans were the only ones doing the asking. My long, newsy letters home often included my own petitions. I asked friends and family to send what I could not get in Uganda but felt I couldn't live without. "Fancy" cooking gadgets like pot holders and potato peelers. Luxury items like cake mixes and sauce packets. Things that were impossible to find in Uganda like brushes and clips for Caucasian hair. And no one got more requests than my best friend, Susan. Years later I cringed (and apologized) when I reread all my letters to her and realized what a pain in the ass I'd been. I once asked her, early on, to send my bicycle. It seems like the asking never ended. Hmmm . . . where have I heard that before?

But Susan forgave me, and just as Sierra's first birthday was approaching, she and her husband, Brad, came for a visit. Of course, I was thrilled—and not just because I knew they'd come bearing all sorts of things that I'd asked for ("a birthday present for Sierra; Little Mermaid decorations so I can make her a birthday party; a new computer battery . . ."). Susan is—and always has been—one of the most astoundingly generous souls I have ever met. And as expected, she and Brad arrived bearing all kinds of goodies for all of us.

We had spared Grammie and Papa the drive to Arua, but assumed that Susan and Brad's kidneys could handle it. They would only be with us for ten days before heading off to climb Mount Kenya. So we took the long drive to Arua, stopping so we could show them as much of the country as possible. Susan quickly exhausted her stash of give-away bubble gum and pencils and made friends with everyone as we straddled the equator, saw the source of the Nile, and had a hyena steal our shoes while camping at Murchison Falls.

On their first morning in Arua, Brad slept in, while Susan and I had coffee and played with the newly toddling Sierra on the verandah. Regina's husband, Steven, stopped by.

"Oh, your friend must buy some of my *adungus* to take back to America," he said when I introduced them. Steven had a sparkle in his eye that he got whenever he met a prospective customer. He had exhausted the local expat market: We all had more of his lovely handmade instruments than we could ever use. "If you see any here that you like," he said, pointing to the assortment of stringed instruments that took up an entire corner of my living room, lined the walls, and decorated the tables, "I can sell you those. I can always make another one for Eve." Steven had been known to resell my *adungus* before. But I had more than I needed.

"Eve, Regina and I have a serious problem," Steven continued.

"Really? She told me everything was fine this morning." But I had already noticed that Regina was as calm and trouble-free as Steven was frantic and perpetually problemed.

"Well, we have to get married," Steven said.

"I thought you two were married already," I said.

"With three kids and a fourth on the way, right?" Susan had chatted with Regina that morning.

"And that's why we need to get married in the church this time.

Years ago, my family gave Regina's family four goats—not a small price," he added, puffing up his chest. "You will no doubt get many goats, too," Steven said, tickling Sierra's cheek. "And we were married by local custom." Pretty much everyone I knew in Arua was married that way. Some more than once.

"Ah, but now we *need* to get married. Married-in-the-church married," he said, pointing to the ring finger of his left hand. "This is the only kind of wedding the church approves of. And that will cost a lot of money." Apparently, Steven's Christian correspondence course frowned on all that out-of-wedlock procreating.

"Okay, so you have a church wedding. That'll be nice. So what's the problem?" I asked.

"Oh, the wedding! The wedding is the problem! It will have to be big and it will be expensive and we do not have the money for a big, expensive wedding!"

"Why don't you guys just elope?" Susan asked. "You know, just go off to church, the two of you, and get married nice and simple. That's what we do in the States if we can't afford a big wedding." Steven stared at her, his eyes the size of cue balls. "Or can't you just make a very small wedding?"

"Oh, NO! We cannot do that. For us to get married in the church, we must invite everyone. All of my clan. All of Regina's clan. All of our friends and neighbors. And, of course, all of the Christians." *I didn't know who all of the Christians were. But I feared there could be a lot of them.*

"So how are you going to pay for this wedding?" I asked.

"Well, we will pray and we will form committees and we will ask God and our friends to help us." And right then and there I knew that Steven's wedding was going to end up costing me.

"You could just pay for their whole wedding, couldn't you?" Susan asked me when Steven had gone. "If I lived here, I'd be handing over whatever I had to whoever needed it." It was probably true, too. Susan was a lot like John in some ways. Aside from both of them being so tall that everyone here just assumed they were siblings, Susan also never seemed to get tired of giving. "I mean, it seems like we have so much and they have so little," she said.

Of course, John knew better than to just give everything away. He lived by the development adage "If you give a man a fish, he eats for a day. But if you teach a man to fish, he eats for a lifetime." He'd stopped handing out fish long ago, preferring instead to arm folks with their own fishing poles and lures, so to speak. But Susan might literally give someone the shirt off her back.

I took Susan to the market with me that day while I did my shopping. I made the mistake of wearing those obnoxious pink pants again (it's not like I had a lot of clothing options), and Zila asked again if she could have them.

"Aw, give her your pants, Eve," Susan chided. "I'll send you a new pair."

"Yeah. Give me your pants, Eve. Your friend will send you a new pair. Nicer ones from America."

"Well, I can't very well give them to her right now," I said.

"Do they sell *kitenges* here?" Susan looked around. We had gotten Susan some *kitenges*—and a lesson on how to wrap them like a skirt—on our road trip when she had figured out how difficult it is for a woman wearing pants to pee discreetly by the side of a barren road.

"Susan!" I knew what she was thinking. "I am not going to take my pants off right here in the market and make a total *mzungu* spectacle of myself." Okay, under normal circumstances, I wouldn't have taken off my pants in the market; I was already a *mzungu* spectacle enough as it was. But Susan has a way of making me do things that I might not otherwise do. And somehow, there I was, with a new *kitenge* wrapped around my waist as I very discreetly (well, as discreetly as possible) removed my pants from underneath as Susan and Zila laughed and high-fived each other in delight.

"Well, here are our pledge budgets," Steven declared the next day, handing Susan and me pieces of paper that contained an inventory of what he and Regina would need for their wedding, along with the cost of each item. I was a little hesitant. I mean, Susan had already talked me out of my pants and she was still here reminding me that we had so much and they had so little. Who knew what she would talk me into giving away next? But this list included meat, fish, cabbages, tea leaves, a suit and a gown, handkerchiefs, socks, and soap. *Why do people keep asking me to buy their toiletries?* Underneath the inventory, "the two-hundred invitees" were broken down as follows: Wedding Team–24; W/Friends Team–10; Bride/Groom relatives–40; Invited Christians–55.

"I see," I said, although the only thing I saw was that 24, 10, 40, and 55 did *not* equal 200.

"What's with the teams?" Susan asked. "Are there going to be relay races at the reception?"

"Relay races?" Steven stared at us blankly. "No, the teams are in charge of raising money. You and John and Sierra are on the W slash Friends team. And, Susan, you may be on the W slash Friends team too."

"Oh, Steven, that is so nice of you. But we won't be here for the wedding. We're heading to Kenya in a few more days and then we're going back home," Susan said. "What is the W slash Friends team, anyway?"

"That is the white friends team!" he said.

A few weeks later, Steven announced that our team had pledged the most money of all the teams. And it was no wonder: The team included Coby and Bernard, Alison, Mark, the Italians for whom Steven's brother worked, their relatives who were visiting from Rome, the Dutch family that had just come from Rwanda and moved into the house where Steven's sister used to work, and any other *mzungu* that Steven came across.

"Woo-hoo! Go white team!" I said.

By the time Steven raised enough money for the wedding, Regina had given birth to a baby boy they named Job, just like Coby and Bernard's second son. This drove me crazy, but made life easy for Sierra, who now called every baby "Yob." During the wedding ceremony, a female relative stood near the front of the church, jiggling Job. Several times during the ceremony, Regina nonchalantly opened the top of her frilly polyester wedding dress and popped Job onto her breast. Always the same breast, I noticed; thus finally solving the mystery of Regina's breast imbalance. I could hardly wait until after the wedding to tell her.

Dear Susan,

Has it really been three months since you were here? Where does the time go? And my how things change! Remember what a quiet, sleepy place this was? Well, here's the latest news from Arua: Three weeks ago, a land mine exploded on the road that you guys were on when John took you out to the village with him. It hit a big water truck and killed two people and wounded two others. A few days after that, an Italian development worker had his leg blown off by another land mine just outside of town, and now most of our Italian neighbors have been evacuated.

Shortly after that, our electricity started going off at 10:00 instead of 11:00. Then we got electricity only every other night. Of course, we have the solar power and the generator, so we're fine. But it is creepy having the power cut off and the military patrolling the streets at night. They haven't announced an official curfew, but they are arresting people who are out on the streets without documents after dark.

The other day, a Sudanese warplane buzzed over Arua. We all watched it and then waited for something to happen. But nothing did. Nothing but more rumors anyway. Among them: Sudan has bombed Uganda; Idi Amin is coming back to save us; a new group of rebels are now targeting the West Nile; the Sudanese government is in cahoots with all the

Ugandan rebel groups and they are all getting together
to invade northern Uganda. Plus, Uganda is about to
have its first presidential election in ten years and
everyone says the instability is going to get worse as the
election gets closer. The tension is killing me. At least
if something—other than rumors—would happen
already, maybe we'd have an excuse to leave early. I
think I might be ready to leave.

I'll keep you posted,
Eve

Chapter Thirty

🌿

The Beginning of the End

"Did you know about the bus they ambushed in the park yesterday?" Coby whispered. "They stole everything and then set fire to the bus with everyone still inside." I shivered even though it was hot outside. Coby and I were sitting in the kiddie pool in her yard while our homemade avocado facial masks dried in the sun.

"Yeah. It's definitely getting worse." I remembered how nervous I was the first time we drove through Murchison Falls National Park with the country director, Stan. But back then the worst danger was that a hungry baboon might reach into your car and steal your lunch. Now, two and a half years later, you risked your life driving through the rebel-held park. Anyone who could afford it flew between Kampala and Arua.

"Are you thinking about leaving?" Coby asked. Our eyes were covered with cucumber slices, but we could hear the squeals of Sierra, Job, and Simon as they chased chickens around the yard, with Cissie and Florence chasing them.

"Lately, I'm often thinking about leaving," I admitted. "What about you?"

"How can I even think about leaving on a day like today?" Coby said.

"That's the frustrating thing about it," I said. "When it's peaceful, it's just perfect here. But whenever something happens I just want to get the hell out of here. You know? What I don't know is how are we going to know when it's really time to leave?"

"Did you hear the gunfire last night?" Coby asked.

"Hear it? Coby, I could have sworn it was in my yard. We jumped out of bed and grabbed Sierra out of her crib and huddled for a half hour in the hallway. I kept thinking 'Call 911. Call 911.' And then, of course, I realized our phone doesn't even work."

"What's 911?" Coby asked.

"Yeah, exactly."

We took off our cucumbers to see our kids running, naked and tan, in the brilliant blue sunshine.

"But it's not all bad," Coby said. "And you're even working now."

"I'm going down to Entebbe to do another close of service conference for the Peace Corps next week," I said.

"Will you take Sierra?"

"I'm thinking of leaving her home. I'm hoping four days without nursing might help her get the idea about weaning. I'm afraid she's planning to nurse until she goes to college."

"If she really needs to nurse while you're away, I'll be here." Months before, Coby and I had agreed to nurse each other's babies if one of us got sick and couldn't nurse. We had even given it a try to see if the babies would cooperate. Job turned his nose up at me, but Sierra happily latched onto Coby and nursed away.

"Oh, Regina and Cissie won't let her starve. They get her to eat whatever they're eating. It's just when she sees me, she insists on nursing."

John took me to the airstrip a few days later. The plane from Entebbe was already four hours late, which was odd, even by Ugandan standards. Finally a helicopter gunship appeared out of the trees. We watched as it circled Arua for half an hour and then continued north toward the Sudanese border. Within minutes the town was buzzing with the news that "the West Nile Bank Front," a new rebel group, had taken over a refugee camp in the area. If this was true, it meant the guerrilla war had now spread to our side of the Nile River. I was terrified.

"You and Sierra should come with me to Entebbe," I pleaded with John. It was starting to seem like there might be something to the rumors after all.

"No. This is nothing. They've been saying this stuff for months. We'll be fine at home. If anything really happens, we'll catch the next flight down."

Reluctantly, I went to Entebbe, leaving John and Sierra in Arua. Usually, I loved conducting COS conferences for the Peace Corps, thoroughly enjoying being the seasoned expat, helping to prepare the departing volunteers for life after the Peace Corps. And, not surprisingly, facilitating these conferences brought a measure of closure to my own Peace Corps experience. But this time everyone was talking about what was going on in Arua. Every day there was another disturbing headline in *The New Vision*. And every night I tried in vain to get through by telephone. And to top it off, my boobs were engorged and killing me!

"You're not really going back there, are you?" more than one person at the conference asked. In fact, none of the Peace Corps volunteers or staff had ever been to Arua. Even before the latest unrest, the American Embassy considered northern Uganda unsafe. Official Americans, like Peace Corps personnel and the Marum family, had always been prohibited from traveling north of Murchison Falls National Park. We used to laugh at that. But I wasn't laughing now.

I returned to Arua and found Sierra still wanting to nurse and the streets of Arua perfectly calm. Whatever rebels had crossed the Nile had been rounded up by people wielding spears, *pangas,* and bows and arrows and turned over to the authorities. But something awful had happened while I was away. Beijing began coughing right after I'd left. The next day she stopped eating and two days later, John found her dead.

"Beijing was coughing" was Sierra's latest sentence, which she repeated over and over, and each time she said it, I cried. John had buried Beijing beneath a mango tree in our compound.

"I am so sorry, Eve," Regina said. "We did not know what to do."

"Beijing was coughing," Cissie said. There were tears in her eyes.

"It's nobody's fault," I said. I vowed not to let them see me cry over a cat. After all, I knew both of them had relatives and friends who'd lost children. Everyone in Uganda did.

But *Mzee* John caught me weeping over the little mound under the mango tree in the yard. "I'm sorry," I said, trying to hide my tears. "I know, it must seem crazy to be so sad over an animal."

"Madam, I think you loved that cat. And so you are sad. In Uganda, we understand sadness." A few days later, Erneste brought me some morning glory seeds, which Sierra and I planted on Beijing's grave. And even as we did, I sensed that we wouldn't be there to see them bloom.

Dear Mom,

I think it might be time to get the hell out of Uganda. I'm frustrated as hell and people here seem totally incapable of taking responsibility for their actions and their lives. What is it about this place that just makes people shrug their shoulders and accept their lot? No one seems to be the least bit interested in lifting a finger to change anything—unless there is something in it for them, that is.

Even Saint John is showing signs of frustration. He came home for lunch the other day and just refused to go back to work! It kills me how hard he works to create a project that will really help people and then to see all the idiotic things that his bank manager does to try to line his own pockets at the expense of the project.

And don't even get me started on the state of AIDS prevention efforts up here. I spent last week at a church-sponsored AIDS education workshop where they told these poor kids that condoms that are made in America won't work in Africa! (The Bernoulli theory proves it, they said. Yeah, I know. It makes absolutely NO sense. But the young people at the conference bought it hook, line, and sinker.) I'm still working whenever I can and running the Anti-AIDS Club at the school. But I swear, I don't even know why I bother. Nothing seems to change. It also seems as if AIDS has been so destigmatized here (good) that nobody has to take any responsibility for doing anything that might have caused them to get it (bad). Like does the disease just jump out of the blue and infect people?

Your granddaughter, at least, is wonderful. She's a real source of joy in our lives—some days the only one. Yesterday she stripped off her nappie and ran around the verandah naked with a scrub brush in her hand. She kept squatting down and scrubbing the floor. Then she squatted down and peed on the floor and then scrubbed that. Then she started scrubbing all the chairs. Every time I sat down on one, she'd chase me off and scrub it! She did not learn this type of behavior from me! She's still nursing voraciously. It's a lovely diet—for me. I now weigh 109 pounds and look like tits on sticks!

This afternoon I took Sierra out to a village meeting with John. We were trying to keep her quiet in the back of the crowd, but she kept running around behind the two of us and flinging herself on our backs and giggling. Of course, she quickly became the main attraction of the meeting. But one of the nice things about this place is that no one ever seems to mind. Once the mzungu baby began giggling, everyone was giggling. And it was as if that was the entire point of the whole meeting. Who cares if nothing got accomplished? We're all happy. Let's go home.

Some days I just tell myself, well, at least it's a really lovely little corner of hell.

I'll keep you posted,
Eve

Chapter Thirty-One

Life and Death in Uganda

"You heard about Theodore?" Adam asked as I hopped off my bicycle in front of the bank a few weeks later. I was on my way to the market but stopped when I saw Adam.

"What about Theodore?" I asked.

"Oh, I thought you knew. I thought that is why you came over here." He put his hand on my shoulder. I noticed then that Adam's usual smile was missing. "Theodore was killed in a motorcycle accident last night."

"What? Where?" I stammered. Adam gave me all the details as we walked into the darkened bank. A sign on the front door read "Closed due to death." Inside, bank staff stood dazed, looking like shell-shocked refugees.

"Where's John?" I asked.

"He and the bank manager have gone to the carpenter to order a coffin," Adam told me.

I went over and hugged Susan, one of the bank tellers, and then looked around for Nancy, the other bank teller, who was Theodore's girlfriend. Just a month before, we had all gathered at Theodore and Nancy's apartment to celebrate the birth of their daughter.

"Nancy?" I asked. "How is Nancy?"

"Oh, she is terrible, Eve. Terrible." Susan began to cry. "She is at the apartment. Her people are from here. Her mother is with her."

"Theodore's family? They are from Kabale, right? Do they know?"

I remembered first meeting Theodore when John, Adam, and I took our bank safari shortly after we'd first arrived. We had all liked Theodore immediately and were thrilled when he transferred up to work in Arua.

"The manager got a call through to the bank manager in Kabale this morning. They will get the message to his family. We will have a funeral here this afternoon and tomorrow morning Nancy and her father and the baby will fly with Theodore to Kabale."

"Have some tea." Gloria, the bank's secretary, put a cup of sugary tea in my hand. "Soon we will go over to Theodore's to prepare for the funeral."

When John and the manager returned we all went over to the small brick building where Theodore and Nancy lived in an apartment on the second floor. A large group of people were milling about outside.

"Come inside with me, Eve," Gloria said as she took my arm. "The women are preparing Theodore for the funeral."

"Oh . . ." I hesitated. "I'll just stay out here with John."

"No, no you should come," Gloria said. "Since Theodore's family is not here, we must do the work of the women of his family today."

"I think it's better for me to wait outside." I didn't think I could handle the sight of a bloody, bashed-in, dead Theodore.

"Oh, Eve, it doesn't matter that you are a *mzungu*. Today we are Theodore's clan. You and John and Theodore all came to us in Arua at the same time. And you were his friend. It is fine for you to be in there."

"No, it's not that, Gloria. I'm just squeamish." Gloria looked confused, and I realized that, perhaps, squeamishness was a privilege reserved for those living in more developed countries. "And it's . . . um . . . it's against my religion to touch a dead body." I was desperate and figured I'd be the only Jew Gloria would ever meet.

An hour later everyone went inside and I had no choice but to go. I tiptoed into the sitting room of the apartment, which now had Theodore in the center of it, lying on a bed, covered head to toe, much to my relief, by a bedsheet. A matronly woman sat on the floor beside the bed and periodically waved a long piece of blue cloth over the body. I didn't know if she was helping Theodore's spirit move into the afterlife or just shooing away flies.

John and I were ushered to chairs that were set up just beside Theodore's head. The room soon filled with women kneeling by the bed and moving their lips. I didn't know if they were praying or having lengthy conversations with Theodore. One old woman lovingly caressed his feet.

Why weren't you wearing a helmet? is what I would have asked. But I would have been the only one. Ugandans didn't usually think in terms of what-ifs. Most of the men came in and lifted up the sheet and had a look at Theodore's body. Some stood silently for a few minutes or sat next to John and me. But most of the men moved fairly quickly out to the balcony, where they sat and glumly smoked cigarettes.

"The coffin has failed to arrive," someone came in and announced after we had been sitting around Theodore's body for several hours. Most Ugandan ceremonies involve a generous amount of sitting around and waiting. No one ever seemed to mind. But this was different. We had both a curfew and a decomposing body to consider.

"Why don't we take Theodore, as he is, to the church and begin the funeral," John suggested. "We can send a message to the carpenter to bring the coffin to the church."

After some discussion, ten men and women gathered around the bed and lifted the mattress that held Theodore. Someone handed me Nancy and Theodore's baby and we all followed the mattress carrying Theodore through the apartment, down a twisting, uneven flight of stairs, and through a narrow alleyway to the street. Then, as gently as one can in this situation, they slid the mattress into the back of a Land Rover for an awkward procession to the church.

"Is it so, Eve? Adam's been shot? Is it so?" Coby was flushed as she stood in my doorway early the next morning. I had trouble at first comprehending what she was asking me.

"No, Adam wasn't shot. It was Theodore—you know, the tall,

very friendly guy at the bank. You met him at my house. He died in a motorcycle accident." There were always so many crazy rumors flying around. I was sure Coby had just gotten hers mixed up.

She put her hand on my arm. "Eve, I just heard it from Bernard that Adam was shot last night while going home from Theodore's funeral."

I ran down the road to the CARE office, and the moment I saw John, I knew it was true.

"When did this happen? Why didn't you tell me?" I screamed.

"Don't worry, Eve. He's all right. He's all right," John said. "I wanted to be sure that he was going to be okay before I told you. I knew you would panic. I thought this might push you over the edge." *How well my husband knows me.*

John and I drove to the municipal hospital in the center of town. Anyone with transport usually went to the Kuluva Mission Hospital, where the care and conditions were usually better. I had seen such depressing conditions when I'd been to this hospital before that I was quite surprised to find Adam in a freshly painted, spotlessly clean private room. He was sitting up in bed, on crisp, clean sheets. He was in a chipper mood, his brilliant white smile radiating from his face. On one side of his bed sat his surgeon, on the other sat the resident pediatrician, both good friends of his. If it weren't for the bandages and the ammonia smell, the three of them could have been playing chess, drinking beer, and listening to the radio broadcasts of the OJ Simpson trial, like they had for months.

Adam took one look at my face and took up John's mantra. "I am all right, Eve. I am all right. I am going to be just fine." Both doctors nodded solemnly, but Adam was almost giddy.

"Yes," said the surgeon. "Adam here is a very lucky fellow. The bullet failed to pierce any major organs."

"Yes," added the pediatrician. "And he is lucky that he was on motorcycle rather than on foot. He was able to keep on his motorcycle and ride away from the direction from which the bullets were coming even after one had hit him."

"And lucky that I am friends with the surgeon and know where he lives," Adam added. People regularly bled to death in the hospital waiting room because the staff were reluctant to disturb the doctors at night.

I thought they were going to break into high fives all around. "Well, isn't it lucky that Adam's so lucky?" I screeched. I stormed out of the hospital room, sat down on the cement curb, and cried.

Adam had been shot so close to his own home that his wife, Sarah, later told us that she had heard the gunshots. We had probably heard them, too, but gunfire had become as common a night sound as the chirping of crickets, and unless it was really close, we hardly thought anything of it.

We never found out who shot Adam or why. Like when Stan had been shot just before we'd arrived, we never knew if it was related to rebel activity or just marauding bandits that occasionally popped up in the West Nile. But not knowing made me feel even more frightened.

"Now don't go all mushy on me," Alison said two days later as I hugged her and wiped away my tears beside the runway. After Adam's shooting, VSO gave Alison forty-eight hours to get out of Arua. "I'm just going down to Kampala. You'll probably be down there any day yourself, knocking at my door and begging me to make you some proper crisps."

I noticed a couple of other expat families with what looked like all of their belongings also waiting for the plane.

As I rode my bicycle back from the airstrip, I passed a military truck full of soldiers standing on the open bed in the back. One soldier had his rifle braced against his chest and it seemed like he was aiming at people on the road. For a terrifying moment, our eyes met and I knew he had me in the crosshairs of his rifle scope. *Someone could get shot that way,* I thought as the truck flew by. And then from behind me, I heard the sound of gunfire; as unmistakable as it was familiar now. I put my head down and pedaled home as fast as I could.

"Eve, my dear," Adam said to me when he was released from the hospital the next day. "It just was not what? It was not my time to go. I was not meant to die at that time and in that place." I no longer cared to wait around to find out if I was meant to die at this time and in this place.

Dear Terry and Pauline,

We haven't heard from you in a while but trust you are well. I also trust that you don't miss Arua too much. But we all miss you. A group of us got together for brunch at our house recently. It was a small group; there aren't many of us expats left up here anymore. Pauline, you would have been proud of the bush hostess I've become: I whipped up some vichyssoise and homemade bagels!

Well, it's certainly wild up here in the West Nile. The Kony rebels have been regularly attacking Gulu and Atiac, and ambushing travelers on the road between Karuma and Pakwach. And now we have our very own rebel group, the West Nile Bank Front. All the guerrilla activity has pretty much closed the road to Kampala. The only way in or out now is to fly. Because there are no buses coming from Kampala, we haven't seen a newspaper in days and the only way to get mail in or out is to send it with someone who's flying down. It's sort of eerily quiet here at the moment. And we're just hoping it stays quiet until the election.

John is beginning to ease himself out of the savings and loan project. Adam will take over, and the hope is that within a year, the bank will be able to run the project without outside support. I'll hate leaving this house and the friends we have here, but otherwise I'm more than ready for a change.

Of course, we have no idea what we're doing next.

Remember when we first arrived in Arua and you told me that once the expat bug gets in your system you never want to go home? Well, I thought you were nuts! Back then I could hardly even imagine making it through two years. Now, I can't imagine ever living in the States again.

The termites came out a few weeks back. This year, Sierra was out there with all the other kids, snatching them right out of the air and popping them in her mouth! Who says my daughter isn't Ugandan? Last night, I even enjoyed some (fried) at a party at Adam's house. And this morning, I saw a woman walk down the road—barefoot—carrying her shoes on her head. Okay, so now I've seen—and done—it all. Maybe it really is time to leave.

I'll keep you posted,
Eve

Chapter Thirty-Two

🍂

Standing Fast and Ready to Run

After Adam's shooting, CARE put us on "standfast" status. We were told to keep the tank of our Pajero full at all times and have a bag packed in case we needed to evacuate. I thought "runfast" would have been a more appropriate name. I packed some diapers, clothes, and books for Sierra, our photo albums, my laptop computer and the disks with all my short stories and letters. Then I agonized over whether or not I'd be able to take Berlin.

CARE advised us to drive over the border into Zaire if things got really bad. This raised the question of how much worse was "really bad"? And Zaire, which had its own troubles—most notably an Ebola epidemic and an impending civil war—was known locally as "the Zaire-shaped hole in the middle of Africa."

I asked Regina what precautions she and her family were taking. "Oh, Eve, things are always like this around here. When things are good, we stay here and get on with our lives. And when things are bad, we stay here and get on with our lives."

"My Gina!" Sierra yelled as Cissie chased her into the kitchen where Regina and I were talking.

"My Sierra!" Regina called back. "Look what I brought you." She pulled a small, wrinkly ball from a pocket in her dress.

"Tunda!" Sierra said.

"Sierra now loves *matunda*," Regina said as she cut the little passion fruit and handed half to Sierra, who expertly sucked out the sweet, seedy flesh. I hadn't taught her to do that.

John and I did make plans to leave, though. Since this would be easier if one of us had another job, we both applied for jobs in various countries. We were hoping that John would get another posting with CARE, but that wasn't guaranteed. Meanwhile, CARE asked John to go to Armenia for three weeks to develop a grant for a new savings and credit project, which could result in a job. With Arua's volatility, Sierra and I went down to Kampala while John was away. We stayed in what had now been dubbed "the Sierra Suite" at the Marums' house.

In the meantime, May 9, 1996, fast approached. That was the day Uganda would hold its first presidential elections since 1980. We all held our breath. In the last presidential election, Milton Obote had been charged with voter intimidation and rigging the count. No one inside or outside of Uganda accepted the results, and this led to the years of guerrilla warfare that ultimately ended with Yoweri Museveni ousting Obote and declaring himself president. Now, sixteen years later, Museveni promised a free and fair election, although he himself was the favored candidate.

On election eve, Larry, Elizabeth, and I made a champagne toast to what we hoped would be a peaceful election. Sonja, Paul, and Sierra toasted with chocolate milk. It was love at first sip for Sierra. And when Sierra said "nurse" before bed that night, I offered her a cup of chocolate milk instead. Okay, I know it's not the doctor-recommended weaning method. But I was a desperate woman. And it worked.

Despite our fears, election day was calm, with reports of people in every corner of the country standing peacefully—sometimes for hours—in long lines to cast their ballots. When we ventured out in the evening there were still long lines. But now everyone was waiting to witness the votes being counted. We watched as the paper ballots, with pictures of each candidate next to their printed name, were removed one by one and held up for all of us to see before being tallied on a huge board. It took all night for the votes to be counted this way at polling places all over Uganda. But when Yoweri Museveni was once again declared the president, everyone accepted the results.

When John returned from Armenia, we went back to Arua. I congratulated everyone for their country's peaceful return to democracy. I was sure, now that Museveni had won fair and square, the rebels would go away and things would go back to sleepy dullness for good. But my Ugandan friends said I was being naïve.

"This is the way of Uganda," Adam said. "The violence will return. It is our way here." While I panicked and made plans to leave, my neighbors blithely accepted the violence and carried on with their lives.

We also carried on with our lives while we waited to hear where we would be going next. We were watching a video shortly after we got back, when we seemed to run out of solar energy. This made no sense since it was a perfectly sunny afternoon. John went up to the roof to investigate.

"Guess what I found up there?" he asked when he'd climbed back down.

"A giant marabou stork carcass lying across the solar panels?"

"No. Nothing."

"Okay, then why don't we have any power?"

"Because there's nothing up there. Our solar panels are gone. Someone must have taken them while we were in Kampala."

The next day Arua's police chief came with two officers to investigate. "We are terribly sorry to have inconvenienced our white guest like this," the chief said. "We are taking this case very seriously." And they were, too; they fanned out around the house and snooped and sniffed as if the missing solar panels might be found behind the couch. But after a thorough investigation, for which we had to supply the vehicle and the fuel, our two solar panels were found—in our boy Richard's possession. Despite my reluctance to press charges against him, Richard was taken into custody.

"Do you think, maybe, there's a remote possibility that Richard didn't steal from us?" I asked John. "I mean, after all we've done for him."

"If he didn't steal them, how do you explain our solar panels being found in his compound?"

"Well, he said lots of the other kids are jealous because of all the stuff we've given him over the years and they did this to get him in trouble."

"And the fact that he was the only one who had been alone in our compound while we were away?" John continued. "Eve, don't be naïve."

"After all we've done for him, you really think he'd steal from us?"

John shrugged. "Some people will, I guess. If they're poor and desperate and have the opportunity. Yeah. I know it stinks. But it happens. We have so much and they have so little, Eve."

I still had a hard time believing it. "Did Richard really take our solar panels?" I asked the police chief the next day at the police station. "I paid his school fees. I bought his chloroquine."

"Yes, I understand that Richard was your boy," the chief said. "It was very wrong for him to do this. And by the way, madam, did you bring any food for him? He has been in our custody for two days with nothing to eat."

"Wait a minute! I take him in, pay his school fees, buy him whatever he needs. I took his sister to the hospital, paid her medical bills. When his father died last year, we gave money for the coffin. We went to the funeral. Now he steals from me and I'm supposed to feed him while he's in jail? No, I did not bring him any food!"

"Yes, well, maybe tomorrow you should bring him some groundnuts and tea."

"Well, what's going to happen to him now?" I don't even know why I cared.

"Ah, he has been sentenced to two years of hard labor," the chief said.

"Wow. That was quick!" I said.

"Oh, yes, madam. Uganda has a new constitution." The police chief reached into his desk and pulled out a small booklet. "This is our constitution and in here it says that we may not hold a prisoner for more than forty-eight hours if he has not been found guilty. Uganda is a democracy now and it is very important that we follow the constitution." He proudly waved the booklet in front of us.

"Yes, congratulations on your election," John said.

"In the United States court cases drag on for months or sometimes years," I said. "But how can you manage to do that so quickly?"

"Well, your boy confessed." The police chief smiled.

"He confessed?" I asked. "Two days ago he was still denying he had anything to do with it and coming up with elaborate stories to explain how the solar panels got in his compound."

"Well, in Uganda, we have two important tools for seeing that justice is served quickly. We have our new constitution"—he waved the booklet at me once again—"and we have this." He picked up a thickly knotted tree branch from under his desk. "And together they work very well to bring about justice."

Despite Uganda's recent peaceful elections and the swift resolution of our robbery, CARE had decided that Arua was too unstable for an employee with dependents. We were to be the last CARE family in Arua.

Dear Folks,

Sorry for the form letter, but as most of you know, our lives have been incredibly hectic. The ending of John's project, the search for new employment, uncertainty about the peacefulness of the presidential elections, and rebel activity in Arua has kept us flying back and forth to Kampala the way other people take the commuter train to work! I'm sure you've stopped trying to keep up with where we think we're headed next. I know I have.

For a while, Armenia seemed the likeliest place to end up next. It would be another job with CARE, making the transfer process nice and smooth. And since

John spent three weeks there writing the project proposal, we had a bit of a background about the place, the people, and the project. But as of yesterday, the proposal was still awaiting final funding, so nothing is definite. We'd barely finished eating the cheese and butter from our last trip to Kampala when John got a radio message inviting him to Vienna to interview for the position of Income Generation Officer with the UN in the West Bank (Palestine). So back we went to Kampala, where Sierra and I stayed with the Marums while John bought a white shirt, scraped the mud from his shoes, and flew to Vienna. He was interviewed for an hour and a half by a panel of four people. Then he was eating pastries and drinking real coffee in a Viennese café. Living in Palestine would be exciting, but honestly, I think I've had enough bombings and gunfire to last a lifetime.

When John returned to Kampala we joined the Marums on a camping trip to Queen Elizabeth National Park in southern Uganda for a last safari hurrah. We saw impala, kob, cape buffalo, and baboons by day and were kept awake at night by colobus monkeys, hyenas, and hippos in our camp. And best of all, we were finally able to see the elusive tree-climbing lions! Sierra's newest sentence: "The big cats were sleeping in the tree."

We camped in a spot that, apparently, was favored by hippos. Did you know that more people are killed in Africa each year by hippos than by lions? Well, we do, and now we know why. John was charged by an angry hippo, which he escaped by running through the (thankfully) narrow doorway of the cooking hut. And now I know—firsthand—what to do when you desperately have to pee in the middle of the night but hippos stand between you and the latrine. Thank God John brought us some Pampers from Vienna!

When we returned to Kampala, John had several frantic messages from the Peace Corps. They desperately wanted to interview him for the job of Assistant Country Director in (now hold on to your hat and grab your atlas) Uzbekistan. In case you're looking for it, Uzbekistan is in the southern part of what used to be the Soviet Union, near Kazakstan, Afghanistan, and Tajikistan. In the space of two hours, John was interviewed by the country director, who called from Uzbekistan, and by three different people calling from Peace Corps headquarters in Washington. (Boy, this modern telephone technology they have in Kampala is truly amazing. I can only hope that someday the good people of Arua can benefit from it too.) It looks very positive, and the Peace Corps needs to move quickly as the new person must attend a three-week training in Washington that begins in two months. Uzbekistan is beginning to emerge from the blur as our choice for a next post. We both have fond feelings about the Peace Corps. It is what brought us together in the first place.

At almost two, Sierra is doing grand. The hardest part about leaving here will be separating her from all the people whom she has grown to love. How will we ever say good-bye to everyone who has become a part of our life? I can't even stand to think about it.

John is busy, not just looking for the next job, but finishing up and passing on the old. His deputy, Adam, will be taking over, since CARE has decided not to hire another expatriate to replace him. We think this is good for Adam, who is highly capable, and for the

project, which in order to be sustainable cannot
continue to rely on expatriate expertise.

Well, keep your fingers crossed, and I'll keep you
posted,
Eve

Chapter Thirty-Three

❦

Forever in My Blood

"What do I hear for this roll of toilet paper? It's soft, it's gentle on the bottom, it came all the way from America." Bernard was playing auctioneer. His eager audience was made up of just about all the expats left in Arua and plenty of our Ugandan friends and colleagues.

"I'll give you a dollar," Mark chimed in.

"Heck, I'll give you two dollars!" his younger brother Stephen piped up. We all laughed. Stephen was only two weeks into his summerlong visit to Uganda.

"I've got two dollars for the toilet paper. Do I hear three? John and Eve tell us it's a collectible—left over from the Kennedy administration."

"Well, why didn't you say it was used, then? I'll give you four quid for it," John Hatchard bellowed.

"I'll give you five U.S. cash dollars," said Stephen, waving a five-dollar bill. "I gotta have that toilet paper!"

"Aw, all right. Let the new bottom have it. Heck, I enjoy wiping my arse with *The New Vision,* anyway," Hatchard said.

"Sold! The toilet paper goes to Stephen for five dollars. Good for you and good for Kuluva Hospital!"

With our departure date approaching, John and I had begun the time-honored tradition of all expatriates heading home: the mad giveaway. There was nothing that someone didn't want. We still weren't sure where we were headed, but we'd have at least a brief stopover in the States first. We could replace anything that we had prematurely parted with.

"Eve, I would like to have some of your dresses and some of Sierra's things for my children," Regina had said.

"I would like a dress too," Cissie had practically whispered. "And a cooking pot?" I think that was the most I'd ever heard Cissie say directly, though she chattered away like a bird to Sierra and Regina.

"The two of you can have whatever you want. Take anything. Well, except for my cookbooks. God knows what I'll be cooking wherever we go next."

"What would we do with these useless American things?" Regina laughed. "Your peelers and graters and electric things. Our simple things work better than your fancy American things."

"Better for you, maybe. But you ought to know about us Americans by now!" All three of us laughed.

Mzee John asked if he could have Armstrong. Since we still didn't know where our next post would be, we didn't know if we could bring the dog. But we felt sure that *Mzee* John—who had bonded with Armstrong much as Nassar had in our old house—would give him a good home. Several people asked if they could have Berlin. But that was never an option: I had no choice but to leave Beijing in Arua; Berlin was coming with us.

Over the past two years, I had acquired quite a stash of luxury food items that I doled out sparingly. Somehow I felt secure knowing that if the shit really hit the fan, at least we could enjoy hollandaise sauce and daiquiris while Arua burned. Ugandans had little use for any of that, although Regina and Cissie had both acquired a taste for ranch dressing on everything. But these things—along with books, videos, and Tupperware—were in high demand among expats.

We gave Regina, Cissie, and our *askaris* anything they wanted. Everything else that wasn't coming with us was auctioned off to the highest bidder with all the proceeds going to Kuluva Hospital. The novelty of the auction, which was held at the first of our three farewell parties, totally eclipsed the "farewell" part of the party. Goodies in hand, most people forgot that they had actually come to say good-bye to us.

"What do I hear for this cake?" Bernard was now auctioning off the cake that Coby had baked for the party.

"I'll pay ten dollars for the cake!" a Ugandan friend offered. And before I could stop him, the beautiful cake on which Coby had painstakingly spelled out "Farewell" in colored sugar, went home with the highest bidder. But I was feeling nauseous and really didn't miss the cake. I wasn't sure if the nausea was from sadness, malaria, or the fact that I might very well be pregnant again, not that I bothered trying to get anyone around here to confirm that. I had learned my lesson.

I had come to Arua fully aware that one day I would leave. I wasn't prepared to be a permanent expatriate and had never intended to spend my whole life in a mud village in Africa. But now that it was finally time to say good-bye, I couldn't.

CARE had assured us that professional movers would come up to Arua, pack up our household, and then bring everything down to Kampala where they would be stored in a warehouse until we knew where we were going next. I was certain that was just a joke; as if anything that efficient could ever happen here. I had a dead telephone on my wall to attest to that. But a few days after our auction, the impossible happened: a moving truck arrived at our door. Moving men in neat uniforms cheerily popped out and set about professionally packing up our personal effects. In a few hours, they were on their way back to Kampala, assuring us that our things would meet us at our next post, and I was forced to reevaluate everything I thought I knew about this country.

But later that night we received word that our truck was being held up by rebels in Murchison Falls National Park. I wondered what armed guerrillas would do in the jungle with plates that said "Plate" and bowls that said "Bowl." We kept in radio contact with the driver, encouraging him to try to bribe his way out. But the guerrillas stead-fastly refused the money, claiming they didn't want to get the nasty reputation of extorting bribes from international aid agencies. After nearly a week, the truck was allowed to continue on its way. Perhaps the rebels had rummaged through our things and couldn't figure out where they'd plug in the cappuccino maker.

Meanwhile, in Arua, the CARE staff invited the whole commu-nity to a huge farewell party in our honor. They roasted two goats and served all the beer people could hold. Which was not a lot for me. The all-too-familiar nausea was hanging on and I was pretty sure I was pregnant again. I skipped the medical runaround this time, as well as the prenatal vitamins and malaria prophylaxis. Without all the drugs in my body, I felt significantly better than I had last time.

The entire CARE and bank staffs came to this party, as did all sorts of people from town. Local government officials, the guys from the post office, Zila and a bunch of women from the market all came to say good-bye. They gave us gifts for setting up a new household—woven mats, baskets, and cooking utensils—for which I was grateful, because at the time our household effects were still being held hostage in the park. The Catholic archbishop, who'd met John's parents when they were in town, offered John a dispensation and a Catholic wed-ding. But we declined, knowing all that that would entail. And be-sides, who would pay for the soap?

On our last Sunday afternoon in Arua, we drove out to Regina and Steven's home for one final farewell party. A group of Steven's mu-sician friends were playing *adungus* and drums. A long table was piled high with vast quantities of *matoke,* beans, and potatoes, there was chicken, rice, and a starchy cornmeal paste called *enya*—sure signs of a special occasion. Most unusual of all, there was a loaf of bread.

"Bread?" I asked. "Regina, where did you get bread?" Bread is not part of the traditional Ugandan diet. I had taught Regina and Cissie how to make it, but few Ugandans could bake it since they had no ovens.

"I baked it for you," Regina answered. "In an oven that Steven built."

"My Gina!" Sierra jumped into Regina's arms, while Steven introduced us to the many people gathered.

"This is my mother," Steven said as an ancient woman grabbed my arm. "And this one"—he gallantly bowed toward a woman I recognized from the wedding—"is Regina's mother." Steven continued reintroducing us to a dizzying assortment of parents, in-laws, brothers, sisters, cousins, nieces, nephews, and neighbors, whom we'd met at their wedding. But I hardly remembered most of them. Each one shook our hands and showered us with a chorus of "Thank you" and "God bless you."

Steven led us to an awning that was propped against the side of one of the huts. He motioned John and me toward two wooden chairs that were placed regally in the shade. Balloons and what looked to be pink and blue crepe paper dangled from the edges of the awning. On closer inspection I saw that the crepe paper was actually stiff and grainy Ugandan toilet paper.

Regina carried Sierra into the cooking hut and came out a few minutes later with plastic plates and serving utensils. Sierra toddled behind her, cradling a filthy, tattered doll, its head hanging by a thread. Women bustled about laying more food on the table. The music stopped and Steven asked us all to sit down. Regina with Sierra on her lap, Steven and their children, Cissie and her sister, Coby, Bernard and their two boys all sat opposite us on a mat on the packed dirt. Everyone else sat on mats that fanned out across the compound.

Steven stood and cleared his throat. "We thank the Lord for bringing us together today. And we thank Him for bringing John and Eve and Sierra to us. We ask Him for his continued kindness and sustenance." Steven paused and turned to look at John and me. "John and Eve, you have come here and become part of our lives. We can never repay your kindness and goodness to us. May the Lord Jesus Christ bless you and keep you in His care wherever you go. And may

He bring you back here to us again. We ask these things in the Holy Name of Jesus."

"Amen." The chorus filtered up from the scattered guests.

Regina stood, easily balancing Sierra on her hip. "I will leave the long speeches to Steven. But I want to say something to Eve and John and Sierra." She squeezed Sierra closer to her as she spoke. "Thank you for coming to be with us here in Uganda and especially for coming to Arua. Thank you for all that you have given to me and my family. We will never forget you. And I am sure that I will never again work for a family as good and as kind as yours."

I winced as she said that. Regina had already found her next job. The Dutch family who'd come from Rwanda and didn't seem particularly concerned about Arua's instability, had hired her. They seemed like a nice family, but Regina had already confided to me that the Dutch woman wasn't particularly warm. Regina would do fine, I was sure. But I was worried about Cissie. She was a good worker, but she was so painfully shy that she needed someone to speak for her. I had convinced the Dutch woman to hire both Regina and Cissie together. But I didn't think it would last. Cissie would have to live with the Dutch family, as she had lived with us. She required a fair amount of patience and care. And from what I could tell, the Dutch woman did not seem the type to be interested in coddling her household help.

Regina's mother-in-law stood and spoke in Lugbara. "We know you, Eve and John and Sierra, though we have hardly met," Regina translated. "We know of your kindness to our children Regina and Steven. We have come today to say thank you for coming to Arua. For coming into our lives and for caring about us. And we want you to see from our faces that we are sad that you are leaving."

Regina motioned for me to come stand with her by the food table. Holding a knife together, like a bride and groom, we cut into the loaf of bread she had baked in an oven built just for us. Solemnly, we all took a bite of the bread, which got stuck around the lump in my throat.

"*Awadifo saaru. Awadifo* for everything" was all I managed to croak out before my words were drowned by racking sobs. I wanted to say more. I wanted to tell Regina that what I had done for her and her family was nothing compared to what she had done for me. I wanted to tell her that when I came to Arua I knew nothing and that I had survived only because of her forbearance and help. I wanted to thank Steven for being a pain in the ass and a pleasant diversion all at the same time. I wanted to thank the two of them for bringing their children into our home and into Sierra's life, and for teaching them that they didn't have to be afraid of our pale, furry skin. I wanted to hug Cissie and say nothing. I wanted to tell them all that the thought that we would never see each other again was unbearable, and yet I knew that we would never see each other again.

"Thank you. Thank you" was all I could gurgle out between sobs. This was our last going away party and the first time I had cried. I stood under the toilet paper–bedecked canopy and blubbered. I couldn't bear to look at the faces of the people that I was leaving and so I looked past them, out toward the dried mud huts that dotted the land around me.

"Oh, God," I sobbed. "How can I ever leave this place?"

John stood up and put his arm around me. *"Awadifo saaru,"* he said clearly and dry-eyed. "We thank you for this lovely party and for all that you have done for us in our three years here." I couldn't comprehend how he could do this: How he could leave without totally falling apart. It no longer seemed even physically possible that the next day I would get on a plane and leave Arua forever.

"We thank you most of all for allowing us to be a part of your lives for these three wonderful years. For making our family part of your family. We will never forget you. And we want you to know that you will always, always have family in America."

I leaned back against the cool dried mud of Regina and Steven's home. I looked out upon that red dirt village that had become my village. I looked in awe upon its spectacular, simple majesty. I saw the head-high rows of tasteless maize and the scrawny cows lowing in the heat. I heard the obnoxious, raucous cough of the goats, the constant cluck of chickens, and the roosters crowing as if all day was sunrise. I saw the dirty, sad dogs that were too lazy to get up and bark at a stranger. If, by chance, there ever was a stranger. I took it all in and became painfully aware of what I was leaving behind. And I knew that no matter where we went next, a part of me would always be homesick for Uganda.

I came to Uganda totally unprepared for life in Africa; in many ways, unprepared for life in general. I had been taught by her and tamed by her. I'd fallen into—and out of—love with this place so many times, I'd lost track. I knew in the end, I hadn't changed Uganda one bit. But she had fundamentally changed me. And like malaria, Uganda would live forever in my blood.

Dear Folks,

We recently received three interesting pieces of news in the mail. One was a State Department warning about the unsafe conditions for Americans in the West Bank; one was a news article about rioting in Yerevan, Armenia, along with a State Department warning to all Americans living in Armenia; and the third was a news article from The New Vision, whose headline read: "Rebels Invade CARE office in Arua."

Bet you're glad that we're in Uzbekistan!

I'll keep you posted,
Eve

Acknowledgments

Authors always say that it took all kinds of people to actually write their book. I say it takes one person to write a book, but an awful lot of other people to put up with you while you are writing that book. Thanks is the least that I owe to all of the people who've put up with me—and helped me—as I wrote this book.

First and foremost, John, Sierra, and Jeremiah have been putting up with me—and supporting me—for the full fifteen years that I've been living, dreaming about, and writing this book. I can never thank you enough for letting me be your wife and mother—and a writer, too. So I'll just try to make enough money to put in a swimming pool, a basketball court, and solar panels on the roof. (Anything extra I'll give to worthy causes, I promise, John.)

Christine Pride, my editor, loved it from the very beginning. Thank you for taking such good care of my baby. And the rest of the amazing team at Broadway Books—Lindsay Gordon, Jennifer Robbins, and Anne Chagnot—you made it seem easy. Thanks so much to Liz De Ridder, who did an excellent job copyediting the manuscript, and did her damndest to make me look like a better writer than I am. All remaining grammatical errors are mine—not hers.

My mom, Sheila Brown-Blei, was the first one to say, "Hey, why don't you write a book?" Thanks for the great idea. And thanks for the years and years of encouragement. My father, Mel Brown, you're a *mensch*. And thanks for always asking about it. My two brothers, Barry/Seth Brown (the musician) and Joshua Samuel Brown (the other writer in the family), are incredibly talented in their own right.

Acknowledgments

Thanks for believing in my dream, for arranging the music, and for letting me be the star this time around.

I am blessed with the most wonderful in-laws imaginable. And I want to thank them for making me one of their own. Pat and Jack, Stephen and Terry, Tom and Paula, Joe and Tiffany, Jim and Julie Waite—you're the best. *(And not a murderer in the bunch!)*

Susan Brockmann and Jean Dresley, my bookend warrior women, thanks for being there through it all (and the sequels to come). Nanci Tangeman, a pretty nifty writer yourself, thanks for turning me into a "real writer." Susan Gottehrer, Jacqueline Cincotta, Kathy Moran, Heidi Ziemke, Kate Luscombe, Susan Buhrmaster, and Sheila Littleton (my Oneonta Tribe); Amy Shapiro, Ellen Mitnowsky, and Daphne Bye; and all the members of the Women's Discussion and Libation Society, thanks for listening, caring, and always cheering me on. Susan Blauner and Shirley Vernick, thanks for making the writing much less lonely (and a lot more fun). Elizabeth Bonney, thanks for making everything you touch beautiful, including my amazing website. Jocelyn Donaghue and Beth Taska, I might have turned back if not for you two. Thank you for being advocates when I needed them.

Four long-overdue thank-yous are owed, to Mr. Ron Frank of P.S. 26 in Travis, for telling me—in the fifth grade—that I was a good writer, and for teaching us to dream the impossible dream; to Patrick Jackson, for teaching me that love doesn't have to hurt at all; and to Judith Kuppersmith, Ph.D., and Katherine A. Brunkow, LCSW—for help when I sorely needed it.

And most especially, THANK YOU, Laney Katz Becker—agent extraordinaire—and all the wonderful souls at Folio Literary Management. Laney, you saw the book in the story. And you changed my life . . . again. *Zei gezunt.*

918.66 BROWN-WAITE
Brown-Waite, Eve.
First comes love, then comes malaria :how a
Peace Corps poster boy won
R0112008867   EAST_A

EAST ATLANTA

ATLANTA-FULTON COUNTY LIBRARY